WHO IS MY NEIGHBOR?

WHO IS MY NEIGHBOR?

COMMUNICATING AND ORGANIZING
TO END HOMELESSNESS

PHILLIP K. TOMPKINS

Paradigm Publishers
Boulder • London

Copyright © 2009 Paradigm Publishers

Published in the United States by Paradigm Publishers, 3360 Mitchell Lane, Suite E, Boulder, CO 80301 USA.

Paradigm Publishers is the trade name of Birkenkamp & Company, LLC, Dean Birkenkamp, President and Publisher.

Library of Congress Cataloging-in-Publication Data

Tompkins, Phillip K.
  Who is my neighbor? : communicating and organizing to end homelessness / Phillip K. Tompkins.
    p. cm.
  Includes bibliographical references and index.
  ISBN 978-1-59451-647-4 (hardcover : alk. paper)—ISBN 978-1-59451-648-1 (pbk. : alk. paper)
    1. Homelessness—Colorado—Denver. 2. Homeless persons—Colorado—Denver. 3. Homeless persons—Services for—Denver—Colorado. 4. Shelters for the homeless—Colorado—Denver. 5. Tompkins, Phillip K. I. Title.
  HV4046.D45T65 2009
  362.5'83—dc22

                                                                    2008042254

Printed and bound in the United States of America on acid-free paper that meets the standards of the American National Standard for Permanence of Paper for Printed Library Materials.

Designed and Typeset by Straight Creek Bookmakers.

13 12 11 10 09   1 2 3 4 5

Contents

Artist Craigory Charlesworth depicts Denver's St. Francis Center for the Homeless in a mood piece that captures a sense of time, place, and poignance. (Courtesy of Craigory Charlesworth)

Yes, the greatest dilemmas facing humanity are still landlessness, homelessness, and hunger.... What literature needs most to tell and investigate today are humanity's basic fears: the fear of being left outside, the fear of counting for nothing, and the feelings of worthlessness that come with such fears.

Orhan Pamuk
The Nobel Lecture, 2006

ॐ

PREFACE

This book is a metanarrative of short stories and numbers. Some critics dismiss stories as "anecdotal evidence," while others refer to quantification as reductionism. But all we have are stories and numbers. My purpose is to introduce the stories of homeless people and numbers about them to allow the reader to *learn as I did*, listening to the guests at a homeless shelter speak for themselves. In addition, I provide insights I gained from other people who have studied homeless people and from the rich literature written by people who have experienced being down and out and on the road. This book is almost completely true. It does change names to protect the identity of homeless people.

This unfolding method is also the best way I know to grasp the complexity of the problem. It is tempting to oversimplify homelessness in either of two directions: One is to blame the victim, making homelessness a symptom of weak character; the other is to make it all a matter of economics. I was tempted at times—and it shows at places in the book—to use the second approach. I will show, however, the weakness of giving in to this temptation. Some say the answer is simply to ask the federal government to throw money at the problem. My purpose, again, is to show how *coordinated action* by a diverse set of interests—including each person reading this book—is required.

The book differs in another way from the social scientific literature on social problems. I spend some time evaluating policies of the past and those recently introduced. I want to help find a rational, pragmatic way to eliminate homelessness, not just to study it. During the decade I have worked with and studied homeless people, I became an advocate for them, a role I adopt readily in this book as well.

I also want to bring the reader close to the guests I met at a remarkable institution: the St. Francis Center, a homeless shelter in Denver, Colorado. I provide, again through short stories and numbers, the culture of the organization. For ten years I have worked there as a volunteer one day a week, learning about the people, the problem, the failed policies of the past, and the promising ones introduced and tested in the past few years. I am confident that we are making progress in eliminating the problem.

Some have asked about the meaning of the title. Some encouraged me to include an explication of it in the book: The Parable of the Good Samaritan appears in the New Testament (Luke 10:25–37). In this powerful story a lawyer stood up to test Jesus by asking him how to live in such a way as to inherit eternal life. Jesus asks him in return what is written in the law. The lawyer answers, "You should love the Lord your God with all your heart, and with all your soul, and with all your strength, and with all your mind; and your neighbor as yourself." Jesus compliments him, saying he has given the right answer.

Wanting to justify himself, the lawyer asks, "And who is my neighbor?"[1]

Jesus answers with the story of the Jew who was beaten and robbed and left for dead on the road from Jerusalem to Jericho. Two separate Jews, one a priest, walk by him without offering any assistance. The Samaritan, a foreigner who is not expected to help Jews, stops, treats him with oil and wine, and then takes him to an inn. He gives the innkeeper money to pay for his food, care, and lodging. He promises to return to pay more if necessary.

The lawyer was really asking, "Who is not my neighbor?" The point of the story is that everyone is your neighbor, even foreigners who despise you. The Samaritan gave housing, gave shelter, to a complete stranger, a homeless man.

There are many people I want to thank: Let me begin with Tom Luehrs and Jean Garrison, the top two administrators at the St. Francis Center

(SFC). They have been admirable "bosses" and mentors. They both read a longer version of this book in manuscript form, catching factual errors and making suggestions. To them I add the rest of the full-time and volunteer staff. And of course, the most important people at SFC: our guests.

I want to thank Matthew Nickaloff for reading the first draft of the first three or four chapters and making suggestions. Thanks also to Larry Browning for the same kind of help at an early stage. Not only is Gregory Desilet a good reader, but he also let me test the ideas included in this book against his sharp mind in conversations over the past ten years. Thanks also to Omar Swartz, who wisely edited my two published essays on homelessness. I am greatly indebted to Roxane White, who cheerfully answered my questions, including those about the processes used by a commission she chaired: The Commission to End Homelessness in Denver within the Decade. She also read those passages relevant to her work as the head of Denver's Department of Human Services. Thanks also go out to two perspicacious and helpful editors at Paradigm Publishers: Jessica Priest and Jennifer Knerr. They made the process of acquisition and editing as delightful as possible. Others of their colleagues at Paradigm served me well, including my production editor, Carol Smith, and superb copy editor, Kathy Delfosse.

Finally, I dedicate this book to my colleague, editor, and wife, Elaine:

> *Without*
> *Whom*
> *Not*

CHAPTER ONE
DOWN AND OUT AND ON THE ROAD

It is hard not to notice Betsy Anne when she gets a stool at the corner where she can see and talk to patrons along both parts of the L-shaped bar. She is attractive, with a winning smile displaying perfect teeth, bright green eyes, and a full head of long, wavy dark brown hair. She has a husky Boston accent, likes to talk, sometimes loudly, and liberally sprinkles her discourse with obscenities—laughingly explaining that she is just one of the boys. She was sipping a "Gramma," or glass of Grand Marnier. Her hands are adorned with sterling silver rings. Some of the rings and the silver bracelets on both wrists have turquoise and black onyx stones set in them. Two sterling silver crosses often hang from her neck.

It was in the bar of a neighborhood diner in downtown Denver that I first met Betsy Anne. She took a corner stool near me, smiled, and addressed me as "Dr. Phil," saying she had heard other people refer to me that way.

"What kind of doctor are you?"

I tried to explain what the degree, doctor of philosophy, means, and what I had done at the university. She explained she had only a high school education. She was quieter than usual, asking questions and concentrating on trying to figure me out. She joked about me with a person at her other side, saying, "He doesn't even swear." I judged her to be in the early days of middle age. As she talked, I noticed a light scar that came down her left temple, following the line of her jaw. After listening to me, she began to reveal the outline of her autobiography, casually mentioning, as if talking about jobs she had held, that she had been homeless three different times in her life. I leaned toward her, immediately replying that I was writing a book on homelessness and would like to interview her. She frowned, then said she would do it if I would meet her at a nice place in downtown Denver, buy her some drinks and a bite to eat. I suggested the Broker Restaurant because it is quiet and elegant and is known for its shrimp bowl.

Betsy Anne—not her name—was forty-two years old when we began our first formal interview on March 27, 2006. Then she corrected herself: "I'm forty-three." She is five feet eight inches tall and has a voluptuous, athletic figure. We talked for a couple of hours, trying to establish the timeline of her life, but she would stop periodically to fill in missing segments and then jump forward in her narrative. I learned in the interview, conversations, and a second formal interview on the telephone that she was born in Massachusetts in 1963. She had several siblings, but her mother divorced her father for spousal abuse, and his meager child support left the family in relative poverty.

Betsy Anne married after high school, and her daughter came into the world in 1984. The father, "that sonuvabitch," disappeared, and she never received a cent of child support. She moved in with another man for eight and a half years; he turned out to be "abusive," and so she took her daughter and possessions, under police supervision, out of his place after catching him in bed with another woman. She also complained of an additional indignity—that he had allowed the woman to wear some of her clothes. She dropped her daughter off at her mother's house and lived in a car for a while, her first episode as a homeless person. A friend told her she could ride to Denver with him and stay with his aunt and uncle until she got stabilized. She took him up on the offer and got a job as bartender in a small country town near Denver, sending for her daughter thirty days later. The patrons of the bar made fun of her apparel and accent.

"I told those cowboys they were full of shit," she said with more than a trace of umbrage. The cowboys, in turn, ran her out of the job and out of town. She frowned as she recalled the unpleasantness of it all: "I'm not bad looking and I have nice jewelry. They can't tell me how to dress and talk."

She and her daughter would move twenty-one times during the next twelve months, piling in with friends, at times with mere acquaintances, until their welcome wore out. This was her second episode of homelessness. She finally got a one-bedroom apartment for the two of them, a tough accomplishment because she had neither a rental history nor a credit rating. But she soon began seeing another man who invited her to bring her daughter to live with him in his house. Not long after moving in she found him in bed with another woman. He gave her two thousand dollars and told her to leave.

She got excited in telling me the money allowed her "to get my own place, a beautiful place with two bathrooms and two bedrooms." She was bartending at a new place in Denver, and then she discovered her kitchen was infested with cockroaches. "I was paying six, seven hundred dollars and had cockroaches." She complained to the manager but got no relief, and instead the manager refused to renew her lease. As a result she became homeless for the third time.

She put their possessions in storage and moved into a friend's basement thirty days later. "He changed the locks...." She fell silent, and seemed to be having trouble expressing herself.

"What's wrong?"

"I'm rehashing some bad shit," she said quietly.

It was at this point she had to admit to herself that she had a drug problem. "My drug of choice was cocaine," she admitted, looking down at her drink, but apparently she had tried nearly everything. I stopped taking notes to ask, "Would you prefer that I not write this down?"

"What I did is what makes me what I am."

She wanted me to tell her story.

I asked her why she did drugs. The words now rushed like a mountain stream during a spring thaw. "You get so high there is nothing else. For twenty to thirty minutes there is no pain. It takes away the feeling that you are a total fuckup. I was three thousand miles away from anyone who cared about me at all."

In 1996 she quit drugs—cold turkey. "I wanted more out of life than twenty or thirty minutes of being high. My dollar is worth more than twenty to thirty minutes of no pain. I wanted my daughter to have her own bedroom." She got her own place and began to socialize with local bikers, going with them to the motorcycle rally in Sturgis, South Dakota. On Easter Day in 2003, she had a party for thirty people who had nowhere to go for the holiday, baking turkeys and hams for them. While preparing for the party, she had a bit too much to drink. She got on the back of a Harley with a driver who was drunk. She remembers nothing about that ride until she came out of a "fuckin' coma" six weeks later.

She had a badly broken leg that had been wrapped around a wheel, a tracheotomy, a brain trauma, and other ailments. I mentioned her facial scar. She nodded, "That part of my face flipped up over my eye." The bone broken in her leg became infected. She pulled up her left pant leg to show me where the broken bone had come through the skin, a dark scar about the size of a human hand on her left shin. Without emotion she pointed to what had been her calf. "They moved part of that muscle here," as she moved her hand to touch the outside part of her leg, "so that it would all work." She moved her foot up and down so that I could see how the newly positioned muscle moved the ankle.

Her mother had come out from Boston to spend Easter that year with her and wound up staying until Betsy Anne could get out of the hospital. Betsy Anne's daughter, who had given birth to a child, pulled away from her mother while she was in the coma. Betsy Anne was sad to tell me that she does not know where her daughter and grandchild are today. Her medical bills came to $276,000, "but," she said, brightening, "I had insurance." Her brother in Pennsylvania helped her mightily in many ways, one of which was to find a lawyer so that she could sue the drunken biker's insurance company. Her insurance company was awarded some money, and Betsy Anne was given an annuity that will bring her fifteen thousand dollars in 2009 and other sums of money stretched over a number of years.

Recovering from an accident she thinks should have killed her effected a profound change in Betsy Anne. She now thinks there is a reason for her existence. She wants even more out of life than she did when she gave up drugs. She got a job as head housekeeper at a country club, proud that she has "four people underneath me." She hated cleaning before the accident, but now she loves it and loves to go to work.

She now believes in God and joined a "cool church" in downtown Denver. She says, "My job here is not done yet."

She wore a bright red silk blouse. She was proud to have paid only "three bucks" for it. She does her shopping for secondhand goods at the Association of Retarded Citizens and the Salvation Army, buying her underwear at Target—and only when it is on sale. She saves money by not owning a car, riding the bus to work, stopping near our neighborhood diner-bar to wait for a transfer bus to get from work to home. She is proud that she now reads, if only on the bus (partly to avoid having to listen to other riders), showing me the novel she was reading and later expressing anger because the female protagonist was turning out to be a "bitch." The local bus drivers' union was threatening to strike at the time of our interview, and I was concerned about how she would get to work and back. "Don't worry about me," she said with smiling confidence. "I'm a survivor."

The job, frugality, her new attitude, the court's award, and her brother's efforts all came together to allow her, in October 2005, to buy her first house, an edifice she calls "my little baby mansion." It is a source of great pride to her. It makes her a real citizen with a roof and two bedrooms. As she sips her drink, she is conscious of the time, checking the bus schedule and her watch, alert to the arrival of her bus in an eagerness to get home, take care of her dog, cook dinner, clean up, and watch the tube. "There is so much to do now," she says with solemnity. "For some reason . . . ," she says, shaking her head, and in failing to finish the sentence she invites her listener to contemplate the depth of the mystery of what has happened to her.

Betsy Anne had a recording in her own voice on her telephone at home then that said, "This is Betsy Anne. I still have my house. And I always will."

There were two of us—two attendants in white shirts and pants—in the day room of a ward housing 120 male patients in the Colorado State

Mental Hospital in Pueblo, Colorado, on a sunny summer day in 1956. I had taken the job after finishing my undergraduate degree, to try to save money for graduate school in the fall. I was seated at a desk with a view of the entire day room. A large, hard-muscled, middle-aged patient sat slowly rocking in a chair close to a square column. A silent, vacant man with white hair walked between the rocker and the column, turning sideways to get through the narrow space. The man in the rocking chair was angered by what he must have perceived as an invasion of his personal space. He loudly told the old man not to do it again, but the old man seemed unable to make sense of the warning, and that was confirmed when I consulted the ward's diagnostic file card on him—catatonic schizophrenic. He circled around the day room to walk again through the narrow passage between the column and the rocking chair. The man in the chair got up, turned the older man around to face him, measured the distance between the two of them, and then hit him in the mouth with a solid left hook. The defenseless old man became an unleashed punching bag, flying backward, teeth clattering on the floor. He lay unconscious on his back, blood pumping from his nose and mouth.

New at this job, I watched to see what the other attendant, my senior and the man in charge—thus called the charge—of the ward would do. He moved immediately to subdue the man I shall call John. But John was bigger and stronger than the charge and quickly put the smaller man in white on his back on the floor, gripping the charge's throat with both hands. I moved to break the inmate's strangling hold, but in spite of having been a middleweight college wrestler, I was unable to break the grip. The charge's face was darkening as both of us struggled against John. John's arms and wrists were like steel cables, and later I learned he had had an epileptic seizure during his attempt to choke the charge.

I looked around to see that most of the 120 patients were headed toward us, and I thought my time had come. They came first at me, hands pulling me roughly off their fellow inmate. As I struggled with this insane mob, I heard the alarm ring, and a group of other inmates we called "trusties"—we rewarded them with roll-your-own tobacco and cigarette papers for help in running the ward—fought their way to the center of the action, pulling the attackers off me and pulling John off the charge, then making a human ring of protection around us. Within minutes the attendants from the other wards in the building, responding to the alarm, burst into our day room to bring about order.

In the discussions we had after the incident, the more experienced men stressed that although such incidents had been common in the past, they had become rare since the introduction of the drug Thorazene (chlorpromazine), the drug of choice for the mental hospital. My memory is that most inmates took it.

As a tyro, or newcomer, I was moved from ward to ward on a daily basis, filling in where I was needed. A couple of weeks after the incident, I was assigned to a much smaller ward for violent inmates. It was my understanding that John had been transferred to that ward, so I asked about him. The charge, a plainspoken man, walked me down the hall to John's lower-bunk bed and said, "We're killing him."

"What?"

"Yeah, we're filling him with Thorazene and restricting his movement."

Looking down at John in the bed, I could see that he was bound in a straightjacket that was chained to the bedposts. He was sound asleep even though the rest of the men on the ward were up, dressed, and in the day room. That was the last I saw or heard of John, and I later wrestled with my conscience about his fate. Was the charge telling the truth?

Not long after that troubling interaction the hospital's head nurse— later I would see an uncanny physical and rhetorical resemblance to the corresponding role in Ken Kesey's *One Flew over the Cuckoo's Nest*—called a special meeting of all the attendants at the facility. The head nurse was blunt: "We have to be more careful with the Thorazene. We're killing inmates; they're dropping like flies."

She went on to explain that Thorazene was stronger than had been realized. The intended effect was to calm the patients, but it did more than that. It slowed down all of the bodily processes … until … they … stopped … working … and the patient died. She said that doctors would examine all the patients to make sure their dosages were correct, but more importantly, we attendants had to do a better job of monitoring them after administering their dosages in the morning. We had to make sure that all of them got up from chairs in the day room and engaged in some sort of movement. Yes, said the head nurse, they had to be more active.

Inexperienced, I was surprised by the frank revelations and directions given us—even though it was in oral form, not written (no doubt for legal reasons). Back on the wards, the more experienced attendants scoffed at the recommendations. Later we did begin to see psychiatrists on the ward, but they spent little time per patient reviewing dosages, seeing a handful of inmates before hurrying on to other work. In addition, we attendants had little time to spare for monitoring the patients. We got them out of bed, saw that they were showered and dressed. We got them into a cafeteria without choices, for such decisions would have paralyzed many of the patients and would have thus made supervising a meal an eight-hour job. We also had to shave them, give them their meds, and move them into the day room. How could we watch 120 men closely enough to make sure their bodily processes were not slowing down?

I can't refrain from mentioning one other incident at the hospital before trying to relate my experience on the wards to that of being a volunteer in a homeless shelter. I met a young inmate who seemed normal. Not only did he have smooth social skills, but he dressed differently than the other inmates did, eschewing the bib overalls, blue-collar shirts, and work boots for creased slacks, sport shirts, and shiny loafers. One day in conversation we drifted from the day room to the dormitory room where the men slept. He sat down on a bed, so I sat down on another one so that we would be facing each other. I was curious: *Why is he in here?*

"Why are you in here, Jack?"

Jack—that was not his name—began his narrative by saying he had been trained in a martial art, jujitsu, as I recall. One night, he continued, he was drinking in a bar on the Western Slope of Colorado. A man sitting next to him picked an argument, then pulled a knife on him, or was it a gun?

Jack said he used a martial arts technique to disarm the man and throw him against a wall. He then walked out of the bar. He was arrested the next day by the police and charged with manslaughter because the man had died of a broken neck. Jack said he made a calculated decision to plead guilty by reason of insanity because being committed to the mental hospital in Pueblo was infinitely preferable to a sentence to the State Penitentiary in Cañon City.

I nodded, thanking him for his explanation, and got up. *He is big enough to throw me against the wall,* I thought as we walked back to the day room. He seemed relieved at having told me his story, at having unburdened himself, and pleased that I had accepted his story as credible. I was nonetheless skeptical enough to check with a reliable source in the Office of Medical Records. She gave me a different story. Jack had taken his car to a service station to have some work done. He asked how long it would take and got an estimate, but when he came back at the promised hour, his car was not ready. Jack picked up a tire tool and beat the mechanic until he fell to the garage floor. Jack continued to beat his head with the tool for forty-five minutes or so, long enough that the mechanic appeared to have been decapitated.

I had been working at the St. Francis Center, a day shelter serving homeless people in Denver, for less than a year when five homeless men were murdered in our city. On the Friday that was the anniversary of my first year as a volunteer, two of our guests wanted to talk about the murders. A short, stocky middle-aged Hispanic man I knew fairly well—his name was Joe Mendoza—said the murderer was a young Hispanic man. Another man interrupted us with his answer to the question of who had killed the men, "There are eight of them." Later in the day, Joe approached me to elaborate in private. He said he had been trying to sleep in a field behind Union Station the night before. There was a drunk lying a couple of feet away. Joe was almost asleep when he sensed someone was standing over him. He looked up, raised a fist—Joe had been a professional boxer—and asked him what was going on. The man, handsome, Hispanic, big, and about twenty-one years old, said, "Sorry, I didn't mean to disturb you." Joe paused, "Phil, what was he doing there?"

"Did he have a weapon?"

"I didn't see one," Joe answered.

I told him the executive director of our shelter, Tom Luehrs, had informed me that the beatings and killings had been administered with a "steel rod or lead pipe." Joe pondered that bit of information, and I had to move on to my next job assignment. Later I would turn this conversation with Joe over and over, wondering if the information might be useful to the police investigation. Shouldn't I encourage Joe to go to the police with the information?

I guessed Joe to be in his late forties. He was short, shorter than my height of five feet nine inches, but stocky, a Mexican American with a brown complexion and a full head of dark hair he brushed back. He was a handsome man despite the slightly flattened nose he'd got as a professional pugilist in Los Angeles. He spoke English fluently without a trace of an accent and was usually in good cheer, smiling and hailing me with a "Hi Phil." Having followed the fight game as a boy and young man, I could speak of another Los Angeles boxer, Art Aragon. Joe nodded and said he also knew Jerry Quarry, a prominent light heavyweight boxer, well.

Joe was always neat and clean, one of the most impeccable homeless men I've known. He pointedly said to me that he didn't mention his boxing experience to other men on the streets. *Like the old gunfighters,* I thought, *he didn't want to tempt anyone to challenge him*; I took this as advice, not mentioning it to others.

Joe was well liked by other people, staff members and guests alike. I hadn't seen him during the late summer, but when he showed up again in the fall, we greeted each other warmly, and in response to my question, he said he had been in Salt Lake City, Utah. I asked if he had heard about the killings. He nodded, and although he said nothing at the time, I think my question may have lighted a fuse. A desire to talk about what had happened to him the night before made him come into the shower room to relate his theory that the killer was a young Hispanic male.

According to my field notes of Wednesday, November 3, 1999, I had learned via local television news that there had been a break in the investigation of the beatings and killings. The *Denver Post* reported that three young people had been taken into custody under suspicion of beating homeless men. Local police officers referred to teenagers who haunted the central street of downtown Denver, the Sixteenth Street Mall, as "mall rats." Some of them were homeless, hanging out in Skyline Park, on Arapahoe Street between Fifteenth Street and Sixteenth Street. Some wore clothing bristling with studs and spikes, attire that shouted their alienation from, even condemnation of, society. My wife and I live a block from the park where they gathered and while walking past them felt more than a bit uncomfortable because of the threatening way they panhandled.

Three days later, the *Rocky Mountain News* reported that six young men had been charged with beating homeless men. One man had been left for dead in the South Platte River. Police sources said the motivation was a turf war between the mall rats and the older homeless men who slept and panhandled in Skyline Park.

My field notes for Thursday, November 12, quoted the headline in the *Denver Post* for that day: "terror stalks homeless," and the subtitle was "Two Headless Bodies Discovered in LoDo" (LoDo is the nickname for lower downtown Denver). The bodies were found in a field near Union Station between Fifteenth Street and Nineteenth Street. This reminded me of my conversation with Joe Mendoza at St. Francis Center two weeks earlier. Another question that came to mind was whether these crimes were committed before or after the so-called mall rats had been arrested. One article said both men appeared to have been dead for some time, and no effort had been made to conceal the bodies.

The *Rocky Mountain News* of that day ran this headline: "Lodo homeless death toll hits 7," "2 More Bodies Found." Neither head was found. The paper also reported that one of the earlier victims, Kenneth Rapp Jr., forty-two, had also been decapitated. Both newspapers ran stories describing the fear and terror among homeless people.

When I left for the shelter Friday morning, November 19, I decided that I should talk to Tom, the executive director, about my conversation with Joe. I believed we should try to persuade Joe to go to the police with his information, particularly his description of the man who may have been the killer. After Joe related the incident to me I saw him talking to Craig, a shelter staff member, raising his fist the way he had in conversation with me, making me assume he was telling Craig the same story. Later that day Craig confirmed that he had heard the same story from Joe.

I saw Craig before Tom that morning, reminding him of what Joe had told us and saying, "In light of the two murders committed in the field behind Union Station, don't you think we should talk to Tom about giving the information to the police, or asking Joe to do so?" Craig agreed. But it was such a busy day I had no chance to talk to Tom and was surprised the day was gone when we gathered around the table for a ritual at 2:00. At that precise moment Tom walked in.

"They think one of them may be Joe Mendoza." *I wonder what he means by "one of them,"* I said to myself. Then it came to me that he meant Joe was one of the headless men in the field.

I sank in disbelief and shock. Although I knew Joe had slept in that area and had been menaced there, it hadn't occurred to me that Joe could be one of the victims, partly because I knew him well, because he was in good shape, a professional athlete trained in self-defense, and because I would have thought that the previous incident would be reason enough to avoid sleeping in the same place again.

Later I would learn from a police officer that Joe Mendoza had not been decapitated; he had been bludgeoned to death, beaten so badly that his head liquefied and seeped into the ground, exactly the modus operandi used by Jack when he beat the garage mechanic to death forty-three years earlier.

Betsy Anne's life is in many ways an apt introduction to this book. We meet in her a real person, not a statistic. A key problem in her story was implicit: the high cost of housing in both Boston and Denver, true of many other cities in the United States. Her life story will help humanize the numbers we inevitably encounter in a book about homelessness. Her story also makes salient the problem of domestic violence and the fatherhood failure in our society—both of which have been producing an increasing rate of homeless women and children. Betsy Anne's response to this illustrates a third danger, the fall into drug use.

Recall that she was homeless *before* she used cocaine and other drugs. Betsy Anne's twenty minutes of ecstasy, as with much drug use, is as much an *effect* of homelessness as its *cause,* contrary to the stereotypical and opposite view of causality. Her escape from drugs is an encouraging lesson for all of us. So too is the fact that she also escaped from homelessness three different times. Although it is treacherously difficult to generalize about homeless people, she does illustrate the fact that most homeless people do get back to a domiciled life. When she most needed help—after the accident—some members of her primary group of family and intimate friends were there. She had social capital, defined by Robert D. Putnam in *Bowling Alone* as "connections among individuals—social networks and the norms of reciprocity that arise from them."[1] Her mother stayed with her; her brother got her an attorney.

Understanding the role of Betsy Anne's medical insurance is important to understanding poverty, homelessness, and their opposites. The excellent medical care she received produced both a recovery and a new sense of *purpose in life,* a new sense of worth, and a new sense of discipline and spirituality. She now wants to connect with her daughter and granddaughter. If it isn't already evident, I want to make explicit my admiration for this life, this story of a woman of grit, accomplishment, confidence, total honesty, good humor, and commitment. I intend to keep track of her as I write this book. I did worry a bit about her need to "chase checks" about the city, running to cover checks before they bounced. She insisted that it would not be right if I didn't include in this account a loan of eighty dollars to cover two checks she wrote during an emergency; and, yes, she did pay me back.

After she paid back the loan, I asked Betsy Anne to make a list of checks she'd written over the past month or so, as a way of helping her manage a bit better. She came to a realization without any further help from me that her Grammas were just about the most expensive drink she could buy. She cut down on them.

The meaning of the second story, my experience as an attendant at the Colorado State Mental Hospital, may seem to be a bit more removed from the social problem of homelessness than the story of Betsy Anne. After I left for graduate school in the fall, I hoped they got the dosages of Thorazene regulated, monitored the inmates better, and stopped killing them, intentionally or unintentionally. When I left in 1956, many of the inmates left as well. Unlike me, they had nowhere to go when they departed. As Alice Baum and Donald Burnes note, the deinstitutionalization of the mentally ill "began in the mid-1950s and was codified into law with the passage of the Community Health Center Act in 1963. The release of the mentally ill from treatment facilities was premised on new scientific developments in understanding the organic nature of mental illness and the development of psychotropic medicine to treat these disorders."[2]

In other words, the use of one of the very drugs we were killing inmates with was a premise in deciding to release them into their own communities. The lesson of my experience, however, was that the new drugs required close supervision by psychiatrists and caseworkers better trained than I and the other attendants. Did the released inmates get that supervision and monitoring? One idea held by classical organizational theory, the span of control, was proposed by L. Urwick and was discussed by Nobel Laureate Herbert Simon. The concept of span of control held that there is a mathematical limit—six or seven—to the number of people a supervisor or manager could oversee.[3] The released inmates did not get that supervision, that key communication link with society.

One person with an excellent perspective on deinstitutionalization is Lars Eighner, who, like me, was once an attendant in a state mental hospital, one in Austin, Texas. He spent five years in the admissions office and before that had worked at a walk-in crisis center. He was forced to resign from his position at the mental hospital for complaining about inhumane treatment of the inmates; a long run of bad luck in finding another job made him homeless. After deinstitutionalization began, he saw people on the street whom he had known in the asylum. Here is his evaluation of the strategy of deinstitutionalization:

> Whether this plan would have worked or not we will never know, for only half of it was implemented. The powers and resources of the central institutions were drastically reduced. But the community clinics were established in only a few places, and where they were established they were inadequate. Many communities did not want mental-health facilities right next door, although their being right next door, in touch with the neighborhoods, was a key aspect of the plan for the clinics. Breaking up the large institutions meant that economies of scale would have to be sacrificed, and neither the legislature nor the communities were willing to fund the clinics at a level that would have offered some chance for success.[4]

Making matters worse, the new wonder drugs were often prescribed where they were inappropriate and ineffective. If a normal dosage didn't work, the physicians increased it. Even when used appropriately, they had side effects that patients resented. Eighner suspected that being a little bit crazy is better than taking the full dosage, but that being a little bit crazy makes one believe she or he can do without the drugs altogether. When it was plain that the plan wasn't working, the institutions no longer had the capacity to handle large numbers of patients. That happened precisely at the moment when more people in the population needed to be hospitalized.

Baum and Burnes make an argument about the baby boomers and the failure of the deinstitutionalization plan in their book *A Nation in Denial: The Truth about Homelessness.* Nearly 76 million babies were born between 1946 and 1964, the two decades after World War II. They would change every institution they entered, from maternity wards to universities to homeless shelters. At the very time the normal distribution of mental illness in their generation would have sent them to the mental hospitals in record numbers, deinstitutionalization made sure there was no place to go. In addition, many of them joined the counterculture and the Beat generation, experimenting with illicit drugs, thus making them vulnerable to the "dual diagnosis" of mental illness and addiction, a condition dreaded by doctors and social workers. The coincidence of an increased population and the closing of mental hospitals contributed to the huge increase of homeless people in the 1980s.

Some of the inmates I served no doubt entered the host of new homeless people. It is conceivable that some of my younger patients might even have become "guests" in the St. Francis Center, the homeless shelter where I have worked as a volunteer for the past ten years.

Although I have changed the names of homeless persons mentioned in this book, I have used Joe Mendoza's real name—and others mentioned in the media—because he became a public figure by virtue of being murdered. I decided to tell his story because it is about a real encounter with a homeless man. In addition, Joe's murder, along with six others during my first year at the shelter, reveals something about the public perception of, and attitude toward, homeless people. Who could hate them so much and why? And why was so little sympathy expressed for them?

Rather than forecast the detailed content of the rest of book in this introductory chapter, I shall instead give a brief description of its overall organization. It is a narrative, a story, of my experience with an unusual organization, a homeless shelter, alternating from time to time with presentations of the history, research, and literature relevant to homelessness. A narrative of anecdotes about an organization or a tribe can reveal something of its culture. After becoming a weekly volunteer at the St. Francis Center in 1998, I began to scratch notes on the back of my work slip, an hourly breakdown of duties from 8:00 a.m. to 2:00 p.m. I began to read the scientific studies on the subject as well as the classic literary works such as George Orwell's *Down and Out in Paris and London*.[5]

When the seven homeless men were killed within the next year I felt the need to investigate the mystery of murder, to look for a theory to explain virulent killers. The narrative offers an experiential resource to readers, to allow them to learn as I did. Soon I realized my volunteering was almost a full-time job because I was serving on committees that did advocacy for homeless people, reading about poverty, and once again doing ethnographic research, a fancy phrase used by anthropologists and other social scientists for studies of a tribe or nation. I had done similar studies in such organizations as NASA and Kent State University, after that institution's tragedy, and had directed doctoral dissertations conducted by graduate students on such organizations as the U.S. Forest Service, the Catholic Church, and an aerospace contractor. All these studies took as a central assumption that communication was a central fact of organization.

While contemplating poverty and homelessness, I discovered a relationship between charity and justice that had to be explored and deconstructed. Writing this book took longer than expected because the homeless tribe wouldn't stand still; nor would the city of Denver, which dramatically changed its policies toward the poor and homeless people. The book grew and grew and moved into new spaces. I found myself observing a naturally occurring experiment. It started with a group called People in Public Places that met at the St. Francis Center and came up with a blueprint for reducing homelessness. A new mayor, John Hickenlooper, was sufficiently inspired by that document to appoint the Mayor's Commission to End Homelessness in Denver within the Decade. The commission attempted to solve Denver's problems and serve as a model for other cities. This remarkable social experiment, now called Denver's Road Home, has been going on for more than two years. Some tentative answers are emerging.

CHAPTER TWO

CHRISTMAS IN THE ST. FRANCIS CENTER

ENTRY, SOCIALIZATION, ASSIMILATION

The fall of 1998 was a season of irony and oppositions. President Bill Clinton announced in early October that the United States had a record budget surplus. On November 20, the House of Representatives began its hearings on his impeachment. On November 6 the Security Council of the United Nations voted to condemn Iraq for noncompliance with arms inspections. My personal concern was with retirement, relocation, and the attendant ambivalent feelings about ending one endeavor while searching for another.

I decided to retire from full-time teaching at the University of Colorado at Boulder. My wife and I moved to Denver's downtown area, buying a loft a block away from the main artery of downtown, the Sixteenth Street Mall, closed to vehicular traffic other than a free bus shuttle connecting the civic center and state capitol in the uptown section with the bus terminal and train station in lower downtown, or LoDo, a section of revitalization and gentrification. We had access, either by the mall bus or by walking, to the Denver Art Museum, the library, the Performing Arts Center, bookstores, restaurants, delicatessens, and other distractions. But there were also street people, panhandlers who could be annoying. We occasionally saw people sleeping in covered bus stops or alleys and on grates. But that didn't prevent us from relishing a largely peripatetic existence.

While shopping around for an urban church, we heard a "mission moment" in which Tom Luehrs, executive director of the St. Francis Center, gave an appeal for volunteers to work in his homeless shelter. I was persuaded by his description of a job offering nothing more than nonmaterial incentives and rewards. So I gave the shelter a call.

I reached Carla, the coordinator of volunteers, and we agreed to meet at the shelter on Thursday, October 29, 1998, to discuss my candidacy as a volunteer. At about 8:45 a.m., I walked in the front door of the St. Francis Center into a large day room full of people. There were two greeters on either side of the entrance. I asked one of them where I could find Carla.

"Phil?" Carla broke into a broad smile. We shook hands, and she invited me to sit on a stool near hers so that I could observe what was happening until a meeting ended and a replacement could relieve her. She was one of the two persons screening the people who wanted to come into the building. My eyes were on the people checking in. I noticed some weatherworn faces with bruises and scars, hands with black and broken nails, skin with black creases and scabs. Some had physical handicaps. Others looked like ordinary citizens. I scanned the great room. I had read enough postmodern philosophy to recognize what Michel Foucault, following Jeremy Bentham, called the "panopticon." This is an architectural design allowing a person in a certain position—such as on my stool—to observe everyone in the hall, an important concept in social control.[1] SFC would not, of course, monitor minute behaviors by an invisible watcher as described by Bentham and Foucault, and yet some degree of discipline is maintained.

Most people were sitting in chairs at long tables, a few asleep with chin on chest, and some with head on table. Others played cards or simply talked, but some sat alone and apart, oblivious to the several hundred people in the room—their hues ranging from white to red to brown to black. Later I would learn that Denver's statistics differed from the national average for homeless people: more whites, fewer African Americans, more Native Americans and Hispanics. Many Lakota Sioux made their way south from the Pine Ridge Reservation in South Dakota to Denver, while some Hopis and Navajos came north from New Mexico.

My field notes indicate that Carla asked entering guests for their TB cards (evidence they had been tested for the disease) and recorded each person's name in a ledger. She had to check a list of people "eighty-sixed" (thrown out) from the St. Francis Center for behaviors proscribed by the center's rules. She would also ask each person if he or she were entering for the first time that day. She explained that she didn't want to count the same person twice because a total number of persons entering the building for the day would be entered on a calendar hanging from the wall not far away. In addition, there was a limit on how many times a person could enter and leave, in order to minimize guests' time on the street outside the center and, thus, the time they were visible to the neighbors.

A large Native American man approached Carla from the world outside with a question: "Have you heard anything about Short Stuff?"

"I've been hearing all morning that she was killed, but it's not confirmed," answered Carla.

"She's one of my best friends," said the handsome man, clearly in pain.

After he moved on, Carla explained to me that even though the staff and volunteers were safe at SFC, the area surrounding it could be dangerous for the street people. Carla speculated that a drug deal might have gone bad. (Happily enough, Short Stuff had not been killed. I later met her, a small, white, attractive woman who stood less than five feet tall. She preferred as a nickname "Little Bit" and was amused, like Mark Twain, by the exaggerated report of her death.)

After thirty minutes Carla's replacement arrived, allowing her to take me through a door into an area that looked like a kitchen, with sink, refrigerator, cabinets, and microwave ovens. There was a telephone, bulletin boards, and a large circular table. She moved me into a private office, seated me in front of a television set, and punched in a videotape: *The Bridge of Hope*. I was participating in what people in organizational communication called entry, socialization, and assimilation (topics defined and researched by the late Fredric Jablin).[2] I was, in short, entering an established organization, one trying to "socialize" or shape me into the kind of contributor it needed and to make me feel at home in a new role and organization.

"There are no clients, only guests at the St. Francis Center," said a talking head. A handsome young white man was shown at his "camp" on the South Platte River that skirts Denver. He said that SFC provided services he couldn't do without. Those services were carefully explained, and as a student of communication I became especially interested in four of them. It is a place where the guests can make and receive telephone calls, receive and send mail, meet friends and make new ones, and get assistance such as help with finding a job, managing their money, handling health issues, and dealing with other important problems.

After the video came to an end, Carla gave me a tour of the huge building. As we walked about, she said that SFC had been open for thirteen years and functioned only as a *day* shelter, between 8:00 a.m. and 2:00 p.m. during good weather, Monday through Friday, and until 4:00 p.m. during bad weather. *It is open to the rhythm of the seasons,* I thought. SFC was closed on Saturday, open half a day on Sunday for some services and an Episcopal service. *There are daily rhythms as well.*

We walked through the great room and out a door onto a walled patio where guests could smoke and park their shopping carts. She showed me a new wing of the building with facilities for classes and meetings. There were separate shower facilities for men and women. There was a laundry with industrial washers and dryers for towels and used clothing the center tried to recycle. There was a clothing room, a place guests could enter with a yellow clothing slip earned by performing a chore for the center, perhaps sweeping the sidewalks in front of the building or mopping the floors inside.

As a person entered the big room, to the left was a large section set off by glass partitions and counters. This was called the mail/storage area, sometimes simply "m/s" on a volunteer's work slip. (Later I was amused by a pun one of the guests made about mail/storage: "That's where they store the males.") There were two places with a break in the glass partitions where I could see guests lining up. At one window they could get access, after establishing their identity, to a walled-off space with shelves holding over four hundred thirty-gallon storage bags, in some cases containing all of a person's material possessions. At the other window, they lined up to get mail and messages.

"Half suffer from mental illness," said Carla, "and some say 90 percent if you count addictions as mental illness." Guests were not welcome if they had been drinking or were high on drugs; nor could they come in if they had been eighty-sixed for breaking the rules of the shelter. The rules were there to show respect for the other, for everyone, guests and staff, in the building. Not unimportantly, I later heard the director say, the rules were also there to help the guests achieve some discipline, a space where they had some order in their life.

I learned some history on the guided tour. SFC was founded in 1983 by the Reverend Bert Womack, a priest working on behalf of the Episcopal Diocese of Colorado, to serve the increasing population of homeless people in Denver and Colorado. SFC was established in a corridor of charitable service organizations such as the Denver Rescue Mission and the Samaritan House. NIMBYism (Not in My Backyard) manifested itself. There was a protest by neighbors when SFC opened; they no doubt feared the shelter would affect their property values and would bring undesirables into their lives.

Father Womack had discovered a niche in the service sector in Denver that SFC would fill. There were shelters where individuals could sleep at night and other places for families, although there have never been enough beds for all the homeless people in the city. There were places where they could get a meal or a sandwich to go, but on bad days there was no place for them to get in out of the weather, let alone have access to the *communication* resources of SFC that kept most of the guests linked at least minimally with society. On a busy day at that time, there might be three hundred guests in the big room.

Carla and I agreed that I would make Friday, October 30, 1998, my first full day as a volunteer. I knew that I would be in training for some time, understood that it would be necessary in order to master the complex rules by which everyone, guest, staff member, and volunteer, played the game. As I walked the eight blocks home, I felt good about joining an organization with such high purpose and high-value premises, which would lead to humane conclusions or decisions, a haven where love and acceptance are shared.

I had been given the opportunity as a young man in 1967 and 1968 to work as a visiting faculty consultant in organizational communication to Wernher von Braun, director of NASA's Marshall Space Flight Center. During this period, the 7,200 employees, civil service workers, were completing the research and development on the *Saturn V,* the moon rocket. Never have I seen people so deeply identified with an organization and its projects. I began to feel it myself, slipping easily into the "we" of inclusion and solidarity. I was making a trip to the moon. The identification altered my identity. Now this process of self-persuasion was happening to me again in regard to my relationship with the St. Francis Center.

On the morning of Friday, October 30, 1998, I walked to SFC with my lunch in a brown bag for my first day as a volunteer. From our loft, I walked the eight blocks to the shelter at 2323 Curtis Street, passing from one world into another, from one social level to another. I walked through the busy and tidy flow of the Sixteenth Street Mall, past several modern high-rise office buildings, then through a semi-industrial area, and finally into a rough section some residents then called the Devil's Triangle. The closer I came to the shelter, the more litter there was on the sad streets and sidewalks. It was a short walk of eight blocks for me and a vast existential distance.

I got to the shelter at 7:15, before it would open at 8:00 to the guests; many were waiting on the sidewalk outside. I excused myself as I snaked through them to get to the door, knock, and gain entry. Carla had told me about a voluntary ritual the staff and some volunteers participated in before the doors were opened to all. After putting on my name tag, I joined in as members of the group each got a handful of salt (blessed by an Episcopalian priest) and a hymnal; we set out marching in single file into nearly every nook of the building, even into the women's and men's showers, singing and throwing salt on the floor and into the corners. No one ever explained all this to me, but I took it to be in part a purification rite, an attempt to bless the shelter, making it ready for the poor to enter.

Then we gathered around a long table in the great room. The coordinator for the day, a young man with long reddish brown hair and beard named Mike, read a passage about Halloween from a book with the title *The Hermit's Handbook*. This precipitated "sharing time." Over the next few weeks, I would come to understand the pattern. Very often there were theological implications to the stimulus material and the discussions of it, and nearly always the discussants tried to make applications to the past work of the center and to that ahead of us in the coming day.

At about 7:45 Mike ended the sharing discussion, picking up a bottle of olive oil, holding it upside down to moisten his finger. Then he turned to the person on his left, tracing a cross with the moistened finger on the palm of each hand, then a cross on the person's forehead, quietly blessing the recipient with words I couldn't hear. The person blessed by Mike repeated the anointment of the person to the left until all had been blessed, and each had blessed another. Mike then asked us all to hold hands as he said a prayer for the day's work.

As a man who had spent his entire career at state universities and thus been made sensitive to the separation of church and state, I'd never participated in, or even observed, religious rituals in my organizational life—except the quasi-religious commencement rituals. Now I found myself marching, singing a hymn, throwing salt, and praying with strangers in a strange place, all before 8:00 a.m.

It is my more carefully considered opinion that these rites and rituals at SFC, including a simpler one at the end of the day, are designed to evoke a commitment, rationale, and discipline through religious symbolism and a sense of "communion" that help forestall the *burnout* experienced in organizations that serve poor and homeless persons.

Mike handed out the work slips to the volunteers. Each hour of the day until 2:00 was printed in the left-hand column, and a room was penciled in on the blank to the right of it. "Showers" was written in on my slip for the first hour, but I was to accompany an experienced volunteer and watch what he did. Cecil, an Episcopalian priest and retired professor of religious studies, showed me the way, unlocking the door the men would enter and then unlocking a supply cabinet inside a square made by tile counters and a door to the clothing room. We stood inside the area described by the counters. He put a towel at the right angle of the L-shaped counters; on the towel he put deodorant, a jar of petroleum jelly, condoms, Q-tips, and toothpaste so the men could help themselves. The lids and caps were placed in the cabinet so that the containers would be less likely to walk out of the shower room. At 8:00 the front doors were opened, and soon we had fifteen or twenty men in the room.

Although we called it a shower room, it was much more than that. As the men came in the door from the big room, they could see an area at the right end of the room with stools on one side and urinals on the other. If they turned to the left they could approach our counters; past the counters were sinks and mirrors on either side of the walls; past that area were four tile benches, facing each other in pairs, where the men could undress for showering, dry off, and put their clothes on; beyond the benches were the showers themselves, four heads on the end wall, and three showerheads on the other two sides forming the end of the long room opposite the toilets and urinals.

The men walked up to the counter and picked up the towels, floor mats, and facecloths Cecil had put out for them. Cecil also sold them razors for a dime, toothbrushes for the same amount, and combs for a nickel. Cans of shaving cream, without tops, were located between the sinks, along with bars of soap on trays mounted on the walls. The walls of the shower had dispensers of a green liquid the men used as shampoo and body soap. There were also trays for bars of soap.

As the men undressed in the area with the benches, many revealed stigmas, from the Greek word for bodily marks: Fresh wounds and old scars abounded; there were many tattoos. A man would approach Cecil with a dirty pair of socks in one hand and ask for a clean, if previously owned, pair. Cecil would give him a clean pair after the man dropped the dirty ones in a bucket half full of water and a deodorant soap.

After a shower or a shave the men used the deodorant stick, wiping it on the towel first and then on their armpits, sometimes on the outside of their shirts. I didn't know what to think when the first man asked Cecil for "smellgood," making it sound like one word. Cecil understood him to be asking for aftershave lotion or cologne. In the dressing area there was a plastic clothing basket where the men dropped their dirty towels, as well as dirty clothes we would wash, dry, and place in the clothing room for recycling. Under a square hole in the counter was another clothing basket for the men to put items in on their way out. When a basket was full, Cecil carried it back to the laundry, returning with a basket of clean towels, floor mats, and facecloths.

At nine o' clock we moved on. I went to the great hall, to "m/s," short for "mail/storage," to observe that operation. I sat on a stool to watch how the staff and volunteers helped our guests, who formed two lines. A guest who wanted to get his or her storage bag would line up at the window closest to the storage room, ask to get the bag, giving his or her last name and then first name. The worker would dive into a box of yellow forms, arranged alphabetically by surname, and if the form was found the worker would ask the guest for the last four digits of his or her Social Security number. (I later learned to ask Hispanic guests without Social Security numbers for their mother's maiden name, which was written on the form.) If the name and numbers agreed, the worker took the guest into the storage room to get the bag from the shelves, which were arranged along all four walls with two sets of shelves standing back to back in the middle of the room. The worker checked the name on the bag's tag, and if the names matched, the worker accompanied the guest back out to the great room.

What if the worker couldn't find the guest's form in the file? It might mean that the worker would have to do some emotional labor that we all came to dread: informing the guest that the bag had been purged because he or she failed to renew it within thirty days. Some guests anticipated the cruel news and handled the situation with equanimity. Others, however, showed a variety of emotions, such as dejection and anger that *everything* was lost.

When a guest was done with his storage bag, he or she returned to the same window to return it to the proper space. The worker accompanied the guest to return the bag, and I learned from watching that there was a rule that a worker may take only one guest at a time into the storage room.

What happened to the space vacated when a bag was purged or a guest no longer needed the space? All bags had to be returned by 2:00 p.m. on weekdays when mail/storage closed. Any empty spaces after that would be listed for reassignment the next morning. I later learned that there was a rush to the storage window the next morning when the shelter opened to see if any spaces were available.

I also watched how the workers handled guests at the mail and message window. The guests would ask a volunteer to "check my mail," perhaps for that day's mail, the day before's mail, or mail for the whole week. The guest would say her or his surname and then first name to the worker, sometimes showing an ID if the spelling was unusual. If a guest's last name was, say, Smith, the worker would check the "S" file for envelopes or for colored cards that indicated that a larger package was stored elsewhere. Some guests joked about their good fortune at not getting any bills. At times a person would be deeply disappointed, expecting a Social Security card, a check, or a letter from someone dear. If there was mail, the worker would ask for the guest's photo ID to verify his or her identity. Meanwhile, there was a telephone on the counter that rang with calls from guests asking for a mail check or requesting to renew their storage space, but guests in person took precedence over those on the phone.

At ten o'clock Mike gave me a fifteen-minute break in the room with the round table. A volunteer named Joe with a difficult Polish last name brought fresh doughnuts on Friday morning; another named Jan brought pastries she baked at home. Staff workers put out corn chips and salsa, a tradition at the shelter. There was an urn full of coffee, another with hot water for tea and instant decaf coffee. The break gave me a chance to learn about the others by listening to their conversations.

At 10:15, and every hour after that, I went to a new room to learn how to do a new job. I learned to work behind the counter in the clothing room, where guests lined up to ask for this or that item of clothing. By far the most popular item was a pair of clean blue jeans. (I would later learn that the most popular size of men's underwear was 30–32, which says a lot about the life of homeless, carless people who spend a great deal of time walking and who are rarely in a kitchen surrounded by enticing foods.) A guest asked to see "the jewelry box," going through the costume jewelry in search of something valuable, perhaps an object to wear, pawn, or give to a friend. Guests waiting to get in the clothing room encouraged the gatekeeper to make sure no one spent more than fifteen minutes shopping. "This isn't K-Mart," they said to the people shopping for items hanging from racks. Some guests complained about low supplies, but most seemed genuinely grateful for their new apparel.

In the laundry room I learned how to operate the washers: how much bleach and soap to put in, how to fold towels, and—a complex, demanding art—how to match a dryer full of socks. When we caught up, we went to the donation bin, carried the bags to a table, and began doing a kind of content analysis. Some people collect and then bring us little bottles of shampoo and conditioner they don't finish in motel and hotel rooms, and little bars of soap with a paper wrapper. We get lots of used clothing. I saw workers smelling the clothes, checking whether the donors had given us clean clothes. I was taught, however, to toss any item of clothing into the recycle can if it was stained or ragged or in such a condition that I wouldn't wear it.

From the very beginning, I didn't like this work as much as working in mail/storage, the clothing room, and the men's showers because I enjoyed interacting with the guests. I would learn much from them, engaging in "research conversations," a research method Herbert Kaufman described in his study of the U.S. Forest Service.[3] I asked questions of our guests while walking back to get a bag in the storage room or during a slow time in the showers, taking down their words if the situation allowed, otherwise making notes as soon as possible. During my entry period, the guests knew more about the rules than I did, helping me learn the job, the rules, and the culture.

Mike gave me the early lunch period, from 11:15 to 12:00. I got my brown bag out of the refrigerator, listened to the old-timers talk at lunch, and asked questions. After lunch I wound up in mail/storage again. I sat on my stool watching and listening. After a while, there was a long line at the storage window. I couldn't resist getting off the stool to help. After I got the knack, we seemed to be serving more people faster than before. I felt as though I was making a timely contribution. Then I heard Mike ask me to get back on my stool and watch. He seemed uncomfortable in giving me this message, and so did I. My discomfort turned to chagrin, however, when he said he noticed that I had failed to check the file to verify a guest's Social Security number.

I got back on my stool, needing only a conical hat to personify the perfect dunce. My humiliation gave rise to the flight impulse. What the academic jargon calls "organizational entry/assimilation" threatened to become "disengagement/exit."

But the reader knows that I couldn't have written this book some years later had I fled the organization that day. No, I stayed to learn how better to serve. In retrospect I shouldn't have jumped into action, even though my motives were good, but I now understand how I could have forgotten to check the guest's form before taking him in to get his bag. I was learning partly by *mimesis,* by imitating what I saw other volunteers and staff members do. Some rules at the center can be waived under certain conditions. Over time volunteers get to know some of the guests quite well and can call them by name. When that happens, one doesn't have to check the storage form for Social Security numbers or check the photo ID before giving out mail and messages. I saw others doing it without understanding why, imitated them, was corrected, and learned the lesson the hard way.

There was another voluntary meeting at 2:00, the time mail/storage counter, the clothing room, and the showers all close, and volunteers were welcome to attend or were free to go home. We gathered around the table in our all-purpose room. The coordinator picked a psalm to read, asking one person to read one or two verses, then letting the next person do the same, until we got to the end. After that we discussed the day—"busy" was the key word that day. At the end of the discussion, Mike again led us in prayer, pausing to let us come up with the name of a person to be remembered in prayer for particular reasons. After the prayer we broke up, taking our badges off. They are red, the size of a playing card. In the upper-left quadrant there is a white shield with a red cross in it; the upper-right quadrant on my badge has "phil" in white letters. Under that, again in white, it indicates I am a member of the

VOLUNTEER
STAFF
ST. FRANCIS CENTER

I put mine back in the row for Friday volunteers, said goodbye, walked out the door, and turned right to walk the eight blocks back to our loft.

I began transforming my scratch notes and memories of the day into my field notes, still terribly upset about my gaffe. Over the next several months, I would write about my relationship with the center, the other workers, and the guests, happy to note instances indicating acceptance of me and recognition of contributions I made. Everybody called me Phil at first, but as the guests got to know me better it became "boss," "brother" or "bro," "Felipe" and "amigo" by some Hispanics, and, inevitably, "Dr. Phil."

By late November, I was writing about helping Joe, a fellow volunteer, clean the showers, sinks, and toilets. I was humbled by the work. Joe asked me to pick up the used soap bars on the floor of the shower room. I put on rubber gloves, but the used soap was so slimy I had to wash the gloves from time to time. The stench from the oblong drain was unpleasant. Long hairs were embedded in the mushy soap. *This is service,* I kept saying to myself.

On Friday, December 4, I was trained again in the showers from ten to eleven by Matt, a young biochemist who tested beer at Coors Brewing Company. An African American man asked if he could take a clean towel with him because he lived on the street. I said "no," believing I was following the rule, and Matt backed me up. The man said he'd go ask Mike, the coordinator, grabbing a towel in his hand. Matt asked him not to take the towel with him, but the man left two bags of groceries on the counter as a form of security deposit.

"Fuck you," he said when he returned the towel in anger. "I don't need it."

At the postwork ritual a staff member named Jerry showed us a draft of a list of all the center's rules in the form of "job descriptions."

"What would a social scientist say about that?" asked Cecil, the priest-professor.

"Max Weber was an important sociologist," I said. "He predicted that the rational-legal form of authority based on rules would invade all aspects of our life over time." Jerry laughed good-naturedly.

At ten on that same day I had moved into the clothing room to train at the door. A guest who had told me earlier she was an FBI agent tried to take out a garment already crossed out on her clothing slip. She appealed to my trainer; he supported me.

"They're stealing the slips again and altering them. I didn't take that garment," said the disturbed guest.

I worked the clothing room again in the afternoon, this time at the counter. Jack the chess player came in during a slow period, and I was able to get him to open up. He recognized me from having watched him play chess on the outside boards provided on the median of the Sixteenth Street Mall between Curtis and Arapahoe, just a block away from our loft. I knew enough chess to recognize Jack as an outstanding player. He modestly denied it, saying that if he lived in Russia he would be only an "average" player.

"Chess is why I'm homeless," he said. "I like the game too much." But then he qualified his diagnosis by adding, "Chess and a double hernia."

I asked him to explain what that meant. He delivered a trenchant criticism of what he called the "labor halls."

"Unions?"

"No," he answered, "they sound like unions, but they aren't." He narrated at length how he got his hernias. He took a job with a day-labor company at $5.15 per hour. They took him to a golf course where he and others were directed to drag a plastic sheet into a large hole that would become a pond. It was raining, adding greatly to the weight of the heavy plastic sheet.

"When we showed up, their regular workers were sitting on their backhoes and other equipment, and they wouldn't do the work we were assigned to." That is how Jack the chess player earned his hernias.

Craig, a staff member acting as the gatekeeper, heard our conversation, adding to it "That's why we don't recommend those places to our guests."

On Friday, December 11, Tom lit two advent candles during the sharing discussion. The discussion turned to burnout of service workers. Social workers were described as becoming frustrated in no time because they expect to be able to "fix" poor and homeless people. The implication was that we, the staff and volunteers, knew better than the social workers did. I spoke up, trying to achieve a balanced position. I acknowledged that I had been properly taught at SFC not to try to fix the guests, that it was enough to help them get through another day. And yet, in my reading about the poor and homeless, it distressed me to learn that the poor are multiplying in our prosperous nation and city. The other side of me, I said, wanted to try to fix our policies and legislation. After the discussion, two members of the staff thanked me for my remarks.

I worked the first hour at mail/storage, moving from there to the clothing room at nine, working the door for the first time alone. Lukas, a staff member who had migrated from the Czech Republic to the United States, was working behind the counter. I returned a pair of socks and a pair of pants to him, saying, "That guy had already received those items."

"Good work," said Lukas with a smile.

I worked the showers at ten for the first time without a trainer. It warmed me to hear "Thank you, brother" and "Thank you, Phil" from the men. I put on rubber gloves to pick up used towels some men forgot to put in the baskets because I learned during my training that they sometimes have blood and fecal material on them, a good way to pick up hepatitis and other diseases. My field notes indicate the feelings I had that morning: It was good "walking through my brothers with concern only for the stench (one of my co-workers had admitted to anxiety while doing that job)."

Fortunately we had some smellgood that morning. I poured out some in the hands of a quick-witted Hispanic man who slapped it on his face, saying to an African American man, "Hey Cadillac, you'll want some of this—it has alcohol in it—but don't drink it." Everyone laughed, including Cadillac.

"Why do they call you Cadillac?" I asked.

He slapped a shopping cart—we let guests bring them into the center—and his was the biggest and shiniest I've ever seen. It was full of blankets and other necessities, but it also had several large plastic bags of crushed aluminum cans tied to its sides. Cadillac and others like him could in those days make a fair amount of money (and also benefit blighted neighborhoods) by acting as the scavengers in an important recycling process.

Carla asked me if I could work Christmas Day, Friday, from the sharing at 8:15 to noon, with a Eucharist Service at 9:00. I thought of my family, asking if my wife Elaine and my daughter Emily could come to the service. She said yes, adding that Tom's wife and children had come to the service the preceding year.

I replied that I would have to check with Elaine.

I walked home against the sun, surprised at how warm it was. The radiant heat of the sun at Denver's mile-high altitude makes one feel much warmer than the ambient temperature. An additional sense of warmth came from my increasing security and sense of communion with the staff and the guests.

At the sharing on Friday of the following week, the eighteenth, I brought up the mission statement of the St. Francis Center. Several people said they had read it, a framed copy of fine calligraphy hanging on the wall outside Tom's office. I told them of having copied it so that I could take it home and study it, adding that I thought parts of it might be relevant to the discussion. This is how it reads:

> Mission Statement
> To better proclaim the enabling love of our Lord Jesus Christ to the poor and needy—to those whom our society has labeled "disposable." As our Lord himself became incarnate to the poor, we seek to manifest His love physically with material assistance—feeding the hungry, clothing the naked, sheltering the homeless. In embracing those whom He sends, we embrace Him in His distressing disguise.
>
> Our constant prayer is that as we are experienced, people experience Him in us.
>
> A haven where love, acceptance, and hope are shared.

I wince today at the lexical choice in the first line—"enabling"—because there are critics of SFC who use that as a code word to say we are pimps for bums, winos, and crackheads. The head of a local agency that takes a tough, no nonsense approach to getting people off booze and other drugs says that SFC and agencies like us are *enablers,* making it possible for our guests to survive an irresponsible life of drunkenness and addiction. I guess he wants us to "fix" them whether we can or not. And what would he have us do with those who aren't addicts, those poor souls who are mentally or physically handicapped?

Another reason I brought up the mission statement was that I wanted help identifying the source of one line that sounded familiar: "In embracing those whom He sends, we embrace Him in His distressing disguise."

No one knew the source, but I learned that the founding director of the St. Francis Center, Reverend Womack, would be the celebrant of the service on Christmas morning. Perhaps he could remember where that line came from.

Some staff members were concerned about a dramatic change in the weather. Although the winter had been mild, Tom said, we had lost five or six persons recently to exposure, and sixty during the year 1998.

That evening Elaine and I attended a vigil for homeless people at the civic center in front of the County Building. Arriving at 6:15 p.m., we were surprised by the "Merry Christmas" message on the building and a life-sized crèche, because it seemed to violate the separation of church and state. Some of my colleagues were carrying a St. Francis Center banner. We held signs saying, "Still no room in the inn." Elaine and I decided to leave by 7:30 for a warm meal in the nearby Trinity Grille because the temperature had dropped to eight degrees above zero. Unlike some, we had a warm home to go home to.

The center decided for various reasons to open on a Saturday, December 19, and I agreed to help out because I feared Tom and Carla would have to do it by themselves. After hanging up my coat, Tom asked me if I wanted to open the storage area and run it by myself. I was thrilled to have an important job. My mood was also elevated by the gratitude of the guests, who, because they knew our usual practices, hadn't expected us to open on a Saturday morning. It was a doubly pleasant surprise for them to be able to get in out of the cold and to have access to their belongings. They thanked me more profusely than ever, calling me "brother" several times and "buddy."

I took careful scratch notes of one character walking about, a tall black man dressed in a jacket, three layers of leggings, and a hat with ear flaps; when he stopped walking, he adopted the fashion model's stance, placing his right heel at the instep of his left foot as if in a model's pose, and raised his eyes to the ceiling and began a dialogue with a higher, if invisible, power. He spoke, and then his body language indicated he could hear a response inaudible to me. He shouted and pointed his finger upward. I lost track of him and his inaudible utterances until I saw him walking toward the exit. But he stopped short when he noticed for the first time the small crèche on the counter by the door. He froze. Finally he spoke without voice, but I could read his lips: "Happy Birthday, Lord."

The week leading up to Christmas was frigid, but it warmed up enough on the day itself for me to walk to the shelter. I got a cup of coffee and chatted with Tom about falling financial support from the federal government for homelessness in Denver. He called me into his office to tell me that people in my department at the university had collected money and donated it to SFC in honor of my retirement. I muttered something about knowing "they had such plans."

"Thanks," Tom said solemnly.

"Well, I knew you would know best how to spend it." I felt great about the gift, Tom's attitude, and his expression of thanks.

We let the guests in at 8:45. Elaine and Emily entered the building just before 9:00. The three of us sat on the front row of chairs lined up for the service. The celebrant of the service was Bert Womack and the homily, delivered by Jerry Winterowd, then the bishop of the Episcopal Diocese of Colorado, was short and adapted to the situation. I returned to mail/storage for an hour after the service and could see Emily and Elaine serving cookies, punch, and lemonade to our guests, obviously enjoying the task.

After Reverend Womack changed out of his robe, I asked him about the mission statement. He said he had helped to write it, calling it a "corporate project." I asked him about the "distressing disguise" line, and he said they took it from something Mother Teresa wrote.

"Where?"

"I don't remember."

He told me that his visit to SFC that day reminded him how much he missed the place.

Elaine and Emily drove home after the party, and I walked back at noon. An old man with a runny nose approached me near the Westin Hotel, asking me if I knew of a church where they were serving a free meal. No, I said, but I'd heard that the Denver Rescue Mission was serving three meals that day, and pointed the way for him. He headed off in that direction after wishing me "Merry Christmas."

CHAPTER THREE

THE HISTORY OF HOMELESSNESS

AMERICA AND DENVER

There are two different but overlapping populations of homeless people captured in the title of the definitive history of the subject in the United States: *Down and Out, On the Road: The Homeless in American History,* by Kenneth L. Kusmer.[1] Other books had used one or other of the phrases *down and out* and *on the road* before the historian Kusmer did. George Orwell used the first in his title *Down and Out in Paris and London,* even though that book describes the working poor as well as tramps.[2] Peter Rossi, an American social scientist, used it for a completely different kind of book, a quantitative survey of homeless people in Chicago, *Down and Out in America: The Origins of Homelessness.*[3] There are at least two other relevant books with the word *road* in the title: Jack London's *The Road*[4] and Jack Kerouac's *On the Road.*[5] Because much of the rest of this book deals mainly with those who are down and out, the urban poor and homeless people down on their luck, I would like to examine the other group, those "on the road," to understand the similarities and differences.

There were homeless people in the colonial era, but then they were the "wandering poor" or "vagrants." Although they were noticeable in the late eighteenth century, they grew in number in the 1820s during industrialization, when work became dangerous and grindingly boring. By

35

the 1840s towns and cities were creating rooms for the overnight lodging of the wanderers, and charitable organizations formed to deal with the problem. Homelessness was not a national problem, however, until the 1870s, when many factors combined to produce a new human being— the "tramp." The tramps rode the trains without paying; some bullied train crews and frightened farmers along the railroad tracks. During that period some poor people went on the road, while others—the down and out—gravitated toward the cities. The former were younger and more adventurous, the latter older and more settled. Some had to go on the road to find seasonal work in agriculture and construction.

What were the factors that produced this new actor, the tramp, in American history? First was the Civil War: the Northern troops invading the South traveled in boxcars or cattle cars, just like the animals the cars were designed for. In addition, the men were taught how to forage for peaches, apples, corn, and other food. Foraging soldiers of both forces stripped farms near the railroad tracks. Gradually the line disappeared between legitimate expropriation for biological needs and the theft of valuables. The Union Army thus trained the soldiers to be tramps. As Kusmer points out, the words *tramp* and *bum* come from the Civil War era. Soldiers went on "tramps" of their own; *bum* was a more derisive term for a foraging soldier, its meaning close to that of *vagrant*. Other new words came into being when the tramps and bums took to the road. Tramping soldiers had "colonies," later called "jungles" by the tramping veterans who built fires to keep warm and to cook the food they gathered by foraging and begging from farmers.[6]

After the Civil War there were other factors that contributed to the national problem, one being a severe three-year recession. Two-thirds of the inhabitants of prisons in Massachusetts, Pennsylvania, and Illinois in 1866 and 1867 were veterans of the war between the North and the South. This vagrant population was concentrated in the big cities, but it spread to the countryside and small towns with the expansion of the railroads. The Civil War vets knew how to ride the trains illegally, depending on the generosity of the housed when they could, foraging when they couldn't. They also worked, picking crops and building the infrastructure of the West.

Other than being settled later than cities in the East, Denver had a similar history. One history of Denver begins this way:

"Our camp is beautifully situated on the bank of the river, which is here about 100 yards wide—our tents are pitched in a grove of cottonwood trees that shade us from the scorching rays of the sun," wrote Capt. John Bell, the official journalist of Major Long's expedition, on July 5, 1820. The river was the South Platte and the place was near the mouth of Cherry Creek. The sun was the western sun on a hot summer day and the trees were the only kind of deciduous trees that grew large enough to give shade in what Major Long called the Great American Desert.[7]

Ever since then, that settlement of "Indians, beaver trappers, traders, buffalo butchers, explorers, dragoons, and just plain tourists" that became Denver, Colorado, has had more people than housing to shelter them.[8] In the spring of 2000, I accompanied an outreach worker to this very location to find people camping under bridges, in tents, and under the cottonwood trees.

The gold rush of 1858 brought emigrants (the word *immigrants* came later) from the Midwest and the East, many of whom would become "gobackers," returning to their homes in disappointment and anger over having been misled by the stories of rich ores in Denver and the surrounding area. There was a silver rush to Georgetown, a short drive today from Denver on Interstate 70. Those who rushed there were disappointed when they realized that no one knew how to extract the riches from the dross. People in Denver lived in mainly wooden structures, in addition to the tents and huts and log cabins. A fire fanned through those incendiary structures in 1864, making many people homeless. Legislation specified that brick and stone had to be used in starting anew, making Denver a mason's heaven ever since.

An economic blow was delivered to the dusty town of Denver when the Union Pacific Railroad decided in 1886 to build across the plains of Wyoming rather than up and over the mountains of Colorado, delaying growth and "progress." This would delay also the arrival of the new tramps reaching Denver by rail until 1870, when the Denver Pacific Railroad tapped the transcontinental railroad at Cheyenne, Wyoming, laying track south to the city that would become the official capital of Colorado in 1881. Thus would the tramps first find their way to Denver.

A method was found to extract silver profitably, and Denver experienced a booming decade in the 1880s, but the panic of 1893 hit Denver in July. Ten banks failed, real estate values collapsed, mortgages were foreclosed, and the town seethed with unemployed. Denver established a camp for the unemployed at the foot of Sixteenth Street, in River Front Park, not far from today's beautiful and busy Confluence Park. There was a tent city of sorts, with enough of the canvas tents to shelter four hundred; another two hundred slept in the grandstand. The city fed up to one thousand people a day for two weeks. Today, ironically, that area, still called River Front Park, is a recently developed complex of fashionable condos, shops, and restaurants.

The history of Colorado is a cyclical one of boom and bust: Both the extraction and tourism industries are subject to ups and down, and information technology recently was added to the list. Even though I can't find a dictionary to prove the etymological connection, the word *panhandling* is in *my* mind related to panning for gold. Indeed, using a pan with a handle may have served two purposes: finding ore in the streams and finding coins in the city.

Five years after the Moffat Tunnel was blasted and bored through the Continental Divide in 1927, Denver would become a center in its own transcontinental rail route—just as the Great Depression was producing another wave of tramps and bums to arrive in the city. Although Denver would show intolerance for vagrants (more so if they were people of color), there was a somewhat different attitude toward the hobo culture that arrived in the late 1920s. Hobos worked steadily as they moved about the country, building railroads and working the fields. Vagrants were also homeless but were more likely to engage in criminal activity. It was common to waive the vagrancy fines if a suspect would agree to leave town. "When a 'millionaire' hobo called for a hobo convention in Denver in 1925, the Mayor and head of the tourist board publicly welcomed them. At the convention, hobo war heroes were honored. Still, life for the common hobo remained far from romantic. Frequent encounters with the railroad police and accidents took their toll, with broken limbs and deaths resulting from falls from railroad cars."[9]

Even before the Great Depression hit Colorado, Denver appointed a city chaplain, Valentine M. Higgins, to help anyone in economic trouble, including those with tuberculosis. Easterners who contracted the disease were sent to Denver and Boulder because it was believed the bacillus couldn't survive so well at a mile above sea level, just as Europeans were sent to Switzerland.

Higgins was the head of Human Services without the title, worrying about runaway children, tuberculosis patients, and destitute families. He established a permanent homeless shelter, the Citizen's Mission, which opened in 1929. "By October of that year the mission had fed and provided temporary housing for 12,000. During 1930 meals were given to 67,351 men and lodging to 21,541 homeless."[10] During the Great Depression the Citizen's Mission served meals to six hundred people a day.

Petertown, a colony of ramshackle huts on the South Platte River established in the 1880s, would continue through the Depression and on into the 1950s serving older men. Rules for living there required abstinence from sex, tobacco, alcohol, and cursing. In return, the men would watch over their neighbors, helping those who were hungry, ill, or otherwise in need. Some of the men earned money by becoming scavengers, combing Denver's alleys for items suitable for recycling. By 1938 Petertown had a suburb called the "international settlement" because it contained every "white nationality," and all together there were about a hundred aging men living there. The strict, even puritanical culture of Petertown must have been the reason it was allowed to exist for so long. Indeed, Petertown was a new form of monasticism. Classical monasteries secluded people by gender to a religious life of asceticism. As we shall see, the concept is used in anthropological theory to explain ways of reducing homelessness.

As such, Petertown was safe from the police. Kusmer relates in his history of homelessness in America that while the federal government set up programs during the Depression to house transients, local authorities often dismantled urban shantytowns. When some of the homeless people tried to rebuild them, local authorities tried to prevent them. He then supplied an example: "In Denver, one welfare official reported that when shantytowns were started they were 'immediately broken up by the police, railway agents, or section gangs.'"[11]

World War II sparked a recovery, improving the economic situation to some degree. Hobos and other homeless men enlisted in the armed services or found jobs in defense industries for the duration. Although decreasing in numbers, there were still many people down and out. After the war most of the country was concerned with the concentration of vagrants in a section or two of a city. In Denver, that section was in the oldest part of the downtown area, Larimer Street, a magnet to those on the road and down and out. Consider, for example, Jack Kerouac's *On the Road*.

Kerouac's novel, published in 1957, has had an enormous influence on readers for fifty years. It is a novel that retraces the author's actual trips and takes real persons as its main characters. The narrator, Sal Paradise, is Kerouac, of course, and the pseudonym does reveal the desired destination of his quest. He hitchhikes from New York to be with his friend and sidekick Dean Moriarity (whose real name was Neal Cassady, a resident of Denver and the son of an alcoholic barber who lived on the skid row of the city, Larimer Street). Sal catches his last ride, and as he is dropped off he says, "Here I was in Denver.... I stumbled along with the most wicked grin of joy in the world, among the bums and beat cowboys of Larimer Street." He also refers to our city as "holy Denver."[12] Currently there are tours arranged to see the sites mentioned in the novel. We even have the new Kerouac Lofts, subsidized housing.

The cheap flophouses are now gone even if the Hobohemian-cowboy-Beat culture remains for some. The single room occupancy (SRO) hotels are gone not only from Larimer Street but from other sections of Denver as well. They had been the marketplace's solution to the problem of housing for the poor and the hobos, one room with a bath down the hall shared by other residents. Saloons and houses of prostitution that were part of the culture are gone from Larimer Street as well, brought down by urban renewal and the gentrification of LoDo. The disappearance of the SROs helped increase the population of homeless Denverites on the streets as well as of drifters who arrived by rail, bus, and thumb.

As mentioned above, Kerouac's novel has had a powerful rhetorical influence on young people ever since it was published in 1957. It has inspired others to intensify their disaffiliation with American society and government, encouraged them by example to go on the road in a quest for a new and independent religion and to experiment with drugs in the quest for a new vision of self. Denver itself personified the name of the narrator of the tale, a sad paradise. No doubt many of the baby boomers read and lived the quest of *On the Road*. As we saw in the first chapter, they were part of the counterculture that helped swell the ranks of homeless people in Denver and other cities across the country.

Three more recent books in the quest genre, or perhaps more aptly labeled the "on the road genre," with Denver as the geographical (and spiritual) center illustrate the continuing call of the road, despite the announcements that there are no more hobos. Ted Conover grew up in Denver and went to Amherst College until he decided to leave the academic world to enter the laboratory of life as a hobo. The findings came out in *Rolling Nowhere: Riding the Rails with America's Hoboes,* first published in 1981. (There are two acceptable plural forms for the noun *hobo*: *hobos* and *hoboes.* The word is said to derive from *homeward bound,* which applies to riding the rails, and *hoe boy,* an agricultural worker.) In a new introduction to the paperback edition twenty years later, Conover noted that a new term was coming into usage—*homelessness*—at the time he was describing his quest. He hopped a freight train in St. Louis, Missouri, and rode to Denver, where he was ingloriously arrested for being a hobo while crossing a bridge during a presidential visit to the city. From Denver he caught rides to Utah, to North Dakota, to Montana, to Idaho, and down the West Coast, looping around the Southwest states on his way back to Denver. He was much aware of Kerouac while on the road and writing the book, also expressing his desire to know the brotherhood of the hobos celebrated by Walt Whitman, Jack Kerouac, John Dos Passos, Jack London, John Steinbeck, and others. His concluding paragraph, his last word, is strikingly similar to the conclusion reached by others; that is, the hobo is not one of them. "He is one of us."[13]

Conover's travels as a hobo were a matter of choice, and although he was living in hobo jungles on the road, he clearly distinguished between this new condition of homelessness as a social problem and the romance of the railroad rider. He believed that the hobo was going to disappear because of changes in railroad practices, but another resident of Denver, Eddy Joe Cotton, took off on a journey from Denver on October 24, 1991, ten years after Conover's book first appeared. The essence of Cotton's book is in the title: *Hobo: A Young Man's Thoughts on Trains and Tramping in America.*

Cotton articulates the tension between the wanderers and the stay-at-homes. Most societies seem to experience such strains. One merely needs to reflect on Gypsies in Europe and nomads in other countries and continents. I have heard that drivers of cross-country semitrailers feel superior to workers in eight-to-five jobs who never get to see the world.

Cotton muses about the white picket fence surrounding a home and green grass cut short, a warm image of security. But pickets get kicked in or fall off, and the security disappears if it's not replaced. Bums and hobos get in fights and lose their teeth. Teeth are pickets. I marked that passage in Cotton's book because from my first day at the St. Francis Center, I noted how many had lost one or more teeth. It is an important metaphor because it signals a visible difference between them and us, a sign of deterioration as well as "differentness," including an inability to pay for repairs. Yes, a well-maintained white picket fence is a symbol of home and security.[14]

Two years after Cotton set off on his quest and twenty-two years after Conover's travels began, Mike Yankoski entered the Denver Rescue Mission, a shelter located near the St. Francis Center. (Our guests refer to it as "Jesus Saves" because of the neon sign with those words on the front of the building.) Yankoski had a different motive for going on the road as a panhandling, homeless young man. The subtitle of his subsequent book, *Under the Overpass: A Journey of Faith on the Streets of America,* reveals that his quest was to determine whether he could maintain his deep Christian faith as a homeless man in the streets and shelters.

He and a friend chose to be homeless, but because they had affluent families and credit cards, they were not like most folks who were under the overpass by necessity, stressing again the economic factor for most homeless persons. Yankoski speaks of the difficulty he had in bringing himself to beg the first time and in becoming a street entertainer, and of the humiliations he suffered in trying to find enough to eat. He also reports that he was able to keep his religious faith but lost confidence in organized religion, in the churches across the country that he turned to in a time of need and that turned him away.[15]

The population of homeless persons increased significantly during the recession of the early 1980s, and the recovery of 1983–84 didn't halt the growth, as we have seen, because of deinstitutionalization and the baby boomer bulge. Kusmer speaks of the new homeless people who appeared nationally in this period and continued into the 1990s. We get some insight into this creation, or construction, of human beings from a study of the media done by Richard Campbell and Jimmie Reeves. By studying the *New York Times* index, they found that there were no stories in that newspaper before 1980 under the category of "homeless persons." There were stories about "vagrants." By 1983 there were eighty-two articles and editorials in the newspaper about homeless persons, and only five articles about vagrants.[16]

Had a new kind of person been created by the media? Perhaps not in the ontological sense, but the answer is yes in the semantic sense. We have a new category, a new label, and a new stigma—one slightly less pejorative than vagrant, perhaps. Imagery of homeless people has changed over the years, particularly in the early years of the twentieth century. The moralists of the nineteenth century considered homelessness to be a defect in the character of the individual, such as the irresponsible desire to avoid work. Popular culture would present a changing image, one capable of eliciting more sympathy. William Dean Howells, the influential editor of the *Atlantic Monthly* and a novelist, showed in his fiction how ordinary people could sink into the homeless class in the late 1800s. Industrial capitalism was the catalyst causing men who once tilled the soil to tramp across it looking for food and work.

Henry George had already argued in *Progress and Poverty*, in 1879, that the simultaneous appearance of millionaires and tramps announced the coming breakdown of the American ideal since its founding—a nation of farmers, shopkeepers, and artisans—and its replacement with the despised European society of sharply differentiated social classes, divided between the rich nobility and the poor workers and beggars. Mark Twain would develop this theme in his fictional work. Theodore Roosevelt would use it in his political rhetoric, claiming that the idle rich and the idle poor led wasted lives. Jack London would write about the tramp in a seductive way, using his own tramping experiences to argue that, unlike in his earlier novels in which the theme was man versus nature, his "larger-than-life tramp pits himself against that most prominent symbol of modernity, organization, and capitalism: the railroad."[17] London glorified the vigorous man who could catch a ride on a train with the sedentary rich man, the blond beast riding with the effete easterner.

Fascination is the word for the American public's interest in the symbols and signs allegedly left by hobos. The claim was that markings would indicate which houses or farmhouses were open to appeals for food, which were not. Some former tramps and hobos claimed they never saw them, but the interest on the part of the public remains. On a train trip my wife and I took through New England during the changing of the colors, the public address system called our attention to the many covered bridges. They had recently been refurbished, said the disembodied voice, and the workers found many notes left by tramps in the walls. One could see amused satisfaction in our fellow passengers' response to this bit of information, perhaps representative of a sense of appreciation for conspiratorial communication that might test the generosity of some people.

When the African Americans made the Great Migration north to escape segregation and find jobs, they brought the blues with them as they rode the rails. They sang of not being able to afford the Pullman cars, of needing to ride the rail in the boxcars. Their mothers responded with boxcar blues of their own, bemoaning the sons who rode north and weren't coming back.

Kusmer's book pays considerable attention to the image of homelessness as portrayed by that singular artist, Charlie Chaplin:

> Charlie Chaplin's famous screen persona of the "little tramp," first introduced in 1914, has often been described as a universal symbol of the average person, buffeted by the winds of fate, struggling to survive through the mechanism of humor. At one level this is quite accurate and helps to explain Chaplin's enduring popularity. The description, however, ignores the specific historical context in which Chaplin's tramp

character emerged. In 1914–15, the United States was in the grips of a sharp economic decline, and the number of homeless men applying for lodging at shelters was at an all-time high.[18]

Chaplin claimed he got the idea for the character after having an encounter with a real tramp in San Francisco. He drew on both the positive and negative dimensions of the character, showing him to be willing to accept any kind of work but also capable of pilfering something to eat. Chaplin's little tramp had a lot in common with real homeless men, depicted as riding the rails and sleeping in a shelter. He denounced the development of social classes, depicting millionaires as incompetent fops, whereas the little tramp is ingenious in working his way out of snares and around obstacles. Film had been a distraction for workers until Chaplin's time; now the middle class was turning to it, giving him a new audience to influence.

Chaplin tried to elicit sympathy for the homeless man. Norman Rockwell also adapted his illustrations for the cover of the *Saturday Evening Post* to a middle-class audience. In 1924 his friendly homeless man is visually illustrated as cooking his sparse meal on a stick over a fire in a small can, a lovable dog between his legs watching the process with an eager appetite. He wears a straw hat with a feather in the band, holds a corncob pipe in his mouth. All these details negated the earlier hostile image of tramps and hobos.

In summary, the dual diagnoses of mental illness and addiction in the most populous generation ever, plus deinstitutionalization, plus urban renewal and the disappearance of SROs, plus deindustrialization and falling wages inevitably created the increases in the population of homeless people we experienced in Denver and elsewhere in the United States.

Kusmer's history also devotes a chapter to the new homeless, arguing that there is a difference beyond labels. The number of people sleeping in the streets and shelters doubled between 1984 and 1990.

The new homeless people were much more likely to live in urban streets and shelters. Deindustrialization contributed new people to the category, sons who had expected to follow their fathers into the mills of Youngstown, Ohio, and the factories of Detroit, Michigan. As the neighborhoods crumbled, so did the family businesses that served the fairly prosperous workers.

As we have seen, deinstitutionalization and the baby boomers added to the numbers of those in the shelters and on the streets. The destruction of skid rows added more. The new homeless families are invisible to the domiciled people because they are more likely to be in shelters much of the time.

Kusmer sees racial factors as well. They began in the 1950s when unemployment among blacks was twice that of whites. It has remained in that ratio since. Add to that the disappearance of inexpensive housing because of highway construction and urban renewal, and it is clear why a higher percentage of blacks than whites are homeless.[19]

William Julius Wilson has written penetratingly about this subject in his book *When Work Disappears: The World of the New Urban Poor,* using an analysis of networks in what he calls "strong" and "weak" neighborhoods. When the factories shut down and the jobs disappear, selling crack cocaine, a relatively cheap narcotic, became an alternative way to make money. The drugs entered the neighborhoods. So did guns. People withdrew from society, became fearful of leaving the safety of their homes. Social isolation, however, is practiced as an adaptive strategy, and Wilson illustrated this phenomenon with an ethnographic study in a densely populated housing project in Denver. Parental fears about safety affected the degree of their children's interaction and involvement with their neighbors and created skepticism about other parents and their children. Thus, economic factors associated with closed mills and factories affect the stability and connectedness of human networks in a negative way, adding momentum to an increase of crime, delinquency, and homelessness associated with those factors.[20]

Did a "new homeless" appear in Denver as well as in the other cities Kusmer and Wilson discuss? Franklin James of the University of Colorado at Denver has conducted surveys of homeless people in cooperation with the Colorado Coalition for the Homeless (CCH). In 1995 he referred to that research as suggesting that "Colorado is experiencing significant shifts in both the numbers and demographics that quantify homelessness."[21] The numbers increased and the demographics changed because there were more homeless families and children than ever before. An increase in the number of homeless children is particularly alarming. As we shall see, a new administration in Denver would try to reverse the trends among what we now call homelessness.

CHAPTER FOUR
MOTHER TERESA, LIMINALITY, AND ABEYANCE

Reverend Womack was right when he remembered that the striking phrase in the SFC mission statement—"in His distressing disguise"— came from the writings of Mother Teresa. I was lucky to prove him right with the first book I consulted, a biography by Kathryn Spink: *Mother Teresa: A Complete Authorized Biography*. It seems Mother Teresa didn't write much except letters. In a letter of advice to her nuns, she wrote that taking care of unwanted children was difficult. "The work with them is more difficult than with the lepers, but they are Christ in his distressing disguise."[1] The expression can be found in several of her letters quoted in the biography.

The book provided another perspective on my new avocation of working with the poor. Mother Teresa was criticized by some in the West for speaking about the "poverty of the rich" and for idealizing material poverty. Spink concluded that it was not poverty itself that Mother Teresa admired, quoting this passage to illustrate and support her interpretation: "The beauty is not in poverty but in the courage that the poor still smile and have hope, in spite of everything.... The poor represent the greatest human richness this world possesses and yet we despise them, behave as if they were garbage."[2] And there is a somewhat different perspective in this statement by Mother Teresa quoted in the book: "If there are poor in the world it is because you and I don't give enough."[3]

Spink's book was just one in a small library I had begun to acquire as a result of becoming a volunteer at the St. Francis Center. For example, I bought and read four biographies of Francis of Assisi, the patron saint of our shelter, and Erving Goffman's *Stigma: Notes on the Management of Spoiled Identity,* finding a connection among them and perhaps even a connection with the "on the road" literary genre.

I came to admire Francis, born around 1182, even though I remain agnostic about the reports of miracles involving him. Three million people each year make the pilgrimage to his tomb, and yet the magnificent basilica dedicated to him contradicts what he stood for.

Karen Armstrong asserts that Francis's life was dedicated to imitating Christ as exactly as he could. He had been born into a prosperous family and led a dissolute life as a young man. He wanted to be a troubadour, a traveling poet, and in this desire we can see he had the fever to go on the road. After embracing a leper, Francis experienced a conversion that persuaded him to give up all property to live as a "homeless mendicant," a homeless beggar. The stigmata, the five wounds on hands, feet, and torso that appeared on his body and that were said to be similar to those on the crucified Jesus, have become highly controversial over the years but are interpreted convincingly by Armstrong as Francis's final *identification* with Jesus. As Armstrong noted in the foreword to Adrian House's biography of St. Francis, although many of us admire his exemplary life, "we prefer to keep clear of beggars and the like."[4] Armstrong is convincing in both her theology and her sociology: Yes, most of us do prefer to keep clear of beggars, panhandlers, and the like, even if they are in the distressing disguise of either Francis or Jesus. She also presents a convincing case that Francis is both medieval and modern, one who speaks to those with or without faith.

What does this have to do with Erving Goffman, once called the Kafka of sociology? In *Stigma,* Goffman notes that the Greeks used the term *stigma* "to refer to bodily signs designed to expose something unusual and bad about the moral status of the signifier."[5] Today, he continues, there are three gross types of stigma: (1) "abominations of the body—various physical abnormalities"; (2) "blemishes of character" that can be inferred from the fact of imprisonment, addiction, mental illness, or radical political behavior; and (3) the "tribal stigma of race, nation," religion, and social class. A stigma is important in interpersonal communication because it is "an undesired differentness." We "normals" believe that "the person with a stigma is not quite human," and "we effectively, if often unthinkingly, reduce his life choices."[6]

In an earlier book, *The Presentation of Self in Everyday Life,*[7] Goffman adopted the overall perspective of Kenneth Burke. Burke had developed a theory of human action he called Dramatism. He plumbed the meaning of Shakespeare's observation that "all the world's a stage," arguing that human beings literally *act*. Things move, people act. Our decisions are made with an audience in mind.[8] Goffman adopted this approach in studying how people present the self in different situations with differing audiences. In *Stigma* he analyzes why we normals want to keep clear of beggars and the like.

Knowing that we normals find them to have an undesired differentness, find them not quite human, people with stigmas try to adapt to their audiences, at times trying to "pass" as domiciled people when in their presence. They act as if they are normal, domiciled people.

It should be clear from this perspective that the status of a homeless person is both a cause and an effect of stigmas. Physically handicapped people wind up in our shelter, becoming homeless in part because of their ailment. Social workers tell me, however, that some of their clients become alcoholics *after* they become homeless for, say, economic reasons. There is the case of the SFC guest with long blond hair and a southern drawl who complained bitterly, these many years later, that he had been held back in elementary school and labeled with terms such as *having a "learning disability."* "I don't have a learning disability," he said with a frown, indicating the stigmatizing power of diagnostic terms. He dropped out, wound up on the streets, and found what he called his "drug of choice," whiskey, which he drinks until he passes out in his "camp." It is quite natural that the stigmatized person is alienated and disaffiliated, the very kind of social type Francis and Teresa would embrace.

*   *   *

I found myself on the road during the first five months of 1999, arranging my schedule so that I could be in Denver on Fridays for my day at SFC. I had been invited to give a public lecture and to give a semester-long graduate seminar at the University of Kansas that met a couple of days a week. I shuttled back and forth between Lawrence and Denver. In addition, I was invited to spend a week in March at Baylor University in Waco, Texas, teaching courses and giving a public lecture. In both cases I decided to give the public lecture on the topic of this chapter: "In His Distressing Disguise: Communication and the Homeless."

In my lecture I informed my audience that I had been doing my homework since starting at the center in late October 1998. The rest of this chapter is drawn from that lecture, my version of what I knew about homelessness in the spring of 1999. Between October 30, 1998, and March 16, 1999, I logged two hundred hours at the center; participated in vigils, marches, legislative action, and lobbying workshops; interviewed experts; and filled four legal pads with field notes. I found the poor and homeless people so interesting in their individuality and heterogeneity that I joined the National Coalition for the Homeless, ordering and studying their factual reports and resource books in an attempt to understand homeless people, the supposed Other.

My growing library on poverty and homeless people took up several shelves and lots of file folders. The books and papers are organized under the headings of anthropology, communication, economics, social work, sociology, religion, and, yes, literature. After reading this mélange of research, I concluded that neither an adequate explanation of the new poverty and homelessness nor policy solutions to them would emerge from a single disciplinary perspective; they are truly interdisciplinary phenomena. Nonetheless, I found communication theory and research to be extremely helpful. Nor did I believe that one method of research would work. Quantitative, survey research is needed as much as interpretive and critical studies.

Indeed, essays on homelessness seem obligated to begin with the facts, the numbers. Hard, sharp empiricism is necessary here, but the numbers cannot be exact because of the nature of the phenomena. Homeless people are hard to define and hard to find for "point-in-time" studies that try to count all of them on a given day, no matter where they are. Some, as I know by participating in a census, can't be bothered unless they are offered an incentive, a reward for talking; some, many in fact, are fugitives from the law. These are some of the obstacles to getting an accurate count.

Few studies use identical methods, making geographical and temporal comparisons difficult. As a result, estimates of the number of homeless people in this country at one time ranged from a few hundred thousand to several million, although the latter seems to have been a consciously created "fictoid" made up by the late Mitch Snyder, an early homeless advocate, to get attention. Over the weekend of March 13–14, 1999, while in a motel on the road to Waco, I heard Housing and Urban Development secretary Andrew Cuomo cite a national figure of six hundred thousand in a speech carried on CNN. In 2006 the figure was said to be eight hundred thousand. But there are many more invisible, uncountable homeless people.

To make some meaningful comparisons for my audiences in Lawrence and Waco, I gathered some data myself in early 1999 while working at three Big XII universities, Baylor, Colorado at Boulder, and Kansas. So I tried to compare Waco, Boulder, and Lawrence. A homeless census in 1998 found that Denver and its northern suburbs had almost seven thousand homeless people, including seven hundred in Boulder, a city then of eighty to one hundred thousand people. I conducted an interview with the director of the Boulder Shelter for the Homeless at that time, Robert Mann. He told me that the figure of seven hundred was an underestimate and that a February 1999 study had produced a count of eight hundred.

While visiting the University of Kansas during the first week of February in 1999 to teach my seminar, I dropped in at the Salvation Army one-stop shelter in Lawrence. Someone in the office asked a woman serving as cook, utility worker, and organizational angel to give me a complete tour. In this "Sally," as homeless people call the Salvation Army, a guest can eat a meal, shower, and sleep. My guide showed me where their guests slept, the cots and the box where the individual bedding is stored. They had a capacity of fifty on the basketball court. Recently the number of people sleeping there was in the thirties and growing. She said there had to be three hundred homeless people in Lawrence. Without my asking, she voluntarily told me, with a pained expression, that the rich people on their board didn't want to see the homeless people when they came for meetings, nor did they want to see the "poop" the guests sometimes leave behind.

A person in the office of the Sally gave me the name of Lou Ann Lee, housing programs specialist for the city of Lawrence. I interviewed her in the handsome new City Building on the Kaw River. She was very helpful when she understood my goal, saying it was a natural comparison between Boulder and Lawrence. Each is the seat of the state university in adjacent states, and each had about eighty thousand citizens then; the Board of Regents for the University of Kansas uses the University of Colorado at Boulder as a benchmark in setting salaries and wages. I learned from Lee that Lawrence's most recent point-in-time study had turned up 140 homeless people, but I was also told that at times one could see homeless people huddled under a nearby bridge from a window in the City Building. After my interview I walked to the bridge and crawled under it, only to find no one at home, but I spotted some empty quart bottles that had once contained malt liquor. Painted on the underside of the bridge in neat block letters was this bit of graffiti: "Los Vagabondos, 98." Wondering how many of those vagabonds had been counted in the study, I decided that the figure I got at the Sally was more credible than the official figure.

In preparation for my lecture at Baylor, I got the telephone number of the Texas Network for the Homeless from the National Coalition for the Homeless. I called the Texas Network to ask for data about Waco's homeless population. The staff member who answered said it would be hard, but he promised he would make the effort and get back to me. After several weeks, I called a second time and was referred to the same staff member, who apologized and again promised he would try to gather the data for me, parenthetically adding that a certain "Jimmy Doyle" in Waco knew more about these matters than anyone. While waiting for the call from the Texas Network, I began asking information operators for the phone number of appropriate authorities in Waco. Invariably I got state officials, none of whom could supply me with the desired data, none of whom could refer me to the appropriate city official, and all of whom recommended that I call Channel Six.

"Channel Six? Why?"

It turns out that the people I was talking to were all watching Channel Six's series on homelessness in central Texas. *Who could be their source?* I called Channel Six, located somewhere between Waco and Temple, Texas. The producer of the series referred me to the reporter of the series, Martha Trevino, who in turn referred me to an amazing character named Jimmy Dorrell, not Jimmy "Doyle." Jimmy Dorrell is the director of Mission Waco. I called him and left a message, and when he called me back in Denver the next morning, we had a long talk. He followed up by giving me most of the data I could find on Waco.

Dorrell is also a Christian minister who conducts a church service every Sunday under an Interstate 35 bridge adjacent to the Baylor University campus; his Church under the Bridge has a congregation of between two and three hundred. He invited me to the service there on Sunday, March 14, so I changed my travel plans. A snowstorm forced me to hole up in a motel in Colby, Kansas, for eighteen hours, so I missed the service during my trip to Baylor. Nonetheless, I saw the "church" when I drove to the campus and was able to get together with Jimmy Dorrell at Mission Waco. He gave me a tour of the city and the facilities serving the poor and homeless people in the area. A call to city hall in Waco got me the estimates of Waco's population as 112,000 for 1999 and 113,000 in the census of 2000. Jimmy estimated the homeless population as between 1,000 and 3,000 in 1999. Let's take the middle figure of 2,000. My best estimates for the homeless populations in these three university cities for early 1999 are Boulder, 800; Lawrence, 300; and Waco, 2,000.

The differences would be all the more striking if I use the 140 number I got from the city official for Lawrence and the upper estimate of 3,000 for Baylor. All three communities were university towns that grew to become small cities. How can we understand these differences?

The median family income for each city for 1999 sheds some light (see Table 4.1). Boulder's was $68,700. I didn't record the exact figure for Lawrence but was surprised to learn that it was said to be slightly higher than Boulder's. In Waco the city manager and Jimmy Dorrell estimated it to be $20,000, less than one-third of the median incomes in the other two cities. Here we have some insight into Waco's status as the statistical outlier of homelessness: *Too little income.* And although Waco was larger than the other cities, the difference wasn't enough to account for such significant differences in the size of the homeless population. (When I called in May 2006 to get the population figure, the official at city hall assured me that Jimmy Dorrell was still at Waco Mission, still preaching at the Church under the Bridge, and that the Department of Housing and Urban Development (HUD) had forced the city to create a committee to end homelessness, at least for the chronic homeless people in Waco.)

What about Boulder and Lawrence? HUD has a technical concept that helps—fair market rent. In 1999 the figure for Lawrence for a two-bedroom apartment was $540, and for Boulder it was $827. Jimmy Dorrell told me that nobody knew what that figure was in Waco, but housing costs were much lower, comparable to their lower wages. In Boulder, another explanation emerges: *Housing costs too high.* Boulder is an attractive city with the backdrop of the Flatirons, sheets of rock that resemble my grandmother's iron when upright and not in use. But the higher housing costs in Boulder are to some extent self-imposed. City government adopted a greenbelt policy that prevents building in the foothills above the city and another policy preventing the development

Table 4.1 Population, Income, and Housing Costs in Boulder, Colorado; Lawrence, Kansas; and Waco, Texas, 1999

City	Population	Homeless Population	Median Family Income	Fair Market Rent Two-Bedroom Apartment
Boulder	80,000	800	$69,000	$827
Lawrence	80,000	300	$70,000	$540
Waco	120,000	2,000	$20,000	N/A

of high-rise buildings—anything higher than three stories—that would block neighbors' views of the mountains.

Although the numbers we have here are indeed small samples, a couple of lessons are clear. First, getting accurate and authoritative quantitative data on relevant factors is difficult when studying homelessness and its causes. Second, it is clear that there is a primitive verbal equation behind homelessness rates that doesn't necessarily implicate mental illness, addiction, or laziness: *Income too low and/or housing costs too high.*

Let me repeat a bit of what I said to those audiences in Lawrence, and particularly in Waco, about the first factor, too little income. We were proud during the Clinton administration, I said, because of low unemployment numbers, yet *underemployment* was increasing. Deindustrialization; declining unionism; the increase in the use of independent contractors, temp-labor, and day labor; and management practices I now refer to with Max Weber's phrase, instrumental rationality, were bringing about lower wages, fewer benefits, and less job security. Without medical insurance, almost anyone could drop into destitution after a long, disabling illness. And many did.

A trend was underway then that continues to this day. The absolute number and the proportion of American families below the poverty line were growing. The minimum wage was not raised during the 1980s, and people who were paid at that level were losing rather than gaining ground. One of our leading labor economists, Richard B. Freeman, produced an eloquent little book in 1999, *The New Inequality: Creating Solutions for Poor America,* which I found in the University of Kansas bookstore. In it he proposes that despite the expanding economy at the time, the United States had "cemented its traditional position as the leader in inequality among advanced countries."[9] The inequality was "new" because it reversed the trend toward greater equality we had enjoyed between 1945 and the late 1970s. It was also new because of the effects of deindustrialization, the outsourcing of manufacturing jobs, and the rise of the global economy.

I was particularly irked to read the ratio of executives' salaries to workers' wages. It was 35–1 in 1978, 200–1 only twenty years later, in 1998, inflating to a condition I called an "obscene bloat." The new inequality was creating a two-tiered society, an apartheid economy. In his foreword to *The New Inequality*, Robert Reich, former secretary of labor, endorses Freeman's arguments, showing us why the trends were invisible to so many of us. Americans were segregating by income: "into different towns, using different modes of transportation, employing different public facilities (parks, playgrounds, schools, libraries), and working and playing in different places."[10] Even the comfortable class, people who are in the business of communicating—that is, journalists, academicians, television producers, and politicians—don't see the problem and don't hear about it because we live in a parallel universe, preventing us from noticing its development.

The second tier in the society, sometimes called the underclass, had given up on politics in the late 1990s because they had no sense of ownership, no confidence the system would work for them. Alienated, disaffiliated, and withdrawn, they don't vote, and because they don't go to the polls, the comfortable class—particularly the politicians—ignores them. They suffer from both an absolute and a *relative* deprivation in comparison to the comfortable class. The new inequality posed a threat to our democratic form of government. A distressingly deepening poverty has to be considered as the first economic causal factor in producing an increase in homelessness.

The second economic causal factor was and is the absence of affordable housing. The National Coalition for the Homeless said the United States had reached a crisis situation in the late 1990s. But wasn't the construction business booming? Yes, but builders weren't putting up homes for the underemployed or minimum-wage workers. I asked my audiences to listen carefully to these facts: Between 1973 and 1993, 2.2 million low-rent units disappeared. During the same period, the number of low-income renters increased by 4.7 million. SRO hotels on skid rows have disappeared all over the United States, transformed into expensive condos and lofts. Denver is a prime example of this phenomenon, but here, as elsewhere, the comfortable class sees what took the place of the SROs, *not what disappeared*.

There was some disagreement among social scientists, I noted in 1999, about the percentage of mental illness among homeless people.

The higher the percentage of illness among homeless persons, the easier it is to "medicalize" the problem, say some, and dismiss it as insoluble. The lower the percentage, the more it is our duty to commit financial resources to reduce if not eliminate the problem. My experience as a ward attendant in an asylum in 1956 convinced me that some unfortunate people are genuinely crazy. In graduate school, I was, as a result, singularly unconvinced by the claims about the "myth" of mental illness.

Later I would encounter work by social scientists who wished to simplify the causes of homelessness. The subtitle of one such book by Doug Timmer, D. Stanley Eitzen, and Kathryn Talley reveals their reductionism: *Paths to Homelessness: Extreme Poverty and the Urban Housing Crisis*. They dismiss frequently cited causes, using headings such as "Alcohol Myths" and "The Myth of Dysfunctional Families." Although sympathetic to their emphasis on economics, I concluded that it is a mistake to oversimplify for the reason they gave: "There are political and policy dangers in emphasizing this complex reality."[11] Furthermore, such a stance also oversimplifies the complex coordination required to produce corrective action.

At the time of my lectures, I was intrigued by a communication hypothesis generated by the shelter director I interviewed in Boulder, Robert Mann. His observation was that communication networks of support could be important because although alcoholics, drug addicts, and the mentally ill may have friends and acquaintances, these relationships are superficial and fragile. Peter Rossi had observed, from statistical studies in Chicago, that people on the streets often become estranged from the people who could help, their families.[12] Homeless people lost their strongest communication links. Thus, they lacked the strong, supportive network connectedness that would see them through the difficult periods most of us experience and that would keep them off the streets. William Julius Wilson argues in his book, *When Work Disappears: The World of the New Urban Poor,* that neighborhoods going through deindustrialization can produce ghetto joblessness and the destruction of support networks that once helped individuals find jobs and kept them out of trouble.

I paused in my lectures at Baylor and Kansas University to mention five observations related to my own discipline, communication, even though I had expressed the doubt that a single discipline could *completely* comprehend the problem and possible solutions. I will point out instances in which I have changed or refined my own position since then:

Mass media coverage. I thought the coverage of homelessness in Denver was inadequate for a couple of reasons. First, I had watched it carefully from October 1998 to March 1999 and saw a bimodal distribution in coverage that concentrated on covering our homeless people on Thanksgiving and Christmas, giving less coverage the rest of the time except for unusual circumstances, such as the series of murders of homeless men in the fall of 1999. (Donations also tend to be affected; most arrive during the holiday seasons.) Concern should have been greatest in January, typically the coldest month of the year. This indicates that the coverage is "feel-good reporting," provided to make viewers and readers feel good about seeing poor and homeless people eat free turkey dinners.

A second inadequacy was the decline in the coverage of homelessness, a decline reported by the press itself in an article in *Time* magazine, "Not Gone, but Forgotten?"[13] Stories about homeless people were becoming less frequent, even though the increase in demand for emergency shelter went up over 500 percent between 1985 and 1998. One hypothesis given by *Time* was that the American people had run out of their supply of compassion, a rationalization for ignoring the problem. That explanation would handily place the blame on the audience, not the media. Perhaps the fault was with the media as well the audience.

I had some evidence to support a more centrist position. I heard nothing but praise for Channel Six's coverage of homelessness in central Texas, and because of it, I was able to find the person, Jimmy Dorrell, who seemed to know most about the problems in Waco. Another counterexample would be the response of the reading audience to John Grisham's best-selling 1998 book, *The Street Lawyer,* a well-researched and sympathetic treatment of homeless people in Washington, D.C. And, in line with the Reich quotation above, journalists are members of the comfortable class who, at least at times, live in a parallel universe, unaware of how the other class lives.

Voice. As I mentioned in my speeches, *voice* was one of the emergent or dominating metaphors in our field of organizational communication at the millennium. I used the term in a broader sense because destitute, jobless people had a voice in neither organizational nor societal channels. I held up a copy of the *Denver Voice,* a lively, almost radical tabloid newspaper written and edited by homeless people in Denver. Its low circulation stands as a symptom of the very problem it would solve. If the homeless people had the same voice, and volume, as the comfortable class in the top tier, this would be a more just society. We need leaders, I argued, who can organize the poor and homeless persons so as to give them more voice at a higher volume.

Alienation, rejection, and disaffiliation. My audiences would have been surprised had I not brought up this topic because of a research program I directed on organizational identification. One must be careful about generalizing, but many homeless people suffer from a lack of any apparent identification with organizations. I hear them talking about the Denver Broncos, our National Football League team, but as Irving Rein and Ben Shields observe, discourse about sports is the language of the city.[14] I also hear scathing remarks about the agencies that dump them in temp jobs where they are exploited at the minimum wage; they also complain about the night shelters they frequent.

Kenneth Burke held that the self, the "I," is a unique collection of corporate "We's." Moreover, he wrote during the Depression, "It is *natural* for a man to identify himself with the business corporation he serves."[15] Indeed, it would follow from this theory that identification with "We's" larger than the self makes for a wholesome, healthy "I." Dialectically, said Burke, the opposite of identification is alienation and disaffiliation. Homeless people are alienated from society and its organizations because they no longer find them *reasonable.* Nor do we domiciled people identify with them. This rejection serves as an additional stigma. As Mother Teresa said of her work among the poorest of the poor in Calcutta, "We know now that being unwanted is the greatest disease of all."[16]

Control. This is another topic studied in the research program I participated in for more than twenty years. Almost by definition, urban homeless people are controlled by those in the top tier. As seen above, the homeless people have little or no voice in these matters. Example: The marketplace used to be able to handle tramps and hobos. Chicago had its Hobohemia. Denver had Larimer Street, a cowboy's version of Hobohemia, the haunt of several Beat-generation writers while visiting "holy Denver." Working-class and poor people could afford the cheap rates for one room and a common bathroom down the hall. Senator Robert Taft of Ohio was horrified by a similar, blighted area in his hometown of Cincinnati and was powerful enough to push urban renewal legislation through Congress, paying cities to tear down their SROs and renew themselves with new buildings. There were SROs in other areas of Denver; one such area was torn down to build a convention center. Nothing was built to replace the SROs.[17]

The displaced persons were forced into camps along the South Platte River and emergency shelters in the Devil's Triangle. The homeless were complaining in 1999 about police "street sweeps" they believed were planned to prevent the comfortable class from having to see them or, worse, interact with them. Once, while training to clean the showers, I was eager to get the men out of the room so we could start spraying the place with a disinfectant. The one man remaining, combing his long wet hair at the mirrors, turned toward me, glanced at my name tag, and said, "The invisible world of the homeless, eh, Phil?"

"Why did you say that?"

"Because most people don't see us and don't want to see us." I thought the remark was out of place, perhaps because it happened to be pointed at me, but reflecting on it later, I had to grant its validity.

The organizational dimension. In a conversation we were having about college students one day, Kenneth Burke remarked that there is a period in life in which young people have to accomplish three objectives: Find a permanent sex partner, find a job, and find a place to live acceptable to the sex partner. Later I elaborated on these existential necessaries by saying that if the first objective had not been achieved, one faced the dilemma of either staying with Mom and Dad, finding a room of one's own, or turning to any of the variations of homelessness, such as piling in with friends or sleeping in shelters or on the street.

I had found by 1999 that there was a theory of homelessness that took similar premises. It is presented in Kim Hopper and Jim Baumohl's "Redefining the Cursed Word: A Historical Interpretation of American Homelessness," the first chapter in a book published by the National Coalition for the Homeless: *Homelessness in America*. Hopper and Baumohl deem the word *homelessness* to be an "odd-job word, pressed into service to impose order on a hodgepodge of social dislocation, extreme poverty, seasonal or itinerant work, and unconventional ways of life."[18] They develop their theoretical scheme by means of two concepts borrowed from anthropology and historical sociology: *liminality* and *abeyance*. The first, liminality, is from a Latin word for threshold. Anthropologists use the word for a number of "states of passage" that a member of a culture must pass. One such example Hopper and Baumohl give is the one Burke called finding a permanent sex partner; they use our society's approved term *marriage*, noting that most of the passages are prescribed by ritual. Other states of passage would be apprenticing to a profession or preparing to take religious vows. No matter how rigorous the passage, how uncertain it is, there is the expectation that one will return to a settled life. The passage occasionally stalls, putting a person in limbo, a space of forgotten confinement. Liminality is the sometimes dangerous passage from one social status to another.

Abeyance, the second concept in the framework, recognizes that in any society there are a limited number of desired status slots available (fewer jobs, for example, than applicants). Abeyance mechanisms or measures are devised to absorb the surplus or redundant people. Although Hopper and Baumohl don't use the example, organized labor in the United States historically supported education at all levels so as to keep students in abeyance longer, because of the finite number of jobs. Abeyance measures might be government programs such as the

Civilian Conservation Corps and the Works Progress Administration during the Great Depression, organizations that hired surplus workers as a way of creating status slots. The essence of the theory is "that what unites the phenomena gathered up in the term homelessness is liminality (resolved or stalled) and abeyance gone awry."[19]

Some of our young people get stuck in the passage from parents' home to one of their own. Some never get unstuck, although their situation is more often a cycle of moving in and out of the streets. Or they suffer a setback that forces them from their own domicile back into their parents' home. If that option is closed, they will wind up on the streets as one of our organizational economy's surplus people.

Other institutions feel some responsibility for providing supplemental status slots, abeyance, for the surplus and redundant among us: "Whether these surrogate occupations are provided under the auspices of the state (frontier settlements, public works, compulsory education), the church (monasteries, breakaway religious orders), or even countercultural groups (communal experiments), the effect is the same. Such measures provide for—and control—redundant people who, in their restive idleness, might undermine social order."[20] State governments used to provide abeyance for the mentally ill but got out of that business. Since then, they have been particularly aggressive in building substitute housing for the dangerous in the architecture of the penitentiaries. The military has provided both substitute jobs and housing to keep young people in abeyance.

In my speeches to those academic audiences, I was critical of academics in organizational studies for paying attention only to those who got jobs, but perhaps I was misguided. One of the defining characteristics of organizations identified by Max Weber was the ability to *exclude people from entering them*. Scientific Management, known as Taylorism after its founder, preached to management to hire only the "first class worker" and reject the rest.

One has to ask, Are the limitations of liminality and abeyance to be found in the society or the system for not providing enough status slots for its young people, or in the inadequacies of those trying to find such slots? The cover of the June 5, 2006, issue of the *New Yorker* takes a position on the question. It is a cartoon featuring a circle of eleven young men and women in black caps and gowns. All but two faces are white. They are walking around a circle of nine white chairs, eyeing each other suspiciously. In the foreground a white-haired professor or administrator in academic regalia has what seems to be a wicked smile on his face as he lifts his hands from the keys of a piano.

CHAPTER FIVE
SEASONS, CYCLES, AND RELATIVE DEPRIVATION

My field notes in late fall of 1998 and winter, spring, and summer of 1999 contained many references to seasons and cycles. I decided to reread Henry Thoreau's *Walden* for ideas about how to organize my thoughts and observations. I remembered that Thoreau had spent two years in his hut and then condensed them into one. His story begins with moving in during the summer, goes on to building his fireplace in the fall and tells of ice and animal neighbors during the winter, and ends in the spring.

Morning and awakening are thematic images of a daily rhythm as well, and he intended to wake up his readers with a rooster's crow. I thought this would work for me as well, but I abandoned the idea in favor of narrative form because the story kept changing. I had taught Thoreau's work in the classroom, had even published an article about it, but was delightfully surprised upon rereading *Walden* to rediscover its relevancy to my study of SFC. He says that he went to Walden to discover the basic "necessaries" of life, those things he couldn't do without.

About Shelter, capitalized as if to get my attention, Thoreau grants that it is now a "necessary" of life.[1] He considers with approval the customs of Native Americans, making shelters mainly out of materials as nature furnished. Yes, Thoreau finds shelter to be a necessary of life, but he either missed or dismissed a passage in the work of one economist he mentioned in the "Economy" chapter of *Walden*: Adam Smith. Smith analyzed the "basic necessaries" of life while inventing the theory of capitalism in *The Wealth of Nations*:

> By necessaries I understand not only the commodities which are indispensably necessary for the support of life, but what ever the customs of the country renders it indecent for creditable people, even the lowest order, to be without. A linen shirt, for example, is strictly speaking, not a necessary of life. The Greeks and Romans lived, I suppose, very comfortably, though they had no linen. But in the present times, through the greater part of Europe, a creditable day-labourer would be ashamed to appear in public without a linen shirt, the want of which would be supposed to denote that disgraceful degree of poverty, which, it is presumed, nobody can well fall into, without extreme bad conduct. Custom, in the same manner, has rendered leather shoes a necessary of life in England.[2]

The notion that something nonessential could nevertheless be considered a necessity within a particular context—as a linen shirt was a basic necessity for a wage laborer—has become known as "relative deprivation," but the wording Adam Smith used in the quotation above could have been used by Erving Goffman to define his notion of a stigma (as introduced above). John Cassidy synthesized the results of research on relative deprivation in 2006. Samuel A. Stouffer and W. G. Runciman did pioneering research on the topic in World War II and in the 1960s. Recent research indicates that people whose neighbors are richer than they are, are not as happy as folks living with neighbors who have about the same income.

Surprisingly, relative deprivation also seems to correlate with one's health and longevity. Cassidy wrote that Amartya Sen, the 1998 Nobel laureate in economics, "has pointed out that African-Americans as a group have a smaller chance of reaching old age than Indians in the impoverished state of Kerala, who are much poorer."[3] Such studies don't provide causation, only correlations. One hypothesis Cassidy mentions is that relative deprivation produces stress, which in turn can damage the immune system. There is direct evidence for this in studies of baboons and monkeys; that is, the lower members of the hierarchy who are abused by the higher ones have higher levels of a hormone caused by stress and a higher rate of heart disease.

Cassidy quotes another economist, Angus Deaton, as saying that those in a low rank suffer more from stress than people of a higher rank. The greater the number of people and ranks above one, the greater the stress suffered from the threats, orders, insults, and other messages from above. "Individuals who are insulted by those immediately above them insult those immediately below them, generating a cascade of threats and violence through which low-ranked individuals feel the burden, not just of their immediate superiors, but of the whole hierarchy above them."[4]

James Joyce anticipated this phenomenon in "Counterparts," published in *Dubliners,* a collection of short stories published in 1914. With apologies to the literati for summarizing Joyce's great work of art in my humble style, I hasten to make my point by illustration. (The story is, in part, about organizational communication, about what the late Fredric Jablin studied under the rubric of "superior-subordinate communication"; it is about hierarchy, formal and informal channels.) The main character, named Farrington, is called from his desk to the office of the head of his company and is humiliated in a Northern Ireland accent for not having copied a contract by hand in the time ordered. The boss will not hear a justification, shouting the subordinate down. He sends Farrington back to his office to finish the contract by a certain hour that afternoon. Farrington starts to work on the contract but has trouble concentrating because he feels the stress of having been berated by the boss, so he sneaks off to the snug in a pub where he can moisten his throat with a glass of porter. He returns to the office and is summoned to the boss's office again; this time he is belittled before an audience of one, a woman who is a client of the firm. Farrington returns to his desk, picks up his pen and tries to finish the task, but he makes a mistake on a page and has to start over. Glancing at his watch he calculates that he has no chance of copying the contract in time. He leaves again, this time for Davy Byrne's Moral Pub. After drinks he moves on to another pub where, even though low on cash, he stands the group to a round. His friends take advantage of him, ordering whiskey and other expensive drinks. Furthermore, Farrington's reputation as a strongman is shattered when a man named Weathers defeats him not once but twice at arm wrestling. Farrington is now weighed down by his humiliations and is broke and not yet drunk. He takes his tram home. One of his young sons greets him. Farrington's wife has gone to chapel, but the boy offers to prepare his meal. Farrington notices that the fire has gone out. He beats his son with a stick; the boy cries out that if he stops beating him, he will say a Hail Mary for his father.

Hierarchy is the *structure* necessary for relative deprivation to develop, *communication* the necessary process. Orders and threats come down the hierarchy. Moving upward are messages of compliance and flattery. The organizational folk wisdom is that bad news comes down the line; good news goes up. It takes a person of considerable strength to speak the truth to power. The cascade of humiliating messages coming down the line becomes more damaging when each level of subordinate dumps on his or her subordinate, and the messages have a second, relational meaning that puts subordinates in their hierarchical place. Those at the bottom suffer most of all from the cumulative cascades of insults and other messages demeaning their personal worth and value.

At the bottom of the hierarchy in contemporary society are the homeless people, who bear all the forms of stigma. My field notes contain abundant descriptions of these marks and signs. No doubt they have received countless demeaning messages, even if expressed nonverbally, from people above them—putting them in their place. If we can accept the research findings under the heading of "relative" deprivation as well as what observation and common sense tell us about "absolute" deprivation, there is no wonder that these people, carrying all that stress, behave the way they do and live much shorter lives than those of us in the comfortable class.

I learned from graffiti artists in Denver that their work is part of a dialogue or dialectic, part of the totality called urban communication. They are surrounded by visual orders, signs that say "stop," "private property," and "no loitering." So they respond visually by spraying their artistic names, or "tags," on whatever they can find. The city responds in turn by erasing their "tags" and artwork and acting as if it wants to catch and prosecute them, but the detectives have a different priority, spending their time chasing murderers, rapists, and armed robbers. So the dialogue continues. The artists gain respect among their peers for their art and their ingenuity and for talking back. A Denver journalist came to a similar conclusion about this visual language, this dialogue: "Who realizes that, behind the gangster bravado and fuck-the-man attitude, what graffiti really speaks to is a desire to be heard, to be listened to, for the world to know your name?"[5]

To conclude my remarks about Thoreau: I had originally planned to imitate the form of *Walden* by compressing two years at SFC into four seasons, thereby stressing the rhythm of the seasons in pastoral time, as opposed to linear time, but other matters prevented me. For one, I kept learning more and more about homelessness and the shelter. For another, a publisher persuaded me to undertake another book about the accident involving the Space Shuttle *Columbia*.[6] By the time that book was finished—and invitations to lecture brought by the book—the St. Francis Center and Denver and homelessness had changed so much I needed more time to do research. It was clear that the issues of home- lessness and Denver's response to it were so complex that I would have to rely on a narrative form covering the entire ten years. In returning to Thoreau I was relieved to learn that although it took him only two years to gather the observations and thoughts for *Walden*, it took him eight more years to write it.

In case the reader has not yet inferred my method or missed the first paragraph of the preface, I should explain that my method of getting at the truth of the St. Francis Center and its culture is by telling stories. Storytelling and the truth are not necessarily in opposition; they provide a human reality behind the statistics. In my first few months at the shel- ter, I was still learning the rules and methods of following them for my various roles in mail/storage, laundry, donations, the clothing room, and the men's showers. In some cases I explicate the anecdotes; with others I delay, waiting for a chance to generalize about them.

On Friday, New Year's Day, 1999, I got up at the usual time and hiked to SFC. There was only one person standing in front of the center, a rela- tively young Hispanic man who said, "No open today."

"No open today?" I repeated his statement as a question.

He nodded and then his eyes followed mine to the slight bit of movement of a mass under a heap of blankets on the sidewalk. How could I have not gotten the word the week before that SFC would be closed today? Deciding to use this surplus day to learn how others help homeless people, I walked the several blocks to Jesus Saves, or the Denver Rescue Mission. I was taken for a homeless man by a guard when I walked in, probably because of my work clothes. I explained my personal mission, and he waved me into a room with rows and rows of men sitting on layers of clothing and wearing stocking hats. The *Today Show* was on a TV set hanging from the ceiling. An official showed me around, taking me downstairs to a breakfast room for men who are in the mission's rehab program. He stressed that they were filling the beds every night and also emphasized their commitment to help men reclaim their life from alcohol and drugs.

On Friday, January 8, 1999, a week later, I started walking at 7:00 a.m., on a cold, below-freezing morning, arriving at the shelter to find a big crowd waiting to get in. I was becoming familiar with many of the guests, and while working in mail/storage was able to wave quite a few through to get a storage bag without looking up their forms because I was able to call them by name. A white man was anxious for me to search the mail on his behalf.

"I'm looking for a letter about my new eye from a woman who hand paints them in Aurora." He told me his story by question and answer. Three cops had beaten and kicked him so badly, he said, that he lost his left eye. All he knows about it, he read in the newspapers later—with one eye. The articles said he was in the lobby of the Westin Hotel in downtown Denver in a state of inebriation. Someone in the hotel called the police. One cop said the man menaced him with a vodka bottle, and a female cop said he came on to her. Three male cops were fired, he said, but the woman was not fired because she had not been involved in the assault.

"I bring trouble on myself," he said, and answered my questions with a "Yes sir" and "No sir."

In those days I recorded many stigmas in my field notes, such as tattoos under the eyes, missing fingers, and the *pickets*: "Many are missing teeth.

Fresh scars on the face and hands. And the clothes stigmatize some of them. Shopping carts." Yes, with the final entry in my notes I realized at last that the shopping carts our guests used as mobile storage units were stigmas in the eyes of us in the upper tier. So were their backpacks. And the missing pickets metaphorically remind the observer that they have no secure house to go home to or money for dental care.

On the way home that day, I walked to the headquarters of the Colorado Coalition for the Homeless (CCH) at Broadway and Stout Street. Deb DeBoutez came out of her office to help me. Although she was working against some kind of deadline, she gathered up some documents, including a brochure describing CCH as "an organization dedicated to the prevention of homelessness. Founded in 1983"—*revealing date,* I thought, *the very time the* New York Times *began to use the word "homeless"*—"to address the growing problem of homelessness in Colorado, CCH maintains and supports programs that assist homeless families and individuals in finding permanent homes and keeping them." A list of services was given:

- Prevention
- Housing
- Medical Care
- Education and Training

"Why Are People Homeless?" is the title of another document she gave me. The main answers were "Inadequate Income," "Lack of Affordable Housing," and "Other Factors" that included domestic violence, mental illness (including an estimate that one-third of single adult homeless people suffer from some form of severe and chronic mental illness), and chemical dependency.

A copy of a PowerPoint presentation she gave me included the results of a census conducted on June 15, 1998, a point-in-time study that sought homeless people wherever they might be for an interview. The total for the Denver metropolitan area for that day was 5,792 persons. In answer to the question "Where did you spend last night?" 1,699 said they had been in an emergency shelter; 1,391, in transitional housing; 810, staying with family or friends; 551, on the streets; and so on. Their education: 30

percent lacked a high school diploma, 19 percent had some college, 4 percent had either a BA or BS, 1 percent had an MA or MS, and three people had a doctorate. I thanked her for the documents and headed home.

My notes for the following week, Friday, January 15, record what I took to be a methodological innovation. I had from the beginning scratched notes on the back of my work slip, but by this time I realized that it was useful to relate stories and conversations with guests to a member of the staff who had been there much longer than I and who knew the guests better than I. This accomplished a couple of objectives: Staff members often could either confirm or reject the veracity of a story or answer I repeated to them, and it helped transfer "bits" of information into my long-term memory, making it much easier when I got a chance to expand my "scratch" notes into field notes.

I worked the showers from noon to 12:45 and was startled when I got behind the counter to scan the room: *Jesus was taking* a *shower.* I did a double take when a tall, slender, light-skinned man turned around from a showerhead to rinse his back, revealing his long black hair, a Semitic nose, and a long black beard. Talk about a distressing disguise. I later learned his name and inferred that he suffered from some sort of mental disorder because he rarely spoke or showed any emotion. And yet, months later on the Sixteenth Street Mall, I saw him; he recognized me, smiled, and softly said "Pheel," even though I wasn't wearing my name tag.

I also had a long interview that day in the showers with Bill, a highly intelligent and articulate man. Bill began talking about "passing," in Burke's and Goffman's sense, in downtown Denver. Bill said he had no difficulty in passing, didn't feel he had to avoid any parts of the city as a homeless man.

"I wear good clothes," pointing toward a neat pile on the tile bench while he was shaving. "I keep clean," pointing toward the showers. "And I shave every day," running his left hand up the left side of his face. He said SFC had been a haven since he lost his apartment two weeks earlier, on New Year's Day. He praised a doctor at the Stout Street Clinic who diagnosed him as a manic-depressive and who gave him the right medicine for it. The problem developed when he said he wanted to enjoy the Christmas holidays, so he stopped taking the medicine.

"I would stay up for five days in a row, or more, without getting any sleep. Then when I crashed, I'd sleep for almost that long. You can't keep a job that way."

I agreed.

"No, and I was working in the mental health field," letting me know he was aware of the irony.

Bill closed the conversation with another compliment for SFC, kudos for the "Christian principles of the staff." I repeated the conversation in the postwork sharing at 2:00. Joe Brzozowski, the Polish American volunteer whose last name I had finally learned, had walked in during part of the conversation and confirmed my account of the conversation to the others.

My notes indicate that Elaine, Emily, and I saw a performance that week of *Rent* at the Denver Performing Arts Center, a block away from our loft. Knowing in advance that it was an update of the opera *La Boheme*, I was still surprised to realize it dealt so directly with homelessness and was pleased that art addressed the problem.

A week later it was cold again, the sidewalks were covered with ice and snow, and I found a large group of people waiting to get into the shelter; two of them were one-legged, one on crutches, the other in a wheelchair. I was a bit late, the lobby was full, and after knocking to be admitted, I could see through the windows that the group was doing the salt rite. A guest was watching them closely.

"They're doing their walking." Looking at me he asked, "Are they praying?"

"They are purifying the building with salt, and they are singing," I said.

"What are they singing?" he said, straining to understand this behavior.

"They are singing a hymn."

We are as mysterious to them as they are to us, I later thought and recorded in my notes.

While at mail/storage, a white-haired woman asked me to come from behind the counter and walk over to her table. It was slow at that time so I complied. She held up a paperback copy of John Dean's *Blind Ambition,* and told me she had "met the author, who is now a woman working at a shelter for women." She said Frank Sinatra had been the author's mentor, tapping her left temple with her left index finger, saying, "Everything in her mind was put there by Sinatra."

In the sharing period at the end of the day, I said the guests had been "testy" during the day. Mike and others nodded. Cecil asked me to amplify the statement. I did so by narrating an example, an altercation, an inter-racial incident involving shouting between two people. I related another incident at mail/storage; as I was working my way through a bunch of letters looking for mail, the guest asked me questions that I answered, and I may have asked some he answered. Another guest standing at the other window waiting to return his bag said, "Would you end that con-versation, I'm in a hurry."

I admitted to the group that anger had risen in me. I finished looking through the letters, "Not today," I said to the guest I was serving, then walked over to the man in a hurry, gesturing to indicate he was free to carry the bag back into the storage room and put it on its designated shelf. As I accompanied him I said, "I was working, helping that man by trying to find his mail. It is possible for me to talk and listen while looking for a name on an envelope."

"I'm sorry," he said.

My comments sparked a discussion among staff and volunteers about testiness and impatience. Mike, our young coordinator, told another story. He recalled an earlier period when, without health insurance, he visited the East Clinic and learned what it meant to wait in line. "They wait to get in the shelter in the morning, wait to get their bags, wait in line to get their mail, wait to take a shower, wait to get clothes, and move on to other shelters and wait for meals and beds." It was a parable.

I must be patient with their impatience, I thought and later wrote in my notes. "I complimented Mike for his valuable insight. People at the bottom wait in line. People at the bottom wait to be served by superiors, those at the next step up on the big H, or Hierarchy."

On February 12, 1999, Lincoln's birthday, it was only twenty degrees Fahrenheit with snow on the ground when I walked to SFC. After the salt ritual and sharing, I headed off to open the men's showers by myself.

Fifteen men came in to use the showers, five blacks, five Hispanics, five whites.

One of the black men said, "I know what you want, a job at nine or ten dollars an hour you can work at everyday, but you aren't going to find that in Denver."

"I make thirteen dollars an hour," said a two-fingered Hispanic man.

"Oh, sure, robbing convenience stores and robbing banks."

And as he slapped some smellgood on his face, the black man said, "Oh, we'll be undeniable today." We all laughed.

Two days later, Valentine's Day, Sunday, February 14, Elaine and I gathered with others at 1:00 p.m. at SFC for a march: "Have a Heart: A Walk in the Footsteps of the Homeless." We heard a welcome from Jack Real, director of education at CCH, and a prayer by Reverend Lucia Guzman of the Colorado Council of Churches. We marched off to the Stout Street Clinic for a speech by a homeless man, Eric Lind, a spokesman for the community. The speech was advertised under the title "The Experience of Being Homeless." He talked about the complications of trying to make the transition off the street.

"When the minimum wage was first established fifty years ago," said Eric, "it was set at the poverty level for a family of four. Today the minimum wage is $5.15, $2.60 below the poverty level for a family of four: $7.75. If someone were to offer me a job tomorrow morning," he continued, "I would have to worry about the bus fare to get there. I would also have to figure out how to get a shower between now and then." He said waiting in line for a bed in a shelter is a "waste of time," something he didn't do except on the coldest nights. Otherwise he sleeps on the streets. "If all of us came in, there wouldn't be enough beds and shelters. There is more to it than getting a job."

Next spoke Ed Farrell, a doctor who had been working at the Stout Street Clinic (SSC) for five years at that time. He said the clinic was "unique," supplying full medical services, caseworkers, and follow-ups. He said the causes of homelessness were "as diverse as the faces on the planet," and he echoed Eric Lind's theme that getting off the street is far more complicated than following the simple advice, "Get a job."

J. Sebastian Sinisi of the *Denver Post* wrote the next day (February 15, 2000) that two hundred people had joined in the Valentine's Day march, which moved on from SSC to the Holy Ghost Church in uptown Denver, a beautiful Catholic church known for helping homeless people, including passing out sandwiches at midmorning on weekdays. They moved on to Samaritan House, a shelter for individuals and some families supported by Catholic Charities USA.

On Tuesday of that week, February 16, I attended a legislative action day at St. Thomas Episcopal Church, a lovely southwestern structure. Talk about the future was discouraging. Senator Ken Gordon, a Democrat and the minority leader of the Colorado State Senate, gave a speech that was both realistic and somewhat depressing in saying that the new legislature is "more conservative than any of the preceding ones." Members wanted to reduce spending from sixty dollars per day on state prisoners to fifty-one dollars by privatization; aid to needy families would also go down.

Everyone in Colorado was in a state of shock after the violent assault at Columbine High School in a suburb of Denver on April 20, 1999. By the end of that gruesome day, fifteen people had died. The *Denver Voice* for May 1999 carried an unsigned poem, "That Day at Columbine." The last two lines:

> *We grieve for the victims*
> *of flower draped Columbine.*

"Who is behind the killings at Columbine?" asked a guest at the shelter with an eastern European accent and a wiry beard contained by three heavy-duty rubber bands.

"What do you mean 'behind it?'" I asked as we walked back to get his storage bag.

"The guns, ammunition, bombs, all of that. Do you believe two teenagers could do all that?"

I didn't know what to say. A staff member had told me this guest was paranoid. Perhaps sensing my quandary, he asked another question.

"Could you have done that in high school?"

"No."

Paranoid or not, he could ask excellent questions.

On that day I spent the time from 12:45 to 1:00 training in the showers with Joe. It was the second time. I regarded the training sessions as
"hard work" and as the premises to a syllogism. Assigning me to clean
the showers must be on their mind.

Sure enough, on April 30, 1999, my work slip said:

- 12:00–12:45 Shower
- 12:45–1:00 Shower

The coordinator had supplied the conclusion to the syllogism. I joked
with Joe, showing him my work slip and saying they were setting me up
to replace him. He laughed along with me.

Between noon and 12:45, I tried to serve the men towels and other
items, moving out from behind the counter at every opportunity to pick
up towels and sweep the floor from one end to the other. An unpleasant
part of that is sweeping up the soiled toilet paper behind and around the
stools. Chris, the young coordinator of volunteers, came in to see how
I was doing and helped me with that task. I asked why the guests threw
the soiled toilet paper on the floor. Chris answered that immigrants from
Mexico and Central America were socialized not to put paper in the toilets because of primitive sewer systems. Ever since then I have thought
we ought either to supply them with waste containers or put up a sign in
Spanish saying it was OK to flush the paper.

The door was locked then at 12:45 whether the men were finished
or not. The entire area, from the end where the toilets and urinals are,
through the walkway to the sinks and mirrors, through the dressing
area with benches, to the walls and floor of the shower area, all had to be
sprayed with a disinfectant. A staff member and Joe came in to help for
fifteen minutes. At 1:00 Mike brought in three guests who would help
me for about fifteen or twenty minutes, scrubbing toilets and urinals,
cleaning mirrors and sinks, scrubbing the walls of the showers and the
floors throughout with stiff, long-handled brushes. After they left, I had

to hurry to spray all the disinfectant down the three rectangular drains, and then squeegee the water down the drain.

Then it was a race to put it all back together again for Sunday. The shelter was closed on Saturday for a day of rest, and the rush on Sunday morning was said to be frenzied, so I had to replenish floor mats and facecloths, get new rolls of toilet paper in the holders, liquid bath soap in the containers, and bars in the trays. I was one tired shelter volunteer. Chris came in to inspect the place and made a few suggestions. He got a dustpan and brush to show me how to clean the long hair and other debris out of the drainage grates. Mike came in to ask if I had let one of my guest helpers leave early. I said yes, and he said I should keep them all the same amount of time. We tried to be consistent in application of the rules at SFC, *equal* treatment for our guests, treatment we could accept if it were applied to us. I accepted the lessons from the two staff members and felt as though I had that day become a full-fledged volunteer. I've been cleaning the showers ever since. It is a tough job, but it is a source of pride to be one of two or three volunteers to do the job, Joe being a constant all this time as well.

On Friday, May 7, 1999, I heard someone say of a guest that he had run away at the appearance of the police. *What police?*

I asked Tom about it. He said the police were trying to reduce the drug traffic by not letting people gather in front of our building or across the street. "Why now?" Tom said the neighbors were complaining about people milling around the building. He also said somebody was buying up the property around SFC.

"Why?"

Tom answered that a complex of three hundred low-rent units was being torn down to make space for a new project of middle-class housing. Gentrification was moving from the area around the new baseball park, Coors Field, to the area around the shelter. Major league baseball was such a big hit that fans demanded and got bars, restaurants, condos, and lofts, transforming the formerly seedy, industrial neighborhood. Real estate prices soared, making for contested urban space. The ballpark itself provided new jobs for SFC guests as vendors and cooks. Perhaps there was a causal relationship between the appearance of the police and the gentrification process. As I left the building at 2:30 or so, there was a policeman talking with Tom on the sidewalk in front of our building. The man in blue was frowning at Tom, and the one segment of his speech I caught was "We've seen three [drug] deals go down."

Friday, May 14, 1999, was a special day, a memorial service for a homeless man named Jimmy Martinez who had been a regular guest at SFC. Jimmy had fallen out of a moving pickup truck, was put up in a friend's room, and died ten days later. We gathered at 2:00 in the corner of the great room we call the chapel, with brass nameplates on the wall engraved with the names of guests who have died. The guests set up the chairs, two rows of them facing the simple wooden table used as an altar during the Christmas service we had attended. After sixteen or seventeen people had taken their seats, Tom, a former Vincentian priest, placed a vase of spring flowers on the table. He began to speak, outlining how the ritual would unfold. He invited those who knew Jimmy Martinez to speak about him, emphasizing his positive traits. A friend of Jimmy's spoke first; rather, he tried to speak, but sobbed so deeply I couldn't understand him.

A middle-aged man at my left who was not homeless rose to speak about Jimmy.

"I have known Jimmy for forty-nine years. I am his brother. He was forty-nine. I am fifty-four, five years older. And yet I didn't know him as well as some of you," gesturing toward the three male guests on my right, at the opposite side of the audience.

"It was my fault."

At first I thought he meant he was responsible for his brother's accident or death, or both, but his meaning became clear when he said, "I tried to be close, but he was distant. He didn't return my calls or answer my messages." The brother began sobbing and dabbing his eyes. He said he had practically raised Jimmy, recalling the time Jimmy fell off a bicycle when they were on the way to buy candy. He told us to cherish the time we have left in our lives.

A guest rose at my right to speak. He looked clean-cut despite the blue jeans and T-shirt. I had been told that he and Jimmy were close friends, almost inseparable, and even resembled each other enough that staff members confused them at times. The friend spoke without notes at a measured pace, as if thinking through what would become Jimmy's eulogy. He said he had known Jimmy for four years. At first they were friends, then they became close friends. "During those four years we were together three years and eleven months. I am not ashamed to call him my brother," he said, looking at Jimmy's blood brother. The speaker turned from the relationship to the object of his friendship, trying to answer why Jimmy was homeless.

"When I first came to this place, I thought that some of the people don't look like homeless people. Jimmy didn't look homeless; why, he could go down to the Sixteenth Street Mall, and nobody would think of him as homeless." *He could pass.* "I probably knew Jimmy better than anybody, and I don't know why he was homeless. I've tried to figure it out. He was a nice guy, sure he had some run-ins with the police, but that was only about too many glasses of wine." He spoke of their relationship on the road, "trampin' if you want to call it that," in which they wintered in warmer weather, and returned to Denver in the spring.

He said Jimmy "never spoke behind anybody's back, *never complained,*" emphasizing those two words, pausing to let them sink in. "Jimmy spoke warmly of his sister, brother, and parents," helping his parents during illness in their old age. "I'd like to believe Jimmy is in a better place."

The speaker took his seat without showing any emotion. There was a long silence before anyone rose to speak. Finally, a tall Native American rose, but he spoke so softly I couldn't follow him. An elderly man followed him, saying he had been a volunteer at SFC for seven years, and that Jimmy had a "spark." "He was my friend. I don't know if I was his friend, but he was my friend."

Chris, the young assistant director and coordinator of volunteers, said he had arrived at SFC four years ago, anxious about how he would fare in a new job. "Ironically," he said, "Jimmy did what he could to make me feel welcome in this building."

Carla spoke directly to Jimmy's friend, thanking him for his words, and apologizing for confusing the two, yet closing with the warning that she might do it again. He smiled.

Tom inquired as to whether any one else had something to say. No response. He walked to the table, picking up the flowers. "They are diverse and pretty, but they won't last." He invited each of us to take one of the flowers to keep as a memory of Jimmy. He gestured toward the nameplates on the wall behind him, saying Jimmy would have his place there, the better to remember him. "Many don't think of the homeless as persons. I will remember Jimmy's face, the person who just happened to be homeless."

We circled the table and held hands, singing "Amazing Grace." The brother said Jimmy's ashes would be scattered at Fort Logan and that the obituary would soon appear in the newspapers. Cecil later gave me a copy he had clipped from a newspaper, but I don't know which one, the date, or page number.

Jimmy Martinez
    Army Supply Technician, 49
    Jimmy Martinez of Denver, an Army supply technician, died May 10. He was 49. A memorial will be at 10 a.m. June 3 at Fort Logan National Cemetery, 3698 S. Sheridan Blvd., Denver. There will be a cremation. He was born Oct. 12, 1949, in Las Animas. He served in the Air Force during the Vietnam War. He is survived by two sisters, Sylvia Villa, Pueblo, and Connie, Denver; and six brothers, Alfred, Orlando, Eddie and Frank, all of Denver, Paul, Albuquerque, and Richard, San Antonio, Texas.

I had begun to understand the hourly, daily, weekly, and seasonal cycles at SFC; this service added another, the sanctified cycle of life and death in a homeless shelter.

Chapter Six

Police Harassment and Degrees of Being

On Friday, May 28, 1999, I got to the shelter early after walking to work. A staff meeting was still going on around the table in our lunchroom. Tom was talking about a problem that had been troubling me for several weeks: police harassment. I put my lunch in the refrigerator, and while wondering whether I should be privy to the discussion, someone asked me to take a seat at the table. Tom's manner was serious. He said we would have to consider opening the front door earlier than 8:00 a.m. to get the people off the street. He also said we would have to prohibit contractors and other people hiring workers from picking them up in front of the building. My personal feeling was indignation bordering on outrage.

The topic and mood carried over to the sharing discussion in the great room. Someone brought up police harassment of SFC again. Cecil, who had not heard the discussion in the staff meeting, asked for a summary of the situation. "That's a bunch of crap," he said after listening to Tom's narrative. "Do you want me to call the American Civil Liberties Union? I've been a member for fifty years." Tom thanked him, saying he thought it would be premature. I asked Tom for the worst possible outcome, and he said it would be the closing of the center. I expressed my anger, asserting that homeless people had too little space as it is. After Craig said a prayer,

I headed for the showers and was also disappointed by shortages—no Vaseline, no socks, no smellgood. I recalled a conversation with Craig the week before in which he had said that the shortages were due to the season. In the spring and summer people don't worry about homeless people out in the cold.

A man who spoke little English faced me and began a swirling motion with his hand, asking, "Do you have a—to-clean-the-ears?" Yes, I did have some Q-tips, but the absence of Vaseline is serious. Some African Americans have many uses for it. Many of them call it "grease," and they apply it to the body as a lotion, use it to treat burns and wounds, and some use it as a hair dressing. And smellgood is probably the number-two booster of morale, after a hot shower, for many of our guests.

A relatively well-dressed young white man asked me for a towel, face-cloth, soap, and shampoo. Looking at the crowded showers, he handed them back to me, saying he would shower elsewhere.

"Why?"

"Too many tramps."

I wish now I had asked him whether the stress should be on "too many" or "tramps." He did sit down, take off his boots, and wash his feet. When he got up from the bench to walk to the mirror, I noticed he was walking oddly, in a rocking motion that didn't make sense until I saw he was wearing a pair of old leather ski boots.

On Saturday, June 5, 1999, I wrote that Friday had been a slow day at SFC. While walking from mail/storage to the clothing room at 9:00, I asked Chris about the smaller number of guests in the building. His answer was that many guests get a Social Security check at the first of the month, allowing them to check into a motel on Colfax Avenue, called the "longest Main Street in America." Parts of Colfax are quite seedy with cheap motels and prostitutes on the prowl, and that is why some call it "Cold Facts" Avenue. Thus I had discovered another cycle—a monthly one to go along with the seasons and changing weather patterns, donation patterns, media coverage, days of the week, and, as we saw in the previous chapter, life and death. There is also a pattern to the hours of the day. The guests pour in at 8:00 a.m. when the doors are opened, line up to get a storage space if available, to get their bags, and to check yesterday's mail.

They also shower, shave, brush their teeth, and line up for coffee. It slows down around 11:00 when they leave to find a free meal. It picks up again at 1:00 because they know we close down mail/storage at 2:00.

I wrote in my field notes for June 11 that the June 1999 issue of the *Denver Voice* was out, with two articles about the death of two guests. A story on the front page by Eric Lind, who had spoken at the Stout Street Clinic about his homeless existence, was about the fatal stabbing of Milan Dante Hudson on April 24. Lind contrasted the publicity given the Columbine killings with the media inattention to Mr. Hudson's killing.

My field notes also contain the report that I sensed a loss of morale among the staff members. I expressed my sense of these matters to Mike, the Friday coordinator, and he agreed. Indignation and anger are accompanied by the loss of morale. He said he would like to be appreciated by the police, not harassed by them. I got Carla's notes from the SFC town hall meeting in which guests were encouraged to speak up. Some praised the value premise, or rule, of fairness at SFC—someone used the expression "same discipline for all," but some guests complained about inconsistencies in decisions to eighty-six guests. Police harassment emerged as a complaint. The town hall meeting was designed to give homeless people *voice*, as their newspaper *Voice* does, and as does "*La Vos*, Colorado's No. 1 Hispanic Voice—for 24 years," as its slogan goes.

At lunch that day Jean Garrison, the administrative director, told me about a new service that Jerry would be heading, an employment office to help our guests find day labor. I asked her if that meant a change in our policy not to cooperate with exploitative day-labor agencies. She said that it was a temporary solution for short-term survival needs and that we would obtain higher wages for the guests than the temp agencies did. That information was crucial at 1:00 when I worked the door at the clothing room and noticed a broad-shouldered white man, perhaps six feet two inches tall, who looked fit and *presentable* in his clean pants and light blue T-shirt. After checking off the items he had picked up on his clothing slip, I expected him to leave the room. Instead, he moved closer to me, and lowered his voice so that no one else could hear him.

"I just got out of jail. Tell me what to do." There was the look of a frightened animal in his face.

"How long have you been out?"

"About two hours."

"Then you need to find a job," I said tentatively. "We have a new service here to help people find temporary jobs. You need to locate a man named Jerry. Ask the greeters at the door."

He nodded.

At home that day I received a copy of the *St. Francis Sun,* the shelter's quarterly newsletter. I studied carefully the executive director's report about a meeting with neighbors of SFC, one of whom had said, "It's time these people moved somewhere else." Tom's response to those words was, "The poor and the homeless are no longer welcome and certainly no one wants to see them.... The poor are out of places to run to for help or a place to be. We hope to remain here for them as a sign that God still finds them worthy even if our society has banished them. Thanks for helping St. Francis Center continue to accomplish its mission to those who are poor."

Word spread quickly that the police had paid another visit to SFC, harassing Tom. I mentioned to him a paper I'd recently read about the NIMBY syndrome, "not in my back yard." He smiled, having heard the acronym in the circles of service providers in which he worked. The city administration seemed almost paralyzed by fear of neighborhood associations that wanted nothing built in their backyards that would attract the needy or the despised. Several staff members and volunteers talked about NIMBY in the 2:00 discussion of police harassment.

It was with some apprehension that I approached the two-hour shift to clean up the showers. Would I remember the many tasks to be done? Not just to get the place clean, but to make it ready for Sunday as well. I began to pick up dirty clothes and towels as soon as I took over at noon. The stench in the room was the worst I had experienced. The clothes abandoned by one man reeked so badly that his friend, waiting for him to go get a cold beer, made faces and rebuked him loudly. I had eaten an early lunch and thought I would vomit when I bent over to pick up, with rubber gloves of course, the discarded rags. Chris passed through to ask how I was doing. I mentioned the malodorous clothes; he showed me a deodorant spray I promptly put to good use.

By the time we—I had three guests who helped me for fifteen minutes or so, thus earning a clothing slip—had sprayed, scrubbed, rinsed, and squeegeed the place, my hair was dripping wet from the top of my ears down. It was 2:05 before I could turn out the lights and lock up. We read a psalm, talked about the day, and heard a prayer, and I for one turned in quite early that Friday night.

On June 25, I noticed a young man in a security uniform participating in the morning ritual. I didn't understand what he was doing there but later heard from staff members what had led up to his short tenure as a security guard at SFC. Some police officers had been maintaining for some time that we shouldn't let the guests congregate or loiter in front of the building. They also claimed that we didn't have the competence to keep them moving and therefore needed to hire a security guard to do it for us. They even recommended the company we should engage for the service. SFC promptly did so, hiring the very owner of the company recommended by the police, the very man who participated in the morning ritual. At our midmorning break we were incredulous to learn that, ironically, the police had arrested our security guard for a number of unpaid parking tickets.

The first Friday of July was a quiet day. One guest told me that those who got their checks were in motel rooms "drinking, drinking, and smoking crack."

New rules had been adopted by the second Friday in July in response to police pressure. Our guests had to form two lines to enter the building, one for the first half of the alphabet, the other for the second. The greeters record the surnames of the guests who enter, and guests are told that if they leave the building they cannot reenter for two hours.

A smiling officer of the Denver Police Department greeted me when I entered the center at about 7:10 a.m. on the third Friday of July. I turned to staff members for an explanation. My notes say that I believed it was Carla who said that we had agreed to hire off-duty uniformed police officers to sit on a stool near the greeters. "The one this morning is at least friendly." I wrote a parenthetical question in my field notes for the day: "(Is this a conflict of interest for them to harass us into such an agreement?)."

A tall, lean volunteer worker at the storage counter said, "Boy, you sure know how to clear this place out," nodding at the police officer.

"What do you mean?"

"This place is almost empty."

"If we bother them that much, you don't want them in here," answered the police officer. When I got a chance, I repeated the conversation in such a way that the policeman could overhear it. Jerry said the hall was often empty at *this time of year.*

During lunch the discussion somehow turned to SFC and organizations in general. I wanted to avoid playing the professor and making judgments about SFC until I had more evidence, but Craig wanted to pursue the topic. He had reached some conclusions about the rotating coordinators and asked me about it. Others joined the conversation, and we agreed that the center's policy was that there was not a single boss for operations (staff members took turns coordinating the center's activities for one day). Tom was clearly the boss as executive director, and there were a few decisions he made in consultation with Jean, his administrative director, but only after a full discussion in staff meetings. I had walked in on a couple of these, and they were consistent with the description given. They pressed me to comment.

I mentioned Theory X and Theory Y, the somewhat oversimplified categories of management-organization theories. Douglas McGregor had noted that management-organization theory was not consistent. Some theories contradict others. McGregor placed the opposing theories in the X and Y categories. Theory X is the top-down, authoritarian approach that assumes that people are lazy and will not accept responsibility. Theory Y is a bottom-up organizational approach that assumes people will readily accept responsibility if given the chance and that better decisions will be made if people are given *voice*.[1] I also explained a theory I had helped develop, "concertive" control, in which organizations operate by means of autonomous teams that have the authority to make decisions—that is, drawing conclusions from premises—by applying the organization's preferred value premise, whether it be efficiency or the Golden Rule, in concrete cases.[2] I said that SFC leaned more toward Theory Y than Theory X and that I could see evidence of concertive control at SFC. I could also see, I added, evidence that members of the staff and even some volunteers sought, rather than avoided, responsibility. I also remarked on the staff's solicitous practices. They held town hall meetings for guests; for volunteers they had luncheons and sharing meetings in which they kept us informed and asked us for suggestions and opinions. It was not all downward-directed communication. They all seemed to agree with these observations.

The last Friday of July was, according to my notes, the busiest day I had yet worked at mail/storage. If the first of the month falls on a weekend, the government mails checks out so they arrive on Friday. All morning people pressed us in person and on the phone to learn whether or not the day's mail had been sorted. One guest asked me to look for a blue envelope with her name on it, a Social Security disability check. There was a mood of anticipation as the mail was sorted into alphabetical order. I got some big smiles and words of thanks for distributing the checks.

One of our guests uses a wheelchair because he has only one leg. As I checked him out of the clothing room, he showed me a handful of mismatched socks. They are freebies, and the guest doesn't get "charged" for them. "I only need one at a time," he said, explaining why he thoughtfully didn't ask for a pair, making one more pair available for the featherless bipeds who come to our center for socks. I let him keep them.

The August 1999 issue of the *Voice* had an article on the front page reminding its readers of its Beat past. The headlines:

YOU CAN'T PARK HERE

SONNY LAWSON PADLOCKED

JACK KEROUAC'S FAVORITE DENVER SPOT

CASUALTY OF WAR AGAINST THE POOR

At the top of the page was a black-and-white photograph of a wire fence with padlocked gate and a wooden sign inside the fence proclaiming, "sonny lawson park."

The article provides some historical background: "According to some of the residents around Sonny Lawson Park their problems started about five years ago, when the redevelopment of the LoDo area forced many of the less fortunate, i.e., those who could not afford to spend half a million dollars on an apartment in some renovated warehouse, to relocate north of town." The writer, "Mike," talks about the booming real estate market; then comes this line: "So just as greed and self-serving politicians have forced the Catholic Worker soup kitchen to close their doors after twenty years of service, and led to the St. Francis Center hiring off-duty police officers to keep the undesirables out of sight, they also fenced off the park." At the bottom of the page, there is a quotation from *On the Road* about Sonny Lawson Park. Here is the paragraph as it appears in my paperback copy of Kerouac's book:

> Down at 23rd and Welton a softball game was going on under floodlights which also illuminated the gas tank. A great eager crowd roared at every play. The strange young heroes of all kinds, white, colored, Mexican, pure Indian, were on the field, performing with heart-breaking seriousness. Just sandlot kids in uniform. Never in my life as an athlete had I ever permitted myself to perform like this in front of families and girl friends and kids of the neighborhood, at night, under lights; always it had been college, big-time, soberfaced; no boyish, human joy like this. Now it was too late. Near me sat an old Negro who apparently watched the games every night. Next to him was an old white bum; then a Mexican family, then some girls, some boys—all humanity, the lot. Oh, the sadness of the lights that night. The young pitcher looked just like Dean. A pretty blonde in the seats looked just like Marylou. It was the Denver Night; all I did was die.
>
> *Down in Denver, down in Denver*
> *All I did was die.*[3]

The literate homeless people of Denver know their Kerouac. I took a walk to Sonny Lawson Park and sadly observed the padlocks.

Mike was on his honeymoon on August 20 so Chris filled in as coordinator for the day. Cecil was going out to buy a burrito for lunch, so I asked him to pick up one for me. At lunch Cecil reported the man would no longer be able to sell his *comida*, or food, in our neighborhood. The police said the neighbors didn't want the poor Mexicans to collect around his wagon. Cecil said the American Civil Liberties Union (ACLU) might have an opinion on all this pressure. I assumed they would be willing to fight the harassment.

On the last Friday of August 1999, I drove to the center. As I arrived at 7:15, parking in the lot across the street, I observed a uniformed policeman frisking a man on the sidewalk just past SFC.

The building was to be closed to put in a new floor on October 8—my birthday, when I became Phillip's 66—and Carla gave me a heads-up call so I wouldn't again walk eight blocks to an empty building. We also talked about the horrific news reports that four homeless men had been beaten to death. She said two of them were regulars at SFC, and other guests who slept on grates at the First Bank said they had been beaten. Carla said that the police were investigating the incidents and that an officer had interviewed one of our guests about an assault. I told her that I had recognized the photograph of one of the victims, a man I had seen all over downtown Denver, sometimes inebriated, but that I had never seen him at the center.

On October 22, 1999, I had a striking conversation with Tom about the killings. He said he had talked the day before with a police investigator who had advised homeless people to stay off the street at night. The investigator also told Tom the department was treating the incidents as "crime." I nodded, reassured, but upon reflection I found this statement to reveal a profound revelation of bias against homeless men, and I also wondered where they might go to get off the streets, given the limited number of shelter beds.

In his essay "Four Master Tropes," Kenneth Burke wrote, "We could say that characters [in literary works] possess *degrees of being* in proportion to the variety of perspectives from which they can with justice be perceived. Thus we could say that plants have 'more being' than minerals, animals have more being than plants, and men have more being than animals, because each higher order admits and requires a new dimension of terms not literally relevant to the lower orders."[4] Although Burke didn't go this far, it would also seem that some humans have fewer degrees of being than others. Recall that Goffman wrote, "We believe the person with a stigma is not quite human." That is the implication of the investigator's remark that the beatings would be treated as *crimes*. There would be no need to make such a remark after the death of four socialites or four middle-class people. What went *unsaid* is "even though they are homeless, worthless, stigmatized bums."

My daughter Emily was at the time working at the Tattered Cover in LoDo, one of the largest independent bookstores in the country and a Denver institution. She got a call from a young man who wanted to change his address. He wanted to change it from 2323 Curtis, the address of the St. Francis Center, to a new address. As Emily later wrote in an e-mail message to me, she was probably the only person at the Tattered Cover who could have truly understood that call and the motives behind it. "His voice sounded happy and proud and I almost congratulated him, but I didn't want him to know I knew about the shelter. So I just changed his address. Dad, when I told you about it you said that he was not only changing his address, but his degrees of being."

Discussions during breaks and lunches and sharing keep turning inward, perhaps because we were powerless to stop the police harassment and the crimes; we kept returning to the shelter-qua-organization and its practices. Mike, the Friday coordinator, said this about rotating coordinators: It helped avoid burnout. After a day of making decisions, he was exhausted. This made sense to me as a student of organization. Jerry admitted he felt burned out in the employment agency because our guests lacked social and communicative skills. They couldn't manage anger, stomping off the job when they got mad. Then they weren't around to get paid for the time they did work. This made for angry phone calls from employers to Jerry.

On the Friday marking my first anniversary at SFC, an event occurred during the first hour while I was running the men's showers. I couldn't help noticing a showered and clothed African American man shouting at a white man taking a shower. The white man shouted back in a language no one could understand. Then on the opposite side of the room another African American man, naked and shaving his face and head at the sink, began shouting. He was answered by a second white man, a muscular, sculpted young man taking a shower. I couldn't get the drift of the heated exchange, but I felt it might get out of hand, might become violent. I considered dialing the number of the front desk and asking for help, but instead I tried to defuse the situation by calmly calling for them to "cool it."

The first dyad, or pair of communicants, had quieted by then, and the athletic white man shouted, "We shouldn't even be doing this because of that murderer out there." As I've already described in chapter 1, at that period there was a series of murders of homeless men. This morning the word was out that a fifth homeless man had been beaten to death. The young white man walked to the place where his clothes lay on the bench, not five feet from the man shaving. The black man made the first move, saying something I couldn't hear—his face was turned away from me—and reached his right hand to the other. The white man accepted it in his right hand, saying, "Yeah, man, we have to stick together," another allusion to the killer or killers. The two naked men, one black and the other white, stood solemnly shaking hands. It is still a memorable image; years later it is a reminder of how two can identify, can become one in opposition to a dangerous third.[5]

On Friday, November 5, 1999, Tom Hollis, one of the men seriously beaten, came into the showers while I was in charge. (His photo and name appeared in a local newspaper that morning, making him a public figure, and therefore I use his real name.) I'd served Tom for over a year and knew him fairly well, so after he showered and shaved he was interested in talking about his experiences.

He told me that he had been asleep in Skyline Park the preceding month, the part of it closer to Eighteenth Street than the one on the mall. He was roughly awakened with a kick in the back. "I got up with a rock as big as your head and gave one of them some stitches." He said he had six stitches himself on his brow and hairline and eight more on top of his head. They kicked, punched, and hit him "with everything they had," which I took to mean some sort of weapons.

"Did you know them?" I asked.

"No," he replied, "but I identified them to the police."

"How many were there?"

"Seven."

"What do you think their motive was?"

"Thrills."

"Are they connected to the murders?"

Tom answered, "When I asked the officer that question he said, 'We have strong evidence to believe they are.'"

Other men gathered around him, so he said to all who were interested that the young people were beginning to "tell on each other." This word was received with positive enthusiasm. One huge man declared, "And they're homeless by choice."

I'd interrupted composing my field notes for the previous Friday to catch the local news at 5:00 on Channel Four. There were a couple of videotapes of police in the St. Francis Center, one showing an officer passing out yellow leaflets. Mayor Wellington Webb, a tall African American, was shown saying, "The victims are human beings." The chief of police said that the victims were "humans and citizens" and that their deaths were therefore deserving of a thorough investigation.

During a commercial break, I thought about those remarks. Both seemed to be saying that although the seven didn't have all the degrees of being the rest of us enjoyed, they were biological humans; ergo, their fate should be considered a crime. They seemed to assume their audience did *not* consider them to be humans and had to be instructed on the matter in order to justify police activities to catch the perpetrators. Channel Four came back to the story with the news that the police had completed their search "behind Union Station" and that the FBI would help process the evidence.

The police arrested six teenagers to be charged with one of the killings and some beatings of older homeless men. I began to search the social science literature for work about teenage crime. A significant study of youth crime and homelessness had been published in 1997. Researchers interviewed nearly five hundred homeless youth in two very different Canadian cities, Toronto and Vancouver, reporting the results and conclusions in *Mean Streets: Youth Crime and Homelessness,* by John Hagan and Bill McCarthy. After analyzing all the data, the criminologists embraced what is called "Social Capital Theory," or more precisely, "human capital." Human capital is different from financial or economic capital. It adds up to the advantages a person has by virtue of being born into a family that is embedded in a network that supports him or her. It is a person's skills, knowledge, and connections. "It ain't what you know, it's who you know" is a folksy expression of the notion of social capital.

What happens if one is born into a family without such advantages? One will be less likely to do well in school; in general, one's life chances will be significantly lower. The authors integrated within this theory two other, smaller theories. The first, control theory, predicts that those who have reduced familial influence and erratic parenting achieve less success in life. The second, strain theory, posits that explosive, violent families often force the children to leave, to run away to the streets. Once they leave, there is a "downward spiral in the capital positions of young people who take to the street." It is intensified by their experiences on the street. And "we find consistent evidence of relationships between involvement in street crime and lack of food, work and shelter."[6]

It gets worse. Such teenagers may well find themselves embedded in networks that *teach them illegal behaviors*. The youth studied tended to deny they joined gangs; their metaphor of choice for their companions was a "family." In other words, they are part of a social system characterized by the term *criminal capital*. Mentors and tutors abound, ready to teach a young woman how to steal food or panhandle, ready to recruit a young man into the job of selling drugs and ready to teach him the ropes. Ineluctably they get caught, go to jail, and are thereafter marked with another stigma. Stigmas can lead to shame and rage, violence, and repeated crimes and convictions. Hagan and McCarthy report that the prospects for such youth embedded in such a social structure are not at all sanguine. They may well grow into homeless adult criminals. Their only hope seems to be employment, plus the shelter that a job can sometimes buy, and the *discipline* that regular work requires. But the employment opportunities for a labeled, stigmatized, defiant young woman or man are low-paying jobs in the secondary market, and they are hard to find.

It seems quite possible from this theory and evidence that a "family" of alienated youth, emboldened by newly acquired criminal capital, stigmatized and full of rage, could beat homeless men to death.

CHAPTER SEVEN
THE SOCIAL CONSTRUCTION OF KILLERS
BY MEANS OF COMMUNICATION

After the fact of Joe Mendoza's death sank in, I quickly explained to Tom my conversations with Joe and Craig. He replied that I should tell everything I knew to the detective who was on his way to the St. Francis Center. I waited at the welcoming desk, shaken and drained. Tom must have sensed how upset I was, for he suggested I go home and let Craig talk to the detective. My automatic response was, "I feel as though I have to."

When the detective arrived, he asked us if we could identify two men in separate photographs. I didn't recognize the first man, but the detective gave his name and Jean walked to the TB card files to look for records of him. The man in the second photograph was, sadly, Joe Mendoza. I sank again.

Someone retrieved Joe's bag from the storage room. The detective said he would have to go to his car for gloves. "We've got gloves," said Craig. Five or six of us went into the lunchroom to take seats around the table.

The detective said he had, "by coincidence, met Joe at the detox center on November 3." This would have been only five days after my conversation with Joe. *Joe must have gone on a binge after our conversation to wind up in detox five days later.* Joe had walked out in his stocking feet to talk to the detective about an altercation he had witnessed between two other men, and yet the detective said he was impressed by Joe's appearance, by his being so clean and neatly attired. Tom said that was Joe's way.

I narrated the story. The detective took notes when I gave him Joe's description of the man who was standing over him on October 28, 1999. The detective asked Craig if he could add to my statement. Craig said, "No, Phil got it right." The detective asked me to fill out some forms. "May I use my notes?"

"Yes," he said, "contemporaneous notes are more valuable than long-term memory." (He was right. When I got home, I checked my field notes and discovered my conversation with Joe had taken place three weeks earlier, not two weeks.) After glancing at the statement forms, I could see I would need some information from him.

"What is your name?"

"Dale Wallis," he said, spelling the last name.

When I asked for his telephone number he gave me his station and desk numbers.

"How shall I get these back to you?"

He gave me a fax number.

Detective Wallis told the group there was no doubt about Joe's identity. *But there was no head by which to identify him.*

"How do you know?"

"He had some identity on him, and we know by his fingerprints."

"How long had he been dead?"

"The coroner says four to seven days."

By 6:10 a.m. the next day, Saturday, I was at work on the reports for Detective Wallis. I woke up that morning at 4:30 and went to the 7-Eleven store in our building for coffee and both Denver dailies. There were stories about the police investigation, but Joe Mendoza's identity was not reported.

I faxed the report to Detective Wallis on Sunday. At 6:25 p.m. Tuesday evening, Elaine answered the phone and passed it to me. It was Detective Wallis. He asked me if I knew two persons whose names he gave me. I didn't recognize either of the names. He complimented me on the report, apologizing for not acknowledging it earlier. "Busy," was his excuse for the lapse. He noticed that I was a retired professor and that I kept a journal. I took it as a question.

"Yes," I answered, "I do volunteer work as service out of ethical beliefs, and also study homeless people as a social scientist, reading the literature on poverty, homelessness, and now some about violence." He asked me to tell him what I was reading.

I told him I had read a book that won the Pulitzer Prize, *Why They Kill: The Discoveries of a Maverick Criminologist*, by Richard Rhodes.[1] It was, I continued, about a criminologist named Lonnie Athens who developed a theory of steps through which a person would have to pass in order to become a "virulent" killer.

"How did he find it out?"

I told him that Athens, putting his own life at risk, had interviewed violent killers in state prisons. "He even got some of them to describe murders they had denied doing in court. That's how good he is."

"Wow. Give me the author and title of the book."

I did.

"I guess I'll have to read that book." He gave me his pager number, and we ended the conversation at 6:35.

Rhodes's 323-page book is about a book that is only 99 pages long. I moved from Rhodes to the source, Lonnie Athens, and his book, *The Creation of Dangerous Violent Killers*.[2] Rhodes got so interested in Athens, the maverick criminologist of his title, that he provided biographical material about him as well as explaining his theory and applying it to other cases, one of which I was in the best possible position to evaluate.

It was natural that Athens would become interested in violence. His father had been a violent man, a man who once put Lonnie's head in a toilet and flushed it several times. His father choked him by the neck on one occasion until Lonnie got hold of a chair with which to menace his father and achieve a standoff. Although his father continued to beat Lonnie's older brother and his mother, Lonnie was spared. His father encouraged him to fight back, never to run away, and Lonnie used weapons to get his way. With his grandfather's support, Lonnie, a bright student, got into Virginia Polytechnic Institute, where he majored in political science until a course in sociology introduced him to criminology, which became his major interest. The dominant philosophy of science in criminology was logical positivism, a form of empiricism dictating that the methods used were inferential statistics applied to quantitative data. Athens became an expert in statistics, gathered some data of his own—while still an undergraduate—wrote a paper, and was admitted to graduate work at the University of Wisconsin. There he came under the influence of a professor, Marshall Clinard, who in turn had been educated at the University of Chicago, where the faculty in sociology developed a case study approach instead of a statistical one. People like George Herbert Mead and John Dewey developed a pragmatic sociology, and Herbert Blumer, who subsequently moved to the University of California at Berkeley, did work called symbolic interactionism, a communicative approach to sociology and human relations. When Blumer visited the University of Wisconsin, Athens met him and decided to work with him at Berkeley for his doctorate.

Athens set out to understand virulent crime by interviewing virulent criminals. Wardens didn't like sociologists or criminologists poking around their prisons, so they preferred to distribute questionnaires rather than let their charges be interviewed in depth. It was difficult for Athens to gain access to violent criminals. He did get access to enough to complete a dissertation and the book mentioned above, even though in one interview the prison guards set him up to be murdered by one of his interviewees. Athens was able to overturn the desk between them to trap the would-be killer and force the guards to rescue him.

The reader needs to be prepared for the jargon Athens came up with in his theory: He defined four separate stages of "violentization" through which the virulent, violent killers he interviewed had to pass. The first is *brutalization*, a process in which a young person experiences "horrification," that is, witnessing and suffering from violence or its threat from an authority figure. In addition, the authority coaches or teaches the young person to use violence as a form of protection and as a way of getting what he or she wants.

The second step is *belligerency*, in which the young subject asks this question: "What can I do to stop undergoing any further violent subjugation and personal horrification at the hands of other people?"[3] His (most of Athens's subjects are men) answer is to hear and heed the coaching of the authority figure and use violence to prevent his own subjugation.

The third step is *violent performance,* and it has a bit of Dramatism or the theater in it because the subject seeks awe, respect, and fear from his audience. The subject learns the aphorism "If something is worth fighting about it is worth killing over."[4]

The fourth step is *virulency,* a conscious commitment to use violence as a means of interacting with other people. The subject wants others to regard him as dangerous, to take pains not to provoke him. He may become an outcast unless he can find others who are similarly malevolent with whom he can identify.

According to Athens, most boys begin the process just before their teens, and some complete it by their middle or late teens. Each step must be completed to create or "construct" a virulent killer. In fact, we can say that such killers are socially constructed through communication. Violent words and meaningful deeds make up the first step. Each step, with the possible exception of the second, involves interaction with other people, and as I pointed out, the person will experience a commitment to dramatic performance. Coaching is required as well.

The theory also explains how violent criminals are *re*produced. A person who has completed the four steps may brutalize youngsters and coach them in how to be like him. This doesn't necessarily mean that the new subjects will move through the entire set of steps, but the potential or first step is there.

In Rhodes's book about Athens and his work, he applies the theory to prominent killers. One he chooses is Perry Smith, the central figure in Truman Capote's nonfiction novel *In Cold Blood,* in which the Clutter family of four—father, mother, daughter, son—is murdered in their farmhouse in western Kansas while Smith and his partner Dick Hickock were robbing their home. Capote's version describes Smith as a rather poetic type who had a "brain explosion" when he and Dick killed the Clutters. Capote says Perry Smith didn't know what he was doing. Athens was very skeptical of such an explanation.

I was impressed that Athens's theory would prepare him to be skeptical about Capote's romanticized characterization of Perry Smith. When

Capote's book first appeared, I took seriously his claim that he had invented a new literary genre. I had decided when *In Cold Blood* came out in 1966 that a new method of criticism would be necessary to deal with it. How could the traditional methods of explication and evaluation deal with the plot probabilities of a nonfiction novel? Moreover, if the author claimed, as Capote did over and over, that every word in the book was true, critics would have to do some investigating on their own. That is exactly what I did.

As a native Kansan, I was skeptical of some things Capote had to say. So I drove from my home in Detroit, Michigan, to Holcomb, Kansas, to interview the surviving principals in the case, read the newspapers that covered the case from the beginning, and examine legal documents. After all that research, I came to the conclusion that Capote had significantly altered the facts in order to write a book that corresponded with his view of literature, which highly valued and relied on irony. He projected his own personality into Perry Smith, giving Smith the ability to correct the grammar in an article about him in the *Kansas City Star*. Although I can't repeat all the evidence here, the reader can examine my case against Capote in my article "In Cold Fact," which I wrote for *Esquire* magazine in June 1966 and which has been reprinted twice since then.[5] Perry Smith knew exactly what he was doing. He and Dick debated as to which one would begin the killings. I was impressed that Lonnie Athens could smell inconsistency, even mendacity in Capote's characterization, and my evidence—never challenged by Capote—is a validation of the criminologist's skepticism and the power of his theory.

Could Athens's theory help explain the person or persons killing the seven homeless men? The crimes Athens studied were heinous and relatively unprovoked. What we knew about the methods in the murders of the homeless men fit his category of virulent violence. The men were beaten to death, and some were said to have been decapitated, the heads not recovered. But what could be the motive? NIMBYism isn't ordinarily thought of as provoking this degree of violence. Could someone be offended that much by the stigma of homelessness? Could the mall rats have created a reference group, people who persuade each other to think and behave alike, with enough criminal capital to commit virulent crime?

I also found it interesting that Athens's theory of virulent crime antedated and even anticipated the criminal capital theory advanced by Hagan and McCarthy, summarized in chapter 6. Hagan and McCarthy take no notice of Athens's work in their own book—even though some of their ideas and findings are similar to his. The first step in the Athens model is brutalization. The first step in the Hagan and McCarthy model is some sort of strain, including violence, at home. The second step in the Athens model is belligerency, involving a decision to put an end to violent subjugation and to heed the coaching of a criminal coach. A corresponding step in the Hagan and McCarthy model is tutelage, accepting a criminal mentor or tutor. The third step in each model is a criminal act, a performance. The fourth step for Athens is a conscious commitment to violence, and the subject's need to find others like himself if he is not to become an outcast. The Hagan and McCarthy model includes the finding of a "family" of similar souls. Although Athens didn't seek to explain homelessness *and* criminality, his theory could be classified under the rubric of "criminal capital." The models are similar. Notice the reliance of both theories on the communication process. Family communication of a nurturing nature is absent in both models. Violent verbal and non-verbal behaviors are rained on the child; the child either runs away or is kicked out. The preteenager or teenager seeks a new "family." He or she accepts a mentor in crime. The candidate performs a criminal act with dramaturgical effects. Legal sanctions brand or stigmatize the criminal, stimulating additional rage or fury.

Either theory could describe the person who killed Joe Mendoza and the other six men. Either theory, or both, could explain why a teenager or a family of teenagers could have done the beatings and murders. Or there could have been a lone adult stalker, produced by either or both theories, who committed the crimes. Finally, the crimes could have been committed in some cases by a "family" and in other cases by the lone stalker, all of whom could have been "constructed" by processes described in either or both models. *Do the police study such theories?*

Somehow I hadn't heard about the service for Joe Mendoza held at SFC, otherwise I would have been there. I was therefore surprised to see a photograph in the *Rocky Mountain News* showing Tom Luehrs holding in both hands a bible that had belonged to Joe during the service for him and another victim, Harry Redden. There was also a photograph of our Friday coordinator, Mike, in prayer during the service.

On December 3, I worked the door of the clothing room from nine to ten, and one guest hung around the door after getting his clothes. I asked him why. His answer was that he heard we were going to distribute some ski pants. I called Mike to find out. Mike said he could neither confirm nor deny the rumor but gave it away when he said he was "amazed" that the guests had already picked up the news.

I struck up a conversation with a young man waiting to get in the clothing room. We had heard that another man, Kenneth Rapp Jr., was the fifth victim, so I asked the young man about the threat of the murderer. He said the choice to sleep out was a form of "suicide." What if they want to drink? "That is another form of suicide."

I moved back to the showers later in the day while the ski pants were distributed. An African American man who had just finished shaving his face and head looked me in the eye and said, "But I need ski poles to go with the ski pants." I began to laugh heartily, as did some of the men dressing and undressing around him. I called the front desk to say the men wanted ski poles and got a laugh. Then I stepped into the clothing room where Mike was supervising the distribution of the ski pants to say the men wanted ski poles. Mike frowned, "I don't think we can do it," he said regretfully. I smiled and said, "It's a joke." He got it, smiled, and said, "Around here you never know."

I started out in the showers the day after Thanksgiving of 1999 and heard some of the men bragging about how well they had fared the day before. The mood was so good that they could joke about the murder spree. A man who worked for the *Denver Voice* bravely invited the "boogieman" to come to his camp, saying, "I'm ready for you." One man suggested to another that they could work together to catch the killer and share the hundred-thousand-dollar reward posted by an anonymous donor. Without hesitating, the other man said, "There ain't enough money for me. A man who cuts heads off, there ain't enough money for me."

I still had fairly close connections in several departments at the university. A professor of sociology introduced me to a new hire in her department, Daniel Cress. He had been a graduate student at Arizona State University and had worked with faculty members there who had done significant research on homelessness. One was David A. Snow, who with Leon Anderson published an important study of homeless people in Austin, Texas, stressing that some of us are more vulnerable than others to the consequences of bad luck.[6] Dan and I got together for two and a half hours on January 9, 2000. Dan listened to what I had been doing for the past fourteen months or so. He urged me to write a book about the late 1990s stressing how the economic boom had raised the price of housing in Denver beyond the reach of working people, thus influencing the rates of homelessness.

Dan was also a member of the board of Boulder's Homeless Shelter. Most of the people on the staff there, he said, bought into the mental health model of homelessness fostered by the social service industry. His personal plan was to get homeless people out of the shelter and into affordable housing. The board, he said, was planning to move the shelter from north Broadway to south Broadway and was expecting the inevitable NIMBY reaction.

On Friday, January 14, a Hispanic guest in the showers brought up Joe Mendoza. He described him as "courteous" and "helpful," as spending most of his time with white people but being willing to help Spanish-speaking guys with translations. He said Joe carried a big knife and had a bad temper, neither of which I had seen. He hypothesized that Joe got drunk and got into a fight. He didn't believe the rumor circulating that wild animals had devoured his head.

On the last Friday in January, we had a minor emergency at the shelter. Paula is six feet two inches tall or taller, stronger than most men, and intimidating to both men and women. I wrote that she had a mean demeanor most of the time, recalling the time she told Craig, seated on a greeter's stool, "You remind me of my trained monkey," saying it not in jest but insultingly. On that day she was stirring up people in the lobby, perhaps using the "n" word. Craig felt bad about having to call the mental health people; he also felt bad about her resistance to them. (This turned out to be a success story, for after getting a diagnosis and the proper meds, she got subsidized housing, and her personality changed completely; she would return to the shelter to get her mail, with a smile on her face. She also became reconciled with her son. The mental illness theory can't be completely wrong.)

During this period I began to read Walter Wink's *The Powers That Be: Theology for a New Millennium*[7] and David Wagner's *Checkerboard Square: Culture and Resistance in a Homeless Community*,[8] two books with very different starting points that come to similar conclusions. Wink argues that the powers that be constitute a domination system that should be *resisted,* starting with the first level, the family. He analyzes many quotations attributed to Jesus that are critical of the family, concluding that he had "almost nothing good to say about families."[9] Wink's explanation was that the family in those days was patriarchal, practicing male supremacy, the principle of the larger domination system that is made up today of a complex of organizations: businesses, government, and yes, churches.

Wagner, the social scientist, has similar sentiments in his book: "I suggest that street people struggle to survive resisting the dominant institutions of society—the traditional family forms, the demands of employers, and the rules of the state bureaucracy—while at the same time developing alternative forms of social organization."[10]

Both books took similar stands on different platforms, and neither is inconsistent with the two models of criminal capital that explain homelessness and crime. By coincidence, during my next day at the shelter, I was working in the showers when a discussion of day-labor organizations developed among our guests in the showers. The first speaker complained about being driven a long way, to Brighton, Colorado, to do some landscaping and then not being picked up at the end of the day. Another man told of being left at a remote work site and being neither paid for his work nor driven back to where he had been picked up. Others agreed, with both words and body language. The tone of the discussion can be characterized by bitterness and indignation. The consensus quickly developed that such practices weren't fair. The St. Francis Center subsequently brought a suit against contractors who had employed our guests and mistreated them. The court ruled in our favor, a victory for resistance against the powers that be.

At a sharing discussion in February, the group was quiet, so I told them about reading Wink and Wagner and about the similarity of their positions. Could it be that some of our guests were protesting the powers that be and didn't want to become the likeness of the powers? Did they have solidarity in resistance to the powers? Shannon, the caseworker, nodded. Then others nodded. Tom had been at a rally the day before; he had been treated by some of the homeless people as an enemy because he had an important position. When Tom said he wasn't important, they accepted him. Jean thought about it, giving a thoughtful response about a guest who had recently died. She said he had been a charming and courteous man, one who could have been a success, but he preferred to travel and take photographs. His life could be considered a rejection of modern society. She was concerned that if we regarded them as being in protest to the system, then we could avoid any sense of responsibility for their well-being. Later she would add that most of our guests lack the skills to function successfully within the system, such as simple presentational and interpersonal skills. I took all of what was said to mean that some homeless people are protesting and resisting the powers that be, whereas others simply lack the skills and social capital to function within their system. Once again, people who know the community of homeless people best are careful not to generalize about all of them.

While I was making notes about the guests in our shelter in the fall of 1999, an undergraduate student at the University of Colorado at Boulder (CU Boulder), Caley Michael Orr, was doing some research of his own on the effect of seasonal changes on the population of homeless youth in Denver. Although he was doing research a block from my loft, I was unaware of him and his work until I got a phone call from him. I had been referred to him by Patti Adler, a colleague in the Department of Sociology at CU Boulder. Patti and I had served on several dissertation committees, and she knew what I was doing at the shelter in Denver, so she recommended me to be the outside member for a thesis committee on homeless youth.

I asked him to meet me in downtown Denver near where we live. He introduced himself, and after shaking hands, we walked across the street to Skyline Park. This was a meeting place for the mall rats. On the way, he said that he had worked as a volunteer for an organization called Stand Up for Kids in San Diego. When he enrolled at CU, he became involved in a branch of the same organization in Denver that, among other services, served hot food to homeless youth gathered in Skyline Park. Caley helped serve the food, getting to know the "kids," as he called them, quite well. Elaine and I had walked through the park when the kids were congregated, and we felt a bit uncomfortable because they seemed withdrawn and defiant, even aggressive in demanding our "spare change." But with Caley at my side, I walked into their midst without any concern whatsoever because they were so glad to see him. The kids chattered away about what they had done since they last talked to him. One short young woman was elated that she had found a basement apartment for $450 a month, which she was sharing with eight other people.

Caley introduced me to some of the young people and the social service workers in the crowd. *Crowd* is not the right word because within five minutes I made the observation to Caley and some of the social workers that "it's already clear to me that they have a community, a social system." The others nodded. We watched the young people greet each other with sounds of delight. They shared food and clothing with each other after expressing their successes and needs. People identified me as "one of Caley's professors." I met a Brenda from Urban Peak, described on her business card as "a safe place for homeless and runaway youth under 21 years old. We have as many ways to help as there are individuals. We do not judge you, we accept you."

I also met the executive director of Stand Up for Kids, the organization Caley worked for that brought food to the park for the kids. I didn't catch his name but someone called him a "different kind of doctor," so I assumed they meant a medical doctor. Some middle-aged people, including a one-legged man in a wheelchair, began to gather as well. Stand Up for Kids, they explained, fed the young people first, and if there was any food left, they gave it to the older people. I took Caley a block down Sixteenth Street to a Starbucks. I agreed to be the outside member of his honors thesis committee if he would agree to think about some questions I was interested in. He agreed. I stiffened at his answer to one of the questions I had in mind.

I mentioned the seven murders, one of which was charged against the mall rats. He said he had arrived at Skyline Park the day after one of the murders and felt bad when one of the kids was excited to tell him that they had killed a man and gouged out his eyes. It isn't clear to me now as I read my notes whether the person who reported this to him was one of the killers, or was referring by "we" to the group, that part of the "family" or social system, the group that committed the crime.

Before he finished his thesis we learned that two of the mall rats were convicted of killing Melvin Washington: Both teenagers, one was sentenced to twenty-five years and the other got ten years. A guest at the St. Francis Center told me in the showers that "what the court told me with that verdict and sentence is that we're nothing but trash." He saw me taking notes, repeated his words and contrasted this outcome with a hypothetical one in which he came into my neighborhood and killed someone. "We're nothing." I had to agree—Melvin Washington's degrees of being were few in number to the court and many people of society.

Caley brought me a copy of his undergraduate honors thesis in anthropology: "Street Ecology: The Demographics, Adaptive Strategies, and Nutritional Status of Homeless Youth in Denver, Colorado."[11] Knowing my interest in language, Caley gave me a list of jargon he picked up from them:

> "Spanging" = panhandling for spare change
> "Squats" = places to stay or places to take over
> "Wino feeds" = food services for homeless alcoholics
> "Dumpster diving" = foraging for food in dumpsters
> "Dine and dash" = eating at a café or diner and running out without paying
> "Bun runs" = stealing from food delivery trucks

Caley's oral defense was on April 6, 2000, on the fourth floor of the Hale Science Building on the campus of the University of Colorado at

Boulder. In his opening statement, Caley mentioned the cohesive culture of the youth, centered around punk rock, unorthodox dress, squatting, and spanging. Some are there for the culture, some out of desperation because of an abusive home life. Having spent a night on the street in San Diego as part of his training to become a counselor to homeless youth, Caley became interested in adaptive strategies when he discovered one could get cold sleeping out even in Southern California in January.

One of his most remarkable methods was used in estimating the population of homeless youth in Denver in the fall. He used this formula to calculate the population:

$$N = (T1 \times T2) / RC,$$

where T1 = number marked, T2 = total from count 2, and RC = number "recaptured."[12] This is called a "mark-recapture" method; it is used in estimating wildlife populations. Caley's subjects, the kids under the age of twenty-one, would probably have resisted having a tag stapled in an ear, the way deer are marked in Colorado, but he reasoned that getting to know them by their street name would be equivalent. Caley "marked" individuals on two separate occasions, October 3 and 6, 1999, by noting their street names on a list that was compared with a second count. He estimated a fall population of 111, compared to another estimate of 200 made by Stand Up for Kids during the summer. By means of a questionnaire, he found that about 50 percent expected to be homeless over the winter and tentatively concluded that the population drops 50 percent from summer to fall, another 50 percent from fall to winter, and probably picks up again in the spring by an unknown percentage.

Caley also studied their body weight, nutritional habits, and strategies for coping with life on the street. He found that some were malnourished, some used marijuana and heroin, and some may have been dealers as well as users. The chief strategy for making money was "spanging," their portmanteau word for panhandling, "Have any spare change?" I had warned Caley that I would ask him in the oral defense of his thesis whether the kids were better off at home or on the streets. This was a difficult issue for Caley because he was committed to counseling them off the street.

He decided not to address that question in his thesis because he had no questionnaire data related to it, but in the defense he did tell us that one day he saw a kid whose face was badly bruised and asked him what happened. The kid said he had gone home for the night and "my old man beat the bleep out of me." He said he had no numbers for how many had been abused at home, but he was sure that "neglect was the rule."

About the killing of the homeless man Caley said, "It made me sick." The kids' motive was that the victim had been panhandling on what they regarded as their turf. He reported to the committee the incident in which the kid told him the next day that they had killed a man and gouged his eyes out. He said he thought the kid who was convicted was "disturbed."

I brought up police harassment, and Caley quickly responded with several stories, one of which had happened while he was working at Skyline Park the previous Thanksgiving as a volunteer serving the holiday meal. A policeman was sitting in his patrol car monitoring the street meal, so Caley decided to offer him some food.

"I choose to work for my food," the cop said with his arms crossed on his chest. He got out of his squad car and got in Caley's face to say, "You're encouraging them by feeding them." Even the Stand Up for Kids counselors experienced harassment by the police.

We talked about his population estimate. He did think it was conservative, 111 in the fall and half that in the winter when the "summer bunnies" go home because of the cold. Our time was up, and the committee voted high honors to Caley.

Caley went off to do graduate work in anthropology, and although I've lost track of him, I thought of his work often as I saw the city tear down the rock outcroppings of Skyline Park, remaking it into a completely flat, street-level park with grass and patio rock—in short, a panopticon easy to police and with no place to hide. Rumors were that police were aggressive in discouraging Caley's kids from congregating there after the makeover. I have no idea where they went. I never saw them at the St. Francis Center.

I was satisfied that social scientists were beginning to understand homelessness, youthful gangs, and virulent criminals. We can be brought up by our intimate communication network, known as the primary group, to be pro-social, contributing citizens, but we can also be turned toward vulnerability and disaffiliation from a lack of social capital. And Athens has shown us how we can be made into vicious brutes. My studies would lead me in the direction of trying to discover ways of decreasing homelessness and cultivating pro-social behavior.

CHAPTER EIGHT
THE VISIBLE HAND OF COMPASSION

As a member of the Affordable Housing Study Group at St. John's Episcopal Cathedral, I met an incredible couple, Ray and Marilyn Stranske, founders of Hope Communities. Ray gave us a tour of one of the complexes his organization bought and managed, the Kittyhawk and Canterbury Apartments. We met as a group there on April 13, 2000, for a presentation by Ray.

I heard of a miracle that day: Hope's ability to put together a complicated mixture of loans and grants to buy such a place, with 130 units, many of which are then rented below market prices. Standing outside the complex later, I said to Ray that he was trying to alter or correct the market in a positive way, to help deserving people who might otherwise be homeless. He agreed. Today I would say it this way: Hope Communities supplants the invisible hand of the marketplace with the visible hand of compassion. Ray inspired us by saying that Hope seeks in its apartment buildings a community of people with different incomes and that it seeks also to encourage upward mobility, strengthen families, and promote the realization of the potential for greatness in each individual.

A Hope Communities builder spoke to us about encouraging trust by means of providing voice to the residents, even inviting police officers to their meetings. She introduced several residents of the complex. The first man had AIDS, renting one of the four units set aside for such patients. He said he couldn't find affordable housing anywhere else. We heard from other tenants, all of whom said they would be homeless without Hope, and all spoke about the spirit of community and support. It was an inspiring meeting, and the more I thought about it, the more grateful I was for what Hope Communities was accomplishing.

I worked the next day, April 14, at SFC, continuing during my second year to find it rewarding as well. I enjoyed talking to a Lakota Sioux man, one of whose ancestors had been a chief who fought at the Little Big Horn. He was just back from a visit to the Rosebud Reservation in South Dakota. Did he see his family? All but his mother, he said; she had gone to the "Happy Hunting Grounds, the great teepee up there." While I was trying to figure out whether or not he was in earnest, another Native American joined the conversation to confirm that people go to the Happy Hunting Grounds in twos, with someone they didn't know before they made the trip.

Another man walked up to the mail counter and said, "My name is Tumbling Skunk." There are so many unusual names among our Native American guests that I began looking for mail under that name. He smiled and gave his real name. We had a hearty laugh. Good Friday was on April 21 that year. Many guests took notice of the day, and when I mentioned it, they would nod in recognition. We closed at noon, so when Joe and I started cleaning the showers early we had to throw a few regulars out.

In May our showers at SFC were closed for repairs, so Mike assigned me, after I requested it, to go with Chris to the Samaritan House from 10:00 to noon to work in their shower area. We handed out towels, soap, and toiletries to the men as they went into the shower room and showed them where to put their dirty towels when they came out. During a lull I walked into the dorm area and took a tour. There were four men asleep, one of whom I hadn't seen in the darkness until his snore startled me. A pleasant black man waiting for his clothes to dry told me about his woman and his job at a gambling casino in Black Hawk, Colorado. He had high praise for the Samaritan House.

The public address system in this huge complex was constantly in use while we were there. One announcement got my attention, about a ceremony being held honoring the seven homeless men killed the previous fall. A plaque commemorating the slain was to be unveiled.

I wanted to see how people lived rough, out of doors, and an outreach worker associated with SFC, Fawn, needed someone to accompany her on her rounds. According to the rules, she was not allowed to go into the field by herself, so we negotiated a day we could go together. She agreed to pick me up in front of our building at 8:30 a.m. on Monday, June 5, 2000. It was a beautiful sunny Colorado day without a cloud in the sky. We headed straight down Fifteenth Street, parked near the South Platte River, near the *very spot* where Major Stephen H. Long's expedition had pitched their tents in July 1820.[1] We found a large bridge and walked down under it to the wedge-shaped space between the bottom of the bridge and the earth that slopes down to the river. Fawn found someone in there and engaged him in conversation. She hadn't done an outreach trip in a couple of months owing to the loss of her partner, and yet the man recognized her. He answered her questions and had one of his own for her. He had reported to the police the name of a person he suspected of having killed some of the homeless men the previous fall. Had she heard if the police had done anything about it? She said she hadn't.

While she was talking to him, reminding him of services available to him at Stout Street Clinic, St. Francis Center, and other agencies, I realized why I hadn't been able to see him. He had placed a piece of heavy plywood against the side of the bridge, and stabilized it with a large stone on the ground, giving him a protective side wall on his wedge of space under the bridge. She later described him as an old white man, but said she had trouble estimating the longevity of homeless persons because they age faster than their housed counterparts.

We walked to the confluence of Cherry Creek and the South Platte River. We saw "nests" and "dens" under most of the bridges in the area: blankets, sweaters, and other belongings marking a squatter's spot. Fawn pointed out many new gratings put in place since the last time she had patrolled this area. The welded gratings had been ordered by the city administration to keep people out of the wedge-shaped spaces. Similar gratings were also welded to the ends of huge drainage pipes that dump into the river, again to keep people from seeking shelter in them.

In some cases the gratings had been welded on without removing the possessions of the squatters, almost defeating their purpose. That is, as I had learned from several people, Mayor Webb intended his monument to be the cleanup of the Platte River Valley that snakes around and through parts of Denver. Paths were built along the river to facilitate bikers, runners, and those out for a walk. Homeless people and their camps would only be an eyesore for the beautified river valley. But the welded-in bedding and clothing, which could never be retrieved by the owners, would be an eyesore until they rotted, reminders that people slept there in 2000 during Mayor Webb's administration, and as they rotted, they would undermine the city's attempt at that time to make homeless people, and evidence of their being, invisible.

Beneath a bridge under Forty-seventh Street, we found a couple with two dogs. I heard the dogs barking before I saw them. The couple had a camp. The woman was wearing shorts and a T-shirt; she was barefoot, had red hair down to her legs, and was holding both of the dogs back by their leashes. The man was sitting with his back against the concrete slab that supported the bridge. He drank from a bottle in a brown paper sack. The redhead recognized Fawn and listened to her relate information about services available to them.

"I had a job, lost a job."

As we left she called out, "Don't think we have anything against working," which I took as a denial of what might be interpreted as laziness.

Fawn and I talked about the couple after we hiked up the steep slope from under the bridge. Fawn reminded me that this was the place she had told me about while we were parking her vehicle. Somehow the folks under the bridge tapped the streetlight above the bridge for electricity, running a line down under the bridge to their camp. Fawn had seen a picture on the TV, picked up by rabbit ears. As clever as they were, the high waters of the spring runoff of melting snow from the mountains swept away their appliances.

We saw a place that Fawn had dubbed "Needle Creek," a tube that empties into the Platte near the Sally, or Salvation Army shelter. Fawn had earlier walked up on what she estimated to be four hundred to five hundred disposable needles. She called a service agency in city government to clean it up because of the risk to people and animals alike. We came across a small cache of used needles on that day as well.

Fawn drove south along the river on Santa Fe Avenue. We stopped so she could point out evidence of camps and nests and dens. She said one was reputed to be a camp favored by military veterans, who liked to stick together. She then took me to a huge intersection, Evans Street and Santa Fe, parking under the bridge carrying the cars on Evans over it. We walked to the spot where the on-ramp created a wedge-shaped space in which the ramp was a slanted roof. I jotted down items in the camp: empty Magnum 40 beer bottles, a rug, blankets, a paperback copy of Michael Crichton's *A Case of Need,* and a homeless person's guide to Denver and the United States. We walked toward the off-ramp wedge: bedsprings, burned mattress, two dirty cups, rugs, and an audiotape: *The Judds: Wynona and Naomi.*

I bought lunch at the Burrito Company. We found a place in the shade to eat and talk. She thought 50–60 percent of her clients were mentally ill. I said that some sociologists thought this was a way of medicalizing the problem so we wouldn't have to spend any money on it. She listened carefully without responding. After lunch she took me to "Pigeon Shit Bridge," a place near Twentieth Street. When we went under it, we found some human belongings left in a human nest covered by bird droppings.

While composing my field notes that evening, I recalled the dens and nests we had seen and the verse from Matthew 8:20:

> Foxes have holes, and birds of the air have nests; but the Son of Man has nowhere to lay his head.

My experience that day led me to rewrite this, with apologies to Matthew, into some less poetic prose:

> Birds have nests, and foxes have dens; many humans have homes. But some have only nests and dens.

At lunch during my next workday at SFC, I described the couple under the bridge, and then asked each person to explain their behavior. Carla said they had no support system, no network of assistance to help them when they were down. I dubbed this the "catcher in the rye" hypothesis, or a lack of social capital (which I explain in chapter 14). Larry, a volunteer, said they were free spirits, hobos. Joe had an eclectic explanation, including a bad or dysfunctional family, drugs, alcohol, and a willingness to give up. Tim, a young staff member, explained their situation by psychological factors. I mentioned that they lacked housing.

In the day-ending sharing, I was able to relate a success story to my colleagues. A guest I knew asked to get his storage bag. As he carried it out, he turned to speak. I was surprised because he rarely initiated a conversation with me.

"I have a room now."

"Congratulations," I replied.

"I'll be back to see you," he said.

I was touched by his success and his promise not to cut his ties with SFC. The other volunteers and staff members I related this to were pleased by his success and touched by his promise.

Late in the month of June, the Boulder Planning Commission voted 4–3 to approve the relocation of the homeless shelter from 4546 Broadway to a former sorority house at 777 Broadway, near a middle school. The capacity of the shelter would be increased from 68 beds to 136. Had NIMBYism been silenced?

On Friday, July 21, 2000, I learned that the staff had been reorganizing itself because of new responsibilities. Chris had become the coordinator of volunteers. Chris later called me in for a conversation in Tom's office. We talked about the changes. He said he would be taking over the center's newsletter, the *St. Francis Sun,* asking me if I would help him by doing the copy editing. I said yes. I had previously asked him to have the staff consider a recommendation I had made earlier. I thought it would speed up the process of helping people get their bags in storage if we accepted an ID, instead of having to look up people's forms in the file, ask them for the last four letters of their Social Security numbers, and so on. We could compare the name on the tag with the

ID. I asked if the staff had considered it. He surprised me by saying the staff had already approved it: It was a new rule. The organization listened.

In July and August, I met a couple of guests, carnies, who came to town. A woman came in for a shower, admitting with a giggle that although they had a bunkhouse, "we spent last night under the Tilt-A-Whirl." Another guest came into the clothing room and said he was a "ride jock" and ran a ride called the "Ring of Fire." He was debating between blue jeans and black. "They make me break down the other rides. My ride is hydraulic, but the other rides get grease all over them," and for that reason he chose the black pants.

"Do you like to travel?"

"Oh, yeah, and I'm determined to hit all the states before I die. I've hit twenty-eight already."

He slept on a mattress in the backseat of the semi that hauled his ride. They had another trailer containing a huge tank of water and a heater for hot showers. "Tribal wanderers," I wrote in my notes, "on the road."

The most notable wanderer I met at SFC was a man I came to call the Lance Armstrong of the Homeless World, a title he liked so much that he would smile broadly whenever he heard me use it. Lance was a man in his thirties who had arrived in Denver a year earlier. He had a bike with bags that contained his possessions. Fawn told me she bought the bike to get rid of him, to let him ride away from SFC and Denver. I was disappointed to hear we did such things, a "bus ticket therapy" that I had heard other cities used to get rid of their homeless persons.

Lance is different; the explanation I heard from staff members was that he was brain damaged in some kind of accident, perhaps involving a bicycle. He had a sister in South Carolina who worried about him. I hadn't seen him for a long time. That Friday, August 11, 2000, he showed up again. Where had he been?

"Spokane, Washington," he answered. He was standing outside the clothing room during a slow period, and I was inside. I made notes, to his obvious delight, about his narrative. It took him twenty-two days to get to Spokane on his bike. He rested for three days in Helena, Montana, in a rest stop. I tried to picture him pumping up the mountainous terrain of Montana with all that traffic on the highways.

"Were you frightened?"

"No," he said in his abrupt manner, "it was exciting."

"What was the most exciting time you experienced?"

"People in the rest stop gave me the tent and sleeping bag," turning to his bike, parked at its usual spot by the mail/storage area, "on my bike now."

He spent five days in Spokane before heading toward Lewiston, Idaho. He went through the Grand Tetons to Jackson Hole, Wyoming, on his way back to Denver. I expressed my astonishment several times, each time making Lance's suntanned face break into a crooked grin that revealed the missing pickets in his mouth. He began to volunteer other details: the numbers of all the highways he had ridden, the rain and cold weather he hit in high altitudes.

When I remarked on his bicycle shorts, Lance was proud to tell me they were exactly like the shorts the original Lance Armstrong wore when he won the Tour de France. Perhaps I make too much of this, but it seems to tell us something about a mysterious man. Even though he may be brain damaged, Lance does have a hero in the original Lance Armstrong. Our Lance's ride to Spokane and back surely is a homeless man's equivalent of a Tour de France victory. I hoped he got the apartment he wanted. He needed financial support, and the landlady was quite choosy. "I don't drink or use drugs, and I don't have any kind of a criminal record," he told her. Although he slept in city parks, as he told me that day, he did want a room of his own.

We gathered together that August afternoon to read Psalm 111, and after doing so we talked about the day. I brought up Lance's amazing feat. Tom gave me more segments of Lance's life story, how he came to Colorado so he could ride his bike up Pikes Peak.

"Did he make it?" I asked.

"No," Tom answered, "they stopped him going up and gave him a bus ticket to Denver."

And that is what we did, I thought. *We bought him a bike out of town.*

"We're going to talk about him at the 2:45 meeting," said Carla.

"Is he a problem?" I asked.

Carla's nonverbal expression was that a yes or no answer would be too simple. I decided to drop the matter during the sharing discussion to pursue it privately with Carla after the meeting. She walked me to the front door as I left, explaining that the staff needed to discuss Lance's case as a matter of policy, that although he wasn't really in trouble, the center did help buy his bike with the expectation he would not be coming back.

"Isn't that what they did in Colorado Springs?"

Carla hastened to say she resented what they had done in Colorado Springs, said that she didn't agree with bus ticket therapy. The difference in the two cases was that Lance said he wanted to move to Spokane, and the staff believed it was time for him to move on to a new stage of his life. The policy issue was, What should the SFC staff do when such cases arose?

While I was working at mail/storage on August 18, our business was slow enough that I could ask Carla, working as a greeter, what the staff had decided about Lance's case. She said they decided he would be allowed to come into SFC only two hours a day.

"Why?"

"Because he makes people upset. He gets in their face." Even though he hadn't ever upset me, I knew he had a blunt manner of speech that could produce a negative effect on some of our guests. Carla added that they were also trying to get him a place to stay, a room of his own.

Tom gave me an invitation to participate in a brainstorming session at SFC on Tuesday, September 12, 2000, at noon. We would use the time to prepare for a meeting we anticipated the governor would call, a summit meeting on homelessness, in the spring of 2001. The governor, alas, didn't call for the summit.

During a Friday late in August, a chilling incident occurred. I was working in the showers in the morning when Mike's voice came over the loudspeaker announcing that we would be closed for Labor Day but would be back to "normal hours" after that. A presentable man asked me with a sneer, "What are your abnormal hours?" He glared at me.

"You've got me," I said, throwing my hands up as if to surrender. "I don't know," I said, seeing no sense in trying to one-up a guest with a clever question.

A second man on the opposite side of the tile benches did try to one-up him with the question, "What's abnormal to you?"

The first man bristled, turned around in my full view to say, "If you don't like it, you can kiss my ass." Then he dared: "Try me."

The first man walked to the mirrors on the right side of the wall from my perspective behind the counter. The second man began walking toward him. I began to talk, asking them to take it easy, but the first man continued to taunt the other man.

I dialed 17, trying to get the front desk, but the phone produced such a loud screeching sound everyone stopped and looked at me. I believe in retrospect that this accidental feedback may have had a positive effect by interrupting the escalation. I dialed another number, this time reaching Mike. He, Tim, and Craig quickly appeared. Mike, the coordinator, did all the talking, ending the interaction between the two antagonists. The first man presented himself to Mike as an innocent victim, appealing to me for verification. The other man also pointed at me, inviting my perspective. I kept quiet.

After the staff members left, the first man started shaving. Naturally, I watched him and listened to him carefully. He spoke to the man on his right while shaving. Not once but several times did I hear him talking about revenge.

"I don't drink like most of these guys. I'll catch him at night when he's drunk and beat the piss out of him."

When I later repeated this to Mike, a change came over him.

"I never thought of that possibility before, that one of our guests might *prey* on the others, on the more vulnerable ones." We were both thinking of the murders. Now it dawned on me that the first man could have been what Athens described as a virulent killer. A man who could threaten to fight and beat up a man over such a mild provocation seemed to be a paradigm case illustrating the theory. A man who could announce his intention to "beat the piss" out of a man while he was drunk wanted the rest of us to know that he was violent, wanted to create fear if not respect in us.

Nonetheless, the visible hand of compassion at work for Hope Communities gave me hope, a hope that we could reduce homelessness through cooperation among nonprofits plus national, state, and local governments. Collectively, as I explicate in chapter 14, we could become the catcher in the rye. Moreover, I was developing a philosophic base—Existentialism— for my hope.

CHAPTER NINE
AN EXISTENTIAL LOOK AT HOMELESSNESS

The cover of the September 2000 issue of the *Denver Voice*:

The *Voice* remembers

Donald Dyer
1948–1999

George "Billy" Worth
1936–1999

Melvin "Fuzzy" Washington
1952–1999

Milo Harris
1947–1999

Kenneth Rapp
1956–1999

Joe Mendoza
1949–1999

Harry J. Redden, Jr.
1950–1999

Mark Warren Davis
1956–2000

The last name on the list was a new one. Davis was found burned to death by a fire in an open camp, and although the police didn't regard it as a murder, the *Voice* wasn't so sure. In my mind there were still six cases to be solved, getting colder all the time.

And so was the weather. I quote my field notes for Friday, September 22, 2000. "I woke up several times early this morning, the first day of autumn. It was dark when I pulled back the blinds and saw the dark, wet city as a scene from the film *Blade Runner*. The temperature had dropped to 38F during the night; it was 41F and raining as I drove to the St. Francis Center at about 7:15. Some of the guests were miserable when they entered the building, pulling off plastic bags they had used as raincoats. We have few Asian guests, but that day a Korean man still wore his plastic bag when he came in the clothing room in the afternoon, looking for dry clothing."

In conversations with guests that day, I asked, "Did you keep dry last night?" Some said they had gone into a shelter; many others slept out but managed to keep fairly dry, under a bridge, in one case, in a van in another. It would rain all day, and I began to worry about their health. When I walked out of the showers at 9:00, I shouldn't have been so surprised by how many people were in the great room. I was the only worker in mail/storage, and the guests were impatient with the long lines as well as being wet and cold. One man, for example, wanted to open his bag in the storage room, take some clothes out, and put some others in. I told him he had to take his bag into the other room so that I could help people waiting in line. "This is too much," he said.

I nodded at a man standing in line with his bag waiting to put it back on a storage shelf. As he started walking into the storage room, a man asked, "Why did you let him cut in front of us?"

"I'm sorry," I said, "were you here before he was?"

Nods.

But my apology seemed to help. Later, when the man brought his bag back, he said, "You're the man."

It was still raining when I turned on the windshield wipers to drive home at 2:30. Later I dropped in at the bar in Gallagher's Restaurant in our building. I wrote at the end of the notes for the day: "Never have been so physically and psychologically aware of the transition from one season to another."

Two weeks later, Friday, October 6, 2000, it was twenty-eight degrees at 7:30 as I drove to the shelter, the windshield wipers dealing with the drizzle. *They must be miserable.* At the 2:00 discussion after another tough, demanding day, I said, "This must be the hardest time of year for homeless people, autumn, the transition between the summer and winter." Tom and Jean nodded. I continued, "Today and September 22, the first day of fall, were cold and rainy and made our guests miserable." The group agreed. T. S. Eliot wrote that April is the cruelest month, and although that may be true for flowers, I suspect he never lived on the streets in October.

Scratch notes on my work slip record "longest line ever for clothing slips"; the thirty-five people who got clothing between 9:00 and 10:00 constituted a "record," according to our experienced coordinator Mike.

A man gave me trouble all day and walked back into the showers later in the day to announce, "I'll kill the motherfucker who stole my shirt." After he left, a discussion broke out about his remark. At least two men said they would never steal from another homeless man "because they work too hard for what little they have."

"I'd steal from a corporation but not from a man," said a third man while dressing, comfortable with the idea of stealing from the corporate powers that be, artificial persons, but not a real one.

A week later we anticipated it would be a wild and crazy day because it was Friday the thirteenth, with the moon in its full phase. I was troublesome, complaining because we no longer did the salt ritual. I had come to take pleasure participating in it. But at the end of the day, Carla said it had been a quiet one, with only 333 guests admitted, a low number for the season.

An article about time had appeared in the August 2000 issue of the *Voice* under the byline of Elberta, no last name, a regular writer for the tabloid who clearly knew the street people well. She wrote that the quality of time is affected by the schedules of the institutions that affect the homeless people—when they open and close. Those institutions are missions, soup kitchens, libraries, senior centers, and beer joints. The crucial point of the monthly cycle is what she called "mother's day"—the first day of the month, when Supplemental Security Income (SSI), Veterans Administration (VA), and welfare checks arrived in the mail. According to Elberta, even those who don't get checks on the first are excited because others who do get them have promised to treat their friends, and some intend to roll a drunk who cashed one, a perfect contrast to those who would steal from a corporation but not from a real person.

Weather is the major survival factor in the seasonal cycle, autumn bringing unpredictability and winter true hardship. But summer is more dangerous because of the risk of being rolled or attacked. Thanksgiving, Christmas, and Easter "evoke sadness and bitterness," despite the gala holiday meals. Elberta quoted a Christmas lunch patron as saying, "No, I didn't see my people—my children. I had nothing to give them. I don't want them to see how I was living."[1]

Homeless folks often talk about "killin' time." Although she didn't quote Orwell's observation that poverty annihilates time, Elberta came close and even surpassed the other writer with these words:

> Only those new to street life talk of the future as a progression from the past. When concrete goals are spoken, it is often of plans to travel else- where. Goals become associated with space rather than time; the hope becomes that a new location may make a difference in the knowledge that a "new time" will never come. Therefore, when some speak of goals, it is often in terms of going someplace else, like another state or relocating to another area across town on RTD [the local bus service].[2]

In these brilliant observations, she even explains the wanderlust and the fever of the tramps and wanderers, the thrill of going somewhere else, someplace new.

A guest named Karl gave me a seminar in hawking newspapers, seemingly enjoying it as much as I. He got the rhythm of stopping when a new guest approached me, picking up again where he had left off. Hawkers don't pay for the newspapers. The *Rocky Mountain News* and the *Denver Post* give them away. Karl sold the *Post* and had a "lock" on a spot in a suburb, Parker, Colorado, on private property owned by King Soopers, a supermarket grocery chain in Denver. He made $1.25 per paper and total sales over the weekend were $100. The conversation moved from mail/storage to the showers, and I learned he charged twenty-five cents per paper on weekdays, fifty cents on the weekend, so his customers were generous with tips. People in Parker travel on business so much, Karl hypothesized, that they didn't subscribe to the papers, relying on him and other hawkers when they were in town.

Karl understood the economics of newspapers and hawking them. Competition was fierce between the two newspapers. The companies gave the papers to the hawkers without charge in order to increase circulation. Circulation figures determine the fees the advertisers pay. Karl said that when his ankle and foot got better, he would go back to his job as a truck driver.

Another man in the showers joined the seminar. He agreed with Karl's numbers, saying if a hawker who worked weekdays as well as weekends could do quite well.

"Well enough to pay for housing?"

He paused to reflect on the question.

"Enough to pay," he nodded, "if I chose to live that way."

"Then you must choose to live another way."

Again he paused, and his smile turned into speech.

"Yesterday I went to a casino in Central City and lost. Lost a lot."

Now I was nodding. I wished him a good weekend.

"Thanks."

Later, the two newspapers would sign a joint operating agreement, in which the *News* would publish the only paper on Saturday—with an editorial page for the other paper—and the *Post* would return the favor on Sunday, minimizing the competition between the two newspapers and eliminating the need for weekend hawkers, drying up a significant source of income for our guests.

Casey is a tall, slender African American man with some gray hair beginning to show on his well-cropped head. His speech is refined, his manner courteous and a bit dramatic at times. He had a limp when I walked him to get his storage bag. I didn't ask, but he let me know, "I got hit by a bus." He was retreating from someone who was beating him up when he backed into a bus.

Mike gave him a job so that he could earn a clothing slip, and while mopping near mail/storage within earshot of three volunteers, Casey gave this speech:

> I can't seem to get out of this state of homelessness. I try, and yet I can't get out. I stopped smoking crack, but it doesn't get any better. I'm going to start smoking crack again.

We three volunteers spoke at once:

"No," said Liesl.

"No," said Jan.

"No," said Phil.

He sat down next to Jan, a retired schoolteacher who volunteers more than one day a week, and she counseled him at length.

Maybe we do try to fix them at times.

In the clothing room, an African American man was trying to find clothes that could constitute the uniform required for his job doing food preparation at St. Joseph's Hospital.

"Are you going to be able to find your own place?"

"I'm trying. I hope so. I lost my wife, lost my way, lost everything, but I'm trying to make it back."

"You can do it."

"Thank you." Our eyes locked for a long, transcendent moment. I later wrote, "That is why I work here."

I spent an hour and fifteen minutes editing Tom's message for the SFC newsletter. I complained to my superiors that we had a private-business mentality, boasting about growth, more and more guests and services offered to them. A *decline* in customers would be the best measure of our success.

The Affordable Housing Study Group invited a city planner to address us. After talking Denver housing history, new issues, and city efforts, we had a question-and-answer period. I thought the speaker was defensive on behalf of the Webb administration. I later stated my conclusion to two members of the study group: "We are losing ground on all fronts." Both men agreed with me.

On a Friday in November 2000, a cold day in Denver, I was responsible for cleaning the showers after many, many men had used them. Larry, a fellow volunteer, came in at 12:45 to help me for fifteen minutes, and there were still a lot of men in the room, delaying us from spraying with disinfectant. One man in particular I asked to finish his shower, dress, and leave. He showered too long. Larry picked up a red plastic bag and threw it in the trash. I threw other trash in on top of it. When I finally got the man to come out of the showers, I noticed there were red spots all over his body, concentrated mainly on his legs. He walked over to Larry and screamed, "What did you do with my clothes?" The red sack was a biohazard bag with the man's clothing in it. We were able to retrieve the clothes for him. He was in considerable discomfort, shaking and picking at the red sores on his legs.

Our coordinator came in to check on him. Mike had sent the man in for a shower two hours earlier and got too busy to check on him. He gently urged the man to put his clothes on so that we could finish spraying.

"But the lice are dead and I'm picking them out."

The man volunteered to help us clean. Mike gently urged him to hurry with his clothes. The man began rapidly clawing his legs. Even after he got dressed he rubbed his legs and feet. Mike had said he had scabies, but the man said it was lice.

"What do you have?"

"Oh," he shouted at me, "now you're going to talk to me."

I felt bad for the man who showered too long, wishing I could do something to relieve his agony. He told me he slept outdoors and got a case of lice. I couldn't understand everything he said because of his spasms. I apologized to him, lamely saying I had not understood his problem. Mike also apologized and later told me privately that there were some mental illness issues in this case.

November 2000 was a period in which numbers became important. On Friday the seventeenth I wrote down the intake numbers on the calendar for the previous two weeks of the month, the second coldest period in recorded history for Denver. The range was from 381 to 520. The highest numbers are on Monday because the center is closed on Saturday and open only half a day on Sunday. The number for the preceding Friday, November 10, was 482, a high number. We volunteers joked about earning our pay. Mike had explained to me the previous week that cold days put more pressure on the organization because the guests spent more time in the building.

On the shortest day of the year, December 22, 2000, I was pleasantly surprised by the mood of the men in the showers. It was, after all, three days before Christmas, the first day of winter, and they were in good humor. The weather no doubt helped. We had blue skies, a warming sun that would bring us to a high of fifty. A middle-aged black man smiled when I asked him what he needed.

"A shower," he answered.

He attracted an audience as he talked and undressed, folding his pants in cadence with his speech. He sat down and looked across the room at me again, saying, "You must wonder why I am a man of joy."

"Yes, why are you a man of joy?"

"I've known Jesus since I was a boy, when I was nine years old." A heavy Hispanic man putting on his clothes near the tile bench nodded and encouraged the speaker.

"The problems I have are of my own making," he said, and as he paused, the men around him became more attentive.

"The burdens he gives me are slight; the burdens I have created for myself are staggering."

Other men were asking me for this and that so I couldn't follow all the soliloquy, but I had seen a bottle of Brut on our lunch table and assumed it was a Christmas present for our guests. After Jean verified my assumption, I took it with me to the showers.

"I've got some smellgood," I announced, and they came running. I poured it in their cupped palms, sternly cautioning them, "Don't drink it," reveling in the laughter of the men. One man winced as he slapped it on his cheeks.

"Does it burn your face?"

"No, I've got cracks in my hands."

He showed me the cracks. He was a mason by trade, and the bricks and mortar had dried his skin to the point of splitting open.

I began to say "Merry Christmas" to each man as he left the facilities, and most returned the wish, some simply saying, "Thanks," all of this making for a warm hour in the showers.

At lunch I fell into a conversation with Joe Brzozowski. We were becoming good friends and would become regular golf partners. SFC would emerge as a topic of conversation on the golf course or over a coke, beer, or glass of wine at the nineteenth hole. In response to a question at the morning sharing discussion, I had said that I thought our guests had a longer "now" than we did. Joe said he had been thinking about my comment, and he said that our sense of community at SFC made Friday so special that he looked forward to it, and that Friday at the shelter was one long "now," in that he didn't look forward to something in the future. I thought back to a remark he had made a couple of Fridays earlier, something to the effect of how much he "loved this place." I had similar feelings and, in fact, was sad that Cecil had to cut back his hours, leaving at 11:00 instead of 2:00 because of a problem with his neck that made standing for long periods difficult. Cecil was our mentor, a wise and good man. But then we would still have him for three hours each Friday. I wrote about the day that SFC had become part of my identity, a "we," a reference group, a community-of-salvation-in-this-world.

"Lance Armstrong" came into the shelter looking for warm clothing. He said he planned to ride his bicycle to Buffalo, Wyoming, even though it was early January. He had tried to do it the previous week but was stopped short of Casper, Wyoming, by a roadblock. He pitched his tent in weather so cold his drinking water froze, so cold he couldn't get to sleep.

The next entry in my field notes is dated Friday, January 21, 2001, even though it was actually written the next morning, Saturday the twenty-second. Elaine and I had taken a whirlwind trip to Italy with Larry Browning, a friend and professor at the University of Texas, and his wife, Vickie Hoch, an experienced traveler with United Airlines who was our informal tour leader. After seeing Sorrento and the Amalfi Coast, we wound up in the medieval city of Assisi, where we bought a print of *S. Francesco,* a fresco by Giovanni Cimabue in the lower basilica. We had it framed, and Craig, our handyman, hung it in a place of prominence, a central place on the wall behind the mail/storage desk.

I had missed a week because of a bad cold but was assigned to clean the showers. Joe said he should have been assigned to do it, that there should be a rule saying that a volunteer shouldn't have to do that duty after an illness. I suggested to Joe that we should form a union. He smiled. I suggested calling it the Amalgamated Homeless Shelter Volunteers of America, AHSVA for short. He smiled. In that moment was born a movement of solidarity unprecedented—to my knowledge—in the history of homeless shelters.

"They," or "management," were asking us to do more and more, to work harder and harder. Mike said we had set a record for the previous month. Tom confirmed it, saying we had 12,400 guests in December. We had averaged 10,000 per month during the previous year. When I asked for probable causes, Tom said cold weather and fewer day-labor jobs. The recent census of homeless people in the Denver metropolitan area came up with the number seven thousand.

On a Friday in March 2001, Lou, a regular guest, decided to take a pair of cotton pants from the clothing room, even though he said they looked like "joint" clothes. The others in the room broke out in laughter, but I was stumped, not understanding the humor. I pressed Lou for an explanation, and he supplied a verbal equation for me: *Joint* meant *pen,* the second term being an abbreviation for *penitentiary.* They all watched my reaction. I started laughing, and they joined me in appreciation of clothing as stigma.

The Lance Armstrong of the Homeless World forgot to take his meds, had an epileptic seizure, and wound up in the hospital. When I first saw him after that, he was reading an article about eating out.

"Do you eat at restaurants?"

"Yes," he said, giving the name of a Chinese restaurant near the hotel where he had a room.

"They made me pay before I ate when I first went there. Now I can pay after I eat." He paused, adding, "And after someone stole my bike, they gave me a new one, uh, a new used one."

"Some people are good, aren't they?" I asked.

"Yes—when they know you."

Lance changed the subject, saying his brother-in-law had told him that more people were losing their place to live.

"Why?" I asked, wondering what a brain-damaged, epileptic super-athlete would have as an answer.

"Because there are too many people and too few places to live in Denver. Only the people with a lot of money can afford a place to live." He paused. "That doesn't sound right." I couldn't disagree.

I ate lunch, as usual, from 11:15 to 12:00. A city police officer the center hired for security ate with us, a rare event. Quite naturally I inquired about the murders. He said he knew little about them but did know enough, however, to say the newspaper reports got it all *wrong*. The men hadn't been decapitated. They had been bludgeoned to death, to the point that their heads no longer existed, no trace of them. He also said I might not be able to get any information out of the department because the cases were still under investigation.

I went on talking with the others at the lunch. Joe and I resumed our playful discourse about forming a union of volunteers. The staff members began to make jokes about it. Everyone seems to enjoy the irony of volunteers organizing themselves into a union in an organization they loved and identified with, and the irony that they didn't have wages and benefits to bargain about.

How long did it take for me to connect the officer's remarks about the murdered homeless men, including Joe Mendoza, with the victim of Jack, the killer in the Colorado State Mental Hospital? I cannot say. The crimes were separated in time by forty-three years or more. Eventually I did see the similarity. The victims were beaten to death in such a way that they appeared to be decapitated. There was speculation in newspaper accounts that the heads had been eaten by wild animals, but that was later denied. There were no heads left after the bludgeoning killings in Denver, just as the mechanic's head on the Western Slope had been vaporized. What kind of person or persons could commit such atrocities? Could it be a group of highly identified kids who fit the criminal capital model? Was it a virulent killer of the kind Athens described? Or could it be a genuinely crazy person like the man I knew in Pueblo in 1956. By the way, I wondered,

Was he released during deinstitutionalization? Was he still alive? Would the police ever catch the killer or killers?

Mary Hupp, the community minister for and head of the Capitol Hill United Ministries, invited me to give a thirty-minute speech at the annual dinner and meeting of CHUM on February 22, 2001. I was more nervous than usual anticipating the occasion because I'd never addressed an audience of ministers; the title of the speech was "An Existential Look at Homelessness."

I began talking about my experience at the St. Francis Center, moving on to the statistics, emphasizing the steady increase in the numbers of guests at the shelter and the numbers of people counted in the point-in-time studies. The number of homeless persons in Denver had increased by 33 percent during my tenure as a volunteer.

I talked about the reading I'd been doing—the social science research, literature, and theology. I admitted trying to find answers in the work of Martin Heidegger, the German Existential philosopher. His work had inspired me to think of homelessness in new ways.

I began with his idea of *Geworfenheit*,[3] translated as "thrownness." I gestured several times at the audience, pretending to throw a baseball in several directions. All of us experience thrownness, I said, not just the misfits. We don't throw ourselves; we are thrown. We are thrown into the midst of other beings. We don't come to rest; we stay "in the throw." In everyday language: "I like to think of thrownness in the concrete way we become human beings. We come into the world without having been asked if we wanted to enter it, without any say about the time, place, our parents, gender, race, or social capital." I tried to describe the trajectory of our thrownness.

Having been thrown, I continued, we have to fall. Falling was a way of saying that we are lost, lost in a crowd of other beings. What is relevant about our thrownness and our falling is that *we are all homeless beings.* We do not "reside."

According to Heidegger, we are driven to seek some sort of home-coming (he seemed to think doing philosophy was the best way to seek a homecoming), though we never achieve a true homecoming. We are stricken with homesickness. The audience seemed to be convinced by these ideas; at the least, my hearers were taking them seriously.

If we are all homeless and homesick, I asked, what is the difference between those of us who are comfortable in our homes and those who are sleeping on the South Platte River on a February night? What does the ordinary use of the word *homeless* now mean? Here I recalled the mole people of New York City as described by Jennifer Toth in her book *The Mole People: Life in the Tunnels beneath New York City*. When I first read the book, I had doubts as to whether an attractive young woman could descend three stories, armed only with a can of Mace, into the city under the ground. But I voluntarily set aside my critical predispositions when I saw the photographs of mole people in their environment.

I also found several passages in the book useful for my Existential project, including this statement: "Most tunnel dwellers prefer to be called 'houseless' rather than 'homeless.'"[4] This was the distinction I asked my audience of ministers to accept. All of us are homeless and homesick, but the guests at the St. Francis Center are different from us only by being *houseless*. Houselessness is a condition or state we can do something about.

I told the audience I had never ended a speech with a prayer before, but that night I wanted to do so with a petition I had found in the book about the mole people. More than a dozen people who lived in the abandoned train tunnel heard a young woman's screams on a freezing December night. She was in labor. A young Hispanic man named Juan who worked at McDonald's during the day said they should pray:

> Dear Lord, please deliver us this baby safely. His parents are good people. He's done nothin' bad, Lord. He's jus' a baby. He don't mean no disrespect being born underground. We'll take care of him when he's with us. Just deliver him and his mama safely, Lord, and we'll take care of the rest. Amen.[5]

CHAPTER TEN
A CRISIS MEETING AT THE SHELTER

Spring of 2001 had arrived. My field notes had a bit less to say about SFC and more about my involvement with advocacy groups. I was still working in the Affordable Housing Study Group, was involved with the Capitol Hill United Ministries, attended a state conference sponsored by the Colorado Coalition for the Homeless, and would join a new group called Housing Justice! (HJ!). In fact, HJ!'s Education Committee began to meet in an upstairs room at SFC on Fridays, giving me a break from the routine. Although I still played golf once or twice a week, homelessness was becoming at least a part-time job. And although I told everyone I was writing a book about homelessness, I was really writing a set of field notes, a voluminous set of field notes. I'd given speeches and lectures, but the first writing that was published was a letter to the editor on Monday, July 2, 2001.

My letter was in response to an editorial in the *Denver Post* on June 18 titled "Windfall for Housing?" The editorial writer realized that the taxes Colorado voters had approved to pay for their new stadium, Coors Field, home of their new major league baseball team, the Colorado Rockies, had paid off the debt sooner than expected. Why not, the editorial asked, spend the tax money on affordable and low-income housing? Moreover, the sales tax that had built the baseball stadium and that had been extended to pay for a new football stadium would pay off the mortgage in ten years. Why not extend it beyond that in order to spend the money toward affordable and low-income housing? In response, I wrote:

> Re: "Windfall for Housing?" June 18 editorial. It is a great idea to propose that metro-area communities use the unexpected income from Coors Field sales-tax rebates to build affordable and low-income housing, and to extend the tax into the future for such uses. The idea of extending the sales tax used to build Invesco Field at Mile High for the same purpose in 10 years is equally admirable and creative.
>
> Homelessness increased by 33 percent in the Denver metro area between 1998 and 2000; this includes workers at or above the minimum wage. Housing in the affordable category five years ago is now out of reach for many. Let me offer a friendly amendment to the proposal: A grass-roots movement to help provide such housing is now formally organized as Housing Justice! It is a faith-based corporate coalition striving to organize a statewide summit on housing needs—and to create a state housing trust.
>
> The trust will be used to leverage the cost of building affordable and low-cost housing. Why not funnel some of the sales-tax rebates into either a Denver or Colorado housing trust with which to build or rehabilitate housing for the needy?
>
> Phillip K. Tompkins
> Denver[1]

I thought it was a good idea. And I still do—particularly the housing trust or investment fund. Unfortunately, my editorial rhetoric didn't stampede the state politicians into enacting my modest proposal. Colorado is among a minority of states—one of twelve, to be exact—without a housing trust or investment fund.

One sentence stands out in the letter I wrote for the newspaper, the one informing my readers that homelessness had increased by 33 percent in the first two years of my work at SFC. Working at the shelter was highly rewarding, but it wasn't having any impact on the figures. Conditions were getting worse, not better.

While Joe Brzozowski and I were working at mail/storage, Mike asked us to purge the mail, pulling out those letters that hadn't been picked up in a week and returning them to the post office. If we didn't purge them, it took too much time to go through all the letters searching for one person's mail, and we would run out of space. Purging anything, storage bags, mail, or messages is painful, hard, emotional labor, but we had to do it. Later Mike asked me to purge the messages and erase the names from the message board. I got permission to look at the purged messages:

1. From a local dairy: "You are good to go. Come in ASAP." That seemed to be potentially good news.
2. "Call *collect* ASAP re: your train accident." Was he a hobo hurt riding the rails?
3. From a beverage company: "Regarding your application, they want to set an interview for you."
4. "—— wants to talk to you about your brother about a job [*sic*]."
5. "Contact your attorney."
6. From a person two states away: "Would you please get in touch with me? I love you & miss you. Very much. My address is ——. I'd like to see you and talk to you. Hey, I really miss you and still love you. Believe me." This was perhaps the most touching of the messages, and I wondered whether they got back together.
7. "This is ——. I would like a divorce. You know this will not work. Contact me. Thanks."

There were messages from a mother who fell, broke some ribs, and couldn't write. Messages were missed: Did it matter that a man missed the message advising him to take his annual toxological test at the Stout Street Clinic? And what was in all that mail Joe and I purged earlier? I cleaned the showers and was tired at the 2:00 sharing when I asked, "Why are we out of Q-tips, jeans, socks, towels, and smellgood?"

I recorded in my notes a trip the day before to Boulder to have lunch with another undergraduate student, Elizabeth Axelrod, writing an undergraduate honors thesis about interaction among homeless people. Dan Cress of the sociology department at CU Boulder had asked me to serve as an unofficial adviser and outside member of her examining committee. Elizabeth and I met for lunch and talked about her thesis. She worked at the Boulder Homeless Shelter not far from the restaurant and was able to gather some data from guests about their interaction patterns. She had such a small sample that her study was not earthshaking, but she did find that the longer people lived on the streets and in shelters, the less frequently they interacted with family members and close friends. To be sure, they did interact with new friends they met on the street, but these ties were much weaker and more fragile than the ones they had lost.[2] Bob Mann, the director of the Boulder Shelter for the Homeless, had come to the same conclusion in conversation with me much earlier. Peter H. Rossi had come to the same conclusion after a massive statistical study of homeless people in Chicago and the origins of their condition.[3]

All of this was consistent with Athens's modification of Charles Horton Cooley's notion of the primary group; that is, Athens held that the primary group doesn't always prepare the individual to have a pro-social orientation. It sometimes does the opposite, and the individual either leaves or is kicked out, losing any possible support that can save him or her from a life on the streets.

Elizabeth gave me a forty-minute tour of the Boulder shelter. It was an old motel, gated and somewhat remodeled. The intake office and meal room were located in what had been the motel office. What had been the motel rooms attached in a U-shaped structure had been converted into dormitories.

The surprise for me was the fact the facility was used in the summer as transitional housing, a place for people to prepare for more traditional housing. Not until October would it open up again as an emergency shelter. That meant that the liberal city of Boulder, Colorado, had no emergency shelter during the summer and early fall of 2001. Three teenagers had shown up the night before at the shelter without a place to stay, without transportation, and without money. There was no place to put them. Perhaps they found a safe nest or den in the greenbelt of the foothills.

Elizabeth briefed me well, explaining that there were three levels of transitional residents in the shelter. Only the third level, the highest, had the combination to the lock on the gate and with it the freedom to come and go. This is in the area the citizens of Boulder used to call "Dogpatch," an allusion meaningful only to those old enough to remember the comic strip *Li'l Abner*, about a community of hillbillies. (My wife, daughter, and I had lived in a new development in that area.) On December 27, 2001, the *Denver Post* reported that the director of the Boulder Shelter for the Homeless would resign on January 31, 2002, to take a job in Iowa to be close to his son and daughter. Mann told the newspaper it had been a life-altering job: "It's given me a new appreciation for human life. . . . It's helped me to deal with that primal fear of the unknown, of homeless people."

The article related that in 1999, the city nixed his attempt to move from the old motel to a spot near a middle school. NIMBYism triumphed, and Mann was still rankled when he decided to retire. "It's stayed with me, because it did represent a level of economic prejudice that was converted into the vilification of an entire population."[4] Those are harsh words about a community so liberal that conservatives in Denver referred to it as the People's Republic of Boulder, and coming from a man who characterized himself as a conservative, they are equally ironic.

In the two preceding paragraphs I jumped from July 2001 to December 31 of the same year to mention that Mann had announced his resignation, skipping over the nightmare of September 11, 2001. My morning page for that fateful day was written in the afternoon and begins with this paragraph:

> They are calling it the Pearl Harbor of the War of Terrorism. I watched television until 1:30 p.m., satisfied that I understood the symbolism as well as the horror of it. They used our resources—huge airplanes full of fuel capable of flying to the west coast—as bombs to attack the Pentagon, synecdoche of our military might and, the World Trade Center, the site and symbol of our financial power.

Three days later I was still in shock when I showed up at SFC. Again I went to the Samaritan House from 10:00 to 12:00 so that our guests could use the showers there. There was a television set in the room off the showers where we put the baskets of towels, soap, socks, razors, toothbrushes, and other goods. On it was a live broadcast of the service at the National Cathedral. I was moved by it, struck by Billy Graham's remarks about the "mystery of evil" and his honesty in admitting that he had no satisfactory answer to the question of why his God would permit such events. President George W. Bush gave the best speech I'd heard come out of his mouth.

Our guests and the residents of the Samaritan House watched carefully, exhibiting some signs of confusion, but some were showing a genuine sense of patriotism. The next month's issue of the *Voice* would contain much about the attacks, including a long and moving poem by a homeless writer.

On January 4, 2002, I met with the Education Committee of Housing Justice! in the upstairs meeting room of SFC. Tom chaired the meeting, calling for introductions from each participant. He began by giving us the bad news: SFC had had more guests in 2001 than ever before. Angie of MetroCareRing said requests for services from her agency had increased by 33 percent since 9/11, including as always the requests for food, but in addition people in Denver now needed more help for such things as their energy bills, rent, even bus tokens. People being laid off were at risk, she said, of dropping into homelessness.

I mentioned a book I was reading that I got for Christmas from my daughter Emily, *Down and Out, On the Road: The Homeless in American History*, by Kenneth Kusmer, professor of history at Temple University (discussed in chapter 2 of this book). No matter their degree of destitution, the homeless people "are not so different from the rest of us. They never have been. Any genuine effort to end homelessness must begin with a recognition of that essential truth."[5]

It started snowing during that January afternoon, bringing much-needed moisture to our high desert, appreciated, oddly enough, by many of our guests. It is strange, upon reflection, to hear them say, "Yeah, it's tough, but we sure need the moisture," as if they had lawns and gardens to worry about. I mentioned that to friends, following Kusmer, saying they couldn't frame the sentence with "We" as the subject if they were all that different from the rest of us.

On the following Friday, January 11, 2002, Lukas gave us a global perspective on our common concern. During the sharing discussion in the morning, he read from an article in an English-language newspaper published in his native Czech Republic, the *Prague Post*, of November

28, 2001. Prague is a city of 1.1 million people, and its estimated home-less population was three thousand people. By contrast, metropolitan Denver had a population of about 1 million people and nine thousand homeless people (up by two thousand in one year). The biggest city in the world then was Tokyo, with 26 million people, and it had five to ten thousand homeless people. New York, with 16.6 million people, had one hundred thousand homeless people, ten times the number for the much larger Asian city.

What to make of these numbers? Denver had three times more homeless folks than Prague. Tokyo, a city with twenty-six times as many people as Denver, had about the same number of homeless people as Denver did.

"Why?"

Lukas posed the question to me as we looked at the numbers together at lunch. I came up with several answers. One was space. A man I knew had a good job for two years in Japan; he lived in an "apartment" that was one room, with barely enough room to turn around in. Another was economics. Japan had been in what they called the *Heisei* recession since 1991, the worst in the post–World War II era. Corporate bankruptcy and unemployment had created a new type of person, the *hoomuresu,* a neologism borrowed from the English word *homeless,* to distinguish the category from *furoosha,* the bums. "Both bum and homeless designate the Other. But there is a significant difference in connotation. Bums were more tolerable than homeless."[6] The homeless people represented a threat to those domiciled workers living on the margin, those vulnerable to be-coming *hoomuresu* themselves. In short, because Japan has always been much more homogeneous than the United States, there were many fewer Others. One might as well have asked why there were so *many* homeless people in that tight-knit, family-oriented culture. Economics in the form of a long recession gives the other part of the answer.

Lukas, a native of Czechoslovakia, born when it was a socialist state, said there were no homeless people in his homeland during his youth. The system brought most people down but lifted up those at the bottom. Capitalism has created a new kind of Czech citizen, the homeless person. But Lukas, who still has relatives in the Czech Republic, would not have it any other way.

I wound up cleaning the showers that day, getting three helpers at 1:00. A black man with some missing pickets was cleaning sinks and mirrors as I used a scrub brush on the benches and floor in the dressing area. He announced to the three of us his faith in God and said that he was blessed to have a pillow to put his head on at night. He mentioned service and prayer, to which I replied that St. Francis taught that the kind of work he was doing was a form of prayer. He thought about it as he polished the mirror, finally telling us, "I agree."

"In fact," he concluded after another pause, "it's stronger than prayer."

Joe Brzozowski gave me the messages purged that day: missed messages. Thirteen of them advised a recipient to see Deb, a staff member, about "jewelry sale profits" that the guest had earned by making crosses sold at local churches. I hoped that whoever it was had heard about the money some other way and had put it to good use. Five messages advised a guest to "call the nurse at the Stout Street Clinic." A message tried to inform a man of an interview for a room in the Forum, an SRO transitional facility. Another tried to tell a guest about an interview for "permanent housing." Finally, did Jim ever learn that someone had found his wallet and left it in the lost and found at SFC?

On March 15, 2002, we had snow for the third consecutive Friday, not atypical for Denver because March is the snowiest month of the year. Two weeks earlier, several men were sleeping on the sidewalk in front of the building when Mike arrived early in the morning. Miraculously, they were all well. Mike told us later that they had put cardboard on the sidewalk, put their sleeping bags on top of it, and then burrowed into the bags; they later said the snow that fell on them served as a layer of insulation from the cold air.

I checked the intake numbers for the previous two Fridays: March 1: 684; March 8: 626. At ten I was working the showers. I put out some pre-electric shaving lotion as a substitute for smellgood. One man raised the bottle to his mouth as if to provoke me to say, as I had said many times before, always in good humor, "Don't drink it!"

He first smiled, letting it grow into a laugh. Everyone in the room heard the remark and began to laugh, or at least smile. It was a wonderful, communal moment of merriment. This was followed by the wisecracks from the other men, some of which implied they might have once tried to imbibe such stuff. The spirit of the moment continued: Each time a man picked up the bottle, the other men would look at me, smile, and I, fulfilling their expectations, would wink and roar, "Don't drink that." Smiles and laughter softened the room.

But a loftier moment was achieved when Kenneth, an African American man who had been a regular for some time, finished dressing at the end of my counter. We had come to know each other fairly well, and as he donned his clean clothes, he made a joke about looking forward to seeing all the beautiful women at work.

"Where do you work?"

"Children's Hospital. In the cafeteria."

"It must be tough at times," I said.

"Yes, it is tough at times when I make the rounds with food and snacks. There is one eight-year-old girl who was burned over most of her body. Her parents ran a meth lab that exploded. They got out, but left their daughter in it."

The story made me mad, mad as hell.

"She lost all of her fingers and is in constant pain, but when she sees me come in with the snack cart she smiles."

He paused.

"I love that job."

In the 2:00 p.m. discussion, I told the story as a synecdoche to capture the day. Carla said Kenneth had stabilized his life in that job.

Tom had earlier joined us for lunch. Officer Ross walked in to tell Tom he had made a heroin bust.

"Where?"

"In front of the building. I sat in my car and watched the whole transaction. I can't believe they went ahead with it."

Bits and pieces came out as we questioned the officer. He saw the dealer take two plastic bags out of his mouth and give them in exchange for money. He said there was enough evidence to arrest two men.

Good Friday came on March 29, 2002, a short day at the shelter. When Joe Brzozowski and I went in to clean the showers at 10:45, I observed one guest picking up dirty towels and putting them in the plastic baskets. I called attention to him, thanking him for cleaning up after his brothers, and thanked him because it made our job so much easier. When he had completed his self-assigned duties, he tried to buy a toothbrush with a bus token, against the rules: ten cents in cash for a toothbrush, or a razor for that matter, without exception. The three guest helpers, Joe, and I all looked at each other. We all knew the rules. The youngest of the guest helpers said, "He has helped us all."

"And it is Good Friday," I said.

"OK," said Joe, making it final.

I gave him a toothbrush for the bus token.

A few minutes later the man said to the young helper, "Happy Easter." I was walking toward the young helper at that moment, and the man said to both of us, "I love you."

On a Friday in the middle of April, I overheard two guests talking about recent changes. One mentioned that he had to spend more time waiting in line to get food. Both talked about how the day-labor jobs had dried up. One went on at length about the change in the rate of pay. As recently as a couple of years earlier, he could get jobs at $7.00 per hour; today, in 2002, if he could get a job, it paid only $5.15 per hour, the minimum wage. I joined in by quoting from an article in that morning's *Denver Post*: To afford the average rent in Denver, a person would have to earn an annual income of $31,242, or $15.15 per hour. They readily agreed, one adding that even at that there wouldn't be much money left to spend on anything else.

The Lance Armstrong of SFC came in. He now had a room for three nights in a row but had to move out on the fourth.

"What do you do on the fourth night?"

"I ride my bike all night to the east, and then turn around, riding back in daylight." He rode twenty to thirty miles, sometimes reaching the town of Byers, Colorado. He said he had passed out while riding in the mountains recently because the dosage of his meds was off a bit.

On a Friday in October 2002, Tom told us there would be an emergency meeting in the morning. He would try out the briefing on us at 11:00. Symptomatic of the crisis, he said, were the intake numbers for the week—numbers up to the six hundreds, numbers we normally saw only in the dead of winter. I checked them out on the calendar when I started at mail/storage: Monday, 507; Tuesday, 556; Wednesday, 685; Thursday, 579. It was my fourth fall in the shelter, and it was truer than ever before, that October is the cruelest month, not April as the poet said. It was particularly tough in 2002 because of a hot dry summer, a hundred-year drought. A cold front had moved in with snow flurries on Tuesday, providing a nasty contrast for those who lived outdoors without winter clothes. As I helped a guest get his storage bag between 8:00 and 9:00, he was bundled up with a bedroll strapped to his back. I asked him where he had spent the night.

"The river," he said matter-of-factly.

"Did you keep warm?"

"Not so bad."

I showed up at 11:00 with my lunch to hear the briefing. Tom had a six-page handout for us that I took notes on. He talked about the sharply increased numbers, with daily intake numbers of close to seven hundred, compared to an average of four hundred per day in 2000, just two years before. The causes, he said, were a downturn in the economy, fewer jobs, and lower pay. We were seeing more people on the street for their *first* time. Other shelters were full. The Samaritan House was turning away three to ten families a day. Our sources of funding were drying up at the federal and local levels. At the same time, our responsibilities were growing: We now managed transitional housing at the Valdez Home, now called Beacon, which was full; Anchor II, also the site of transitional housing, was about to open after remodeling and expansion. The Catholic Worker Soup Kitchen had become homeless and had been serving two meals a week, on Wednesday and Friday, at the St. Francis Center since August 2001. But, he said, we had tremendous resources to face the crisis: a staff of twenty-one persons and one hundred volunteers, who had contributed nearly twelve thousand hours in 2001.

Volunteers from other days of the week, people I didn't recognize, joined us around the table. They were curious about panhandlers, the people on the mall and those who stationed themselves at intersections with cardboard signs, and how they should respond to them. One that got my attention while driving near the civic center was a cardboard, hand-lettered clever admission that the guy wanted a beer, eschewing the appeal of being, say, a disabled vet or just down on his luck. People smiled at him, and he smiled at them; some gave him donations. The guests called this process of holding up a cardboard with pleas for a donation "signing," or "flying the sign," and I'd thought about making a study of the sad appeals they made. (One of the most interesting I've seen was a cardboard hoisted by a dour young white man with this message: "my wife ran off with my best friend. i need money for a thank you card.")

After Tom said he wouldn't deny all panhandlers, I had to mention a book, one of the best on homelessness I'd read: Lars Eighner's book *Travels with Lizbeth: Three Years on the Road and on the Streets*. I didn't summarize the entire book. Instead, I simply recommended it and stated the author's position on the panhandling question. I shall spend more time on it because it ought to be better known than it is. I discovered the book in 2002, read it, and tracked down the author in Austin, Texas, in order to have a long telephone interview with him. He said that he had had a lovely time visiting the University of Colorado at Boulder, giving a speech and interacting with students who had been assigned to read his work.

Eighner's title reveals that he experienced being both on the road and down and out. He lost his job and found himself homeless in the state capital of Texas and the home of the state university. He didn't associate with other homeless people, avoiding the homeless shelters and hobo jungles. Thus, he didn't and doesn't speak for homeless people; rather, he speaks of the condition of homelessness.

Chapter 7 of his book is "Dumpster Diving." It begins with a lesson in etymology, the origins of the word *Dumpster*. Eighner found that it is a proprietary word of the Dempster Dumpster Company, hence, he capitalizes it throughout the chapter. I wrote in the margin of my paperback version of the book that the chapter is an essay, an ironic tour de force. Much of it deals with a disgusting subject, garbage, but it is written in an elevated, even elegant style. Although he wrote the essay while he was homeless, he retained the present tense when he completed the book, involving the reader in the rules he develops as he searches for the *necessaries* of life.

The rest of the book is also insightful and elegantly written. Chapter 10 is perhaps the best essay I have read on its subject—"Alcohol, Drugs, and Insanity"—and as I return to it now in writing about the book, I find that it best expresses my own conclusions about the subject. Like me, Eighner had worked in a state mental hospital. He was working there when he resigned under threat of being fired. Although he had worked there for seven years, he had always been in trouble for complaining about the abusive habits of the staff, habits that conflicted with the humane published policies. With ten years of experience in the mental health field, he could detect the symptoms of mental illness in others without knowing their histories. There is no gainsaying, Eighner says in the opening lines of chapter 10, that many homeless people are addicted to alcohol or illicit drugs or are insane. But he thought the proportion of homeless people who belong to one or more of those categories is greatly overestimated:

> This overestimation seems to stem from two otherwise opposing views. People who do not want to help the homeless seek to blame the homeless for being homeless. These people see alcoholism, drug addiction, and insanity as character flaws that somehow justify the condition of the homeless. This conservative line of thought is only one step removed from the conclusion that in addition to deserving homelessness, the homeless also deserve whatever mistreatment individuals or society may choose to mete out.
>
> Those who wish to help the homeless, on the other hand, want to find a problem that can be fixed. Admittedly, alcoholism, drug addiction, and insanity are difficult problems, but something can be done for them.[7]

Although Eighner didn't drink with homeless people on the street, he did see enough of it and he talked to enough people to understand that the stereotype didn't always apply. It doesn't ring true, he wrote about the hackneyed story of the social drinker, functioning in society, who has a character flaw that makes him drink more or who encounters something beyond his control that deprives him of the will to be sober. He loses his job, his family, his home, and we see him as a wino passed out in an alley with a brown sack clutched in his hand. Eighner said he found some street winos who had followed this script, but he met just as many in which cause and effect were reversed: "people who claimed to have drunk little or not at all until they became homeless."[8]

Why would someone who had never taken a drink, or who had been a social drinker before, begin drinking on the street? Eighner said he didn't drink because he wanted his wits to be keen at all times to cope with the hazards and dangers of the street, but he could understand the appeal of liquor, giving two reasons that I mention to people when they ask me whether they should give money to panhandlers who might spend it on drink. The first is that "alcohol is a fair anesthetic and its sedative properties can produce sleep in restless circumstances."[9] For many on the streets, it may the cheapest or only anesthetic available to them. The second is that drinking is the only social life homeless people have. They tend to be loners, like Eighner, except when they can pool their resources for wine and beer, find a camp, sit in a circle, and pass the bottle. Eighner is certain that *many of them would be called social drinkers if they were not homeless.* Houses provide a safe and appropriate place for behavior that is unacceptable for houseless people. It was the only society he found on the street, and he avoided it because he wanted to get off the street and back into housing. The person who has hit bottom or is near it drinks alone. That is the person clutching the brown sack in the alley or on the grate or in a nest or den.

Eighner's unique set of experiences, along with his gift for the English language, allow him to recognize mental illness on the street and to understand the institutional constraints of the asylum. His discussion of deinstitutionalization is one of most insightful, and clearly written, discussions I've seen, and for that reason I introduced it in an earlier chapter.

Returning to the briefing Tom gave us at the round table, recall that he said the daily intake numbers had increased to nearly seven hundred in 2002, as compared to four hundred per day in 2000, just two years earlier. Should we infer that a statistically significant proportion of the normal, domiciled population had suddenly fallen from their status as social drinkers to brown bag winos? Or that "normal" people, for some unknown reason, became addicted to crack? Could Denver have had an epidemic of schizophrenia or bipolar disorders that, either alone or in combination with the other two causes, dramatically increased the population of homeless people in the city? Is it not more likely that a downturn in the *economy* had created a loss of jobs and decreased income, while housing costs either stayed at the same level or increased from the year 2000? More and more I was being driven to the answer, the simple equation, that most of the increase in the homeless population was due to *economic* conditions: too little income, and housing too expensive.

The shelter was open only during the morning on Christmas day of 2002. Tim said he was so exhausted when they closed at noon that he went home—the Vincentian House, where he lives with other volunteers—fell asleep, and missed the Christmas dinner. Tom spoke next, saying he worked Christmas morning. He said the shelter was "packed," more people than he had ever seen on a half day. Four fights broke out, all of them between African Americans and Mexicans. Tom was heartened when guests tried to stop the fights. So many people lined up for communion that the bishop had to consecrate more wine. There were so many people waiting to get in, they had had to open the shelter early to get them in off the street.

CHAPTER ELEVEN
THE COLLECTIVE DISCIPLINE OF COMPASSION

During early January 2003, I was concentrating on my keynote address for the Rocky Mountain Communication Association's annual convention in the University Memorial Center, at the University of Colorado at Boulder. My speech was scheduled for January 18, and my topic was the contemporaneous scandals of American corporations such as McWane, Enron, Tyro, and others. McWane, for example, had been the subject of an exposé on January 9, 2003, on the Public Broadcasting Service's (PBS's) program *Frontline*. PBS was assisted by the *New York Times* and the Canadian Broadcasting Company. McWane manufactured sewer pipe, and over the previous seven years the company had amassed more safety violations than all of its competitors combined. Their employees suffered countless injuries—including burns and amputations—and nine of them had been killed at work. The company was also a major polluter.

Part of my analysis of the actions leading to corporate disgrace was based on the work of Max Weber (1864–1920), mentioned earlier in this book in connection with the complex rules of the St. Francis Center. I had studied Weber in graduate classes in the Sociology Department at Purdue University and had kept up my studies over the years, even making an interpretation of Weber as a theorist of rhetoric and communication.[1] It was a reading of Nicholas Gane's book *Max Weber and Postmodern Theory:*

Rationalization versus Reenchantment[2] that stimulated me to see Weber as more relevant than ever.

A burning question for Weber and his time was how to understand and explain "uncoerced obedience." Why do most people do what they are told? This is the kind of question a theorist of rhetoric and communication might ask. Weber's answer was *Herrschaft*, a word that can't be satisfactorily translated into English. It is often translated as "domination" or "authority," but in this context I prefer a more communicative term such as "influence." Weber also developed a fourfold typology of human action, but only the first two types are relevant to this discussion. The first, *zweckrational,* is usually translated as "instrumental rationality"; the second is *wertrationality,* "value rationality." What is the difference? In instrumental rationality,

> the end, the means, and the secondary results are all rationally taken into account and weighed. This involves rational consideration of alternative means to the end, of the relations of the end to the secondary consequences, and finally of the relative importance of different possible ends.[3]

Value rationality is quite different, as it takes its major premises from what Weber called the ultimate values, those unquestioned value premises from which we draw ethical conclusions for action or behavior. In general, Weber believed the ultimate values came from religious inspiration. My prime example is the Golden Rule; in my speech and in a later book chapter I show that a variation of it goes back to Hillel, a Jewish commentator on the law who antedated Jesus. Jesus, of course, also had his version of it. I also quoted a philosopher, James Rachels, who *reasoned* his way to a principle of human action consistent with the Golden Rule.[4]

The *Frontline* broadcast presented an organization as a contrast to McWane: the American Cast Iron Pipe Company (ACIPCO). It also manufactured sewer pipe. This company had an excellent safety record in the same dirty, dangerous business. It had a clean environmental record. *Fortune* magazine consistently ranked ACIPCO as one of the best employers in the United States. The founder of the company made sure that it would function with value rationality because all decisions would be based on the Golden Rule—and it has worked effectively as a philosophy of management ever since. The Golden Rule, therefore, can be accepted as an ultimate value on the bases of religious commandment, philosophic justification, and pragmatic justification.

McWane, Enron, and the other corporate bodies I analyzed in the speech were clearly using instrumental rationality. McWane managers calculated down to the last penny the consequences of obeying or disobeying the safety and environmental laws and rules. They calculated their ends, means, and unintended consequences. Corporate productivity and individual greed were the ultimate values. That is exactly what Weber predicted and feared; it has arrived. ACIPCO, however, using value rationality, competed successfully with McWane without breaking safety rules or polluting the environment.

Naturally I thought of the rules and rationality of SFC. I had come to the conclusion that the prescriptive and proscriptive rules at the shelter were an attempt to achieve what I called the "discipline of compassion." I got the phrase from a speech given by Karen Armstrong at a televised conference called "God at 2000." She said that some mystics reported there was nothing out there, no God they could reach in meditation. Of those who did report reaching God, Armstrong said they were most likely to sense the presence of God in the *discipline of compassion.*

In addition, I began to question everyone I could find at SFC about the rules. I asked them what they thought the rules meant and why they were in place, and I grouped their answers under such terms as "safety to the guests," "fairness" or "universality," and "efficiency." A discussion developed at the lunch table among a fairly large group of staff members and volunteers. After they supplied me with their terms, I asked this of them: "Do you believe SFC assumes that the discipline required in the rules helps the guests cope with the discipline and rationality outside, in the larger society?" Jerry agreed, saying that if the guests learned to be responsible for their behaviors inside SFC, they would be more responsible outside the shelter. Joe B. spoke of accountability; the other Joe, Joe K., a psychological caseworker, agreed that the purpose of the rules is discipline. We noted that there are several meanings of the noun *discipline,* such as "systematic training" and "obedience"; then there is the verb *discipline,* meaning "punishment," as when a teacher "disciplines" a naughty pupil for an infraction. Our rules seemed to be to help the guests at three levels: (1) to let them feel they were receiving fair treatment; (2) to promote obedience to the authority of rules designed to protect them from each other in an evenhanded way; (3) and to promote self-discipline that would carry over when they were out on the streets. I discussed SFC in the keynote address, which also found its way into print in 2005.[5]

The shelter continued to be packed during January. I took down the numbers from the calendar: January 3, 678; January 10, 711; January 17, 697; January 24, 675.

On Friday, February 21, 2003, I was finally able to get an hour of Tom's busy schedule for a formal interview. I had given him a copy of the questions I would ask and requested a copy of the budget. The three largest sources of income for the shelter that year were a grant from HUD, $260,966; donations from individuals, $260,000; and foundation grants, $244,835. The total income was projected to be $1,135,769. The major expenses were salaries, $518,963; rent assistance, $266,280; and health insurance, $115,918. The total expenses were $1,135,769. To my untrained eye, it seemed as if administrative costs were low by the standards applied to charitable institutions. I thanked Tom for being so open with me and began the interview:

> Q1: What are the purposes of the rules at SFC?
> A1: In general we have so many people you think of it as a small society or a community. When you walk in, you need to know the boundaries. They know we will protect their space; others won't bug them. The rules are the same for everyone—it gives a sense of fairness to know the rule will be applied to him in the same way it's applied to me. It gives a sense of comfort if all of us know what's going on. We do get challenged—usually at the door when the greeters have to turn away someone who's been drinking. We have a baseline. We have a level playing field, although we do make exceptions. There is a blind man who comes for the soup kitchen; we let him go to the head of the line and somebody carries his food to where he is going to sit.

Q2: What do you hope to achieve with the guests in regard to the rules?

A2: You make it disciplined in the shelter because the streets aren't like that. There are no rules out there, and bad things happen to you. You have to watch your back. This is an oasis from the streets. It is tough in here, but it is appreciated because you can breathe easy; you're not on guard. You can sit down and not have to watch your back.

Q3: Does it change people?

A3: It does—we change them. If you spend from 6:30 a.m. to 5:30 p.m. here it will change your life. By the way we treat people, we affect them. Some of our guests die after spending years here. They don't have any more money, and they're still on the streets, but hopefully their hearts and spirits are better, and they have more dignity. Just take the showers. I was talking with a woman at a foundation, and she said we are better off simply by washing our bodies.

We don't change the world. The kindness and respect we show them gives them more dignity; I like that. If you are around that all day, it rubs off. I see guests who become generous with other guests. We allow that to happen; it is not out of character.

Q4: Tell me about the physical layout.

A4: I wasn't here when the original layout was considered, but I have taken part in the changes made since then. The most important feature is the big room. Wow, you say when you walk in and see it full of people. What's good about that is you go to the spot [chair] that's open. You sit down with people you may not know. We do have social groups who like to stick together, a sense of belonging. The sidewalls. You can be alone sitting with your back to the wall. I saw a guy yesterday sitting in a corner with his head down, his hand over his eyes and I thought, Richard, I don't think you want me to say hello today. He was saying, "I want to be alone."

The layout is practical. First we have to get as many people in as possible. The greeters more than the police officer are responsible for peace in the room. We have to guard each person's space.

Q5: What about the patio and street?

A5: They are out of sight. [After I explained the panopticon, Tom nodded and continued.] The greeters and coordinator had to be able to see everyone in the big room. That is what I meant by guarding their space, preventing others from doing anything to them—such as playing a guitar in their face. New walls were put in to create office space for the staff who don't need to be under the gaze.

Q6: Does SFC teach discipline?

A6: Originally it was called a Hospitality Center. HUD calls it a drop-in center. We say we have guests. Discipline has a negative connotation, but there is a discipline. It is indirect—so they feel free. A guest told me recently, "I really like my apartment and can drink there. But if I want to come here, I can't drink. I don't drink when I come here."

Q7: About the rules: You said they are intended to achieve fairness, and that the rule is applied to you as well as me, and there is a spiritual underpinning to the rules. Is this the Golden Rule?

A7: I would hope so.

As I reread my notes from the formal interview, I made some marginal notes. Tom talked about the difference between inside the shelter and outside on the streets, he said "there are no rules out there, and bad things happen to you. You have to watch your back. This is an oasis from the streets." In the margin there, I wrote "*anomie*," the term used by Émile Durkheim and sociologists ever since to mean "normlessness." It is dialectically opposite to solidarity or collective integration, thus implying confusion and insecurity. My dictionary of sociological terms also attributes the term *acute anomie* to Sebastian DeGrazia, who used it "to refer to a severe form of anomie in which the value and belief systems of a society or group disintegrate, order collapses for the individual and he is gripped by anxiety."[6]

I had lunch that day with Tim and Craig, staff members. I had asked Craig earlier during a slow moment, "Did you ever have to eighty-six a volunteer?" This was a trick question, a test to determine if the organization really did apply its rules to its workers as well as its guests.

"Yes," Craig had answered, "Tom did. He [the volunteer] was too lenient with the rules. It made it difficult for everyone else."

I brought up the eighty-sixed volunteer again at lunch. "The person couldn't say no. He gave out razors and toothbrushes without charging ten cents apiece." So the discipline applies to the volunteers. It came to me that I had my own example, the time when Mike had had to "discipline" me for not checking the guests' records before letting them get their storage bag. I sat on the dunce stool after that. And he had had to discipline me for letting one guest worker leave the showers before the other two.

On Friday, March 7, 2003, I made an exaggerated demand of "management," on the part of the "union," to see a complete and up-to-date set of rules.

"Union?"

I explained with mocking seriousness that Joe B., another Friday volunteer, had decided to help me organize a union. I was the president and he the vice president. We called it the Amalgamated Homeless Shelter Volunteers of America, or AHSVA. This led to questions about the need for a union; the staff members were not sure how serious I was. I talked about the desirability of having solidarity among the volunteers, the need to correct abusive management practices by means of a formal grievance procedure, and, of course, the need for collective bargaining. They now realized from my overacting that it was meant in humor, and the union became a long-running joke at the shelter: *What will the union say about this?*

I had made an appointment for Thursday, March 13, 2003, to tour the Samaritan House (SH) to better understand how other shelters functioned. When I entered the building, I asked for Father Michael, the director of the shelter. He was paged; he appeared and gave me a friendly and informative thirty-eight-minute tour. The Samaritan House provided a wide range of important services, particularly to homeless families. On the third floor I saw the section called the Respite Program, six beds set aside for homeless people released from hospitals. He showed me twenty-one small rooms for families, holding about one hundred people. Everyone had to leave the building by 9:00 a.m. to look for jobs or apartments or both. Everyone had a chore to do each day. The residents could stay for three months, and they had to save 95 percent of their income during that time. SH also helped them with the rent deposit when they found an apartment.

There were playrooms for the children. Some of their "couple of hundred" volunteers watched the kids or tutored them in the evenings to give the parents some time together. Father Michael gave me an intermittent lecture on the history and details of the institution. SH had a staff of forty-five and had been open since 1983. The facility was built by Catholic Charities USA. On the second floor I saw satellite offices of the Stout Street Clinic and the city's social services, bringing services to homeless people where they are. There was also a counseling office and a large recreation room. Although he said in response to my question that they had no NIMBY problems, he later volunteered a rumor he'd heard, namely, that SH, SFC, and the Denver Rescue Mission would be forced to move. "This is expensive land." I'd heard that rumor before.

They served seven hundred meals a day—nearly everyone ate breakfast. They had an employment office. Father Mike—as other people called him during my tour—said there was a national trend toward getting their guests into small groups for counseling and educational purposes. He showed me the schedule of their meetings for the week.

We descended to the first floor where Father Mike pointed out the women's dormitory—we didn't enter it—which had fifty beds. He also pointed out the men's dormitory, saying I was welcome to inspect it, but I told him I'd seen it on the two times we brought our male guests from SFC to shower when our shower room was being repaired.

He also showed me the staff kitchen and conference room where they could get away, if only briefly, from the needs of the guests. They had three hundred beds for the people who had three months to find a room of their own. Vets could stay for a year. Before walking outside he showed me the lobbylike room for the overflow beds. He also pointed out the mats people could sleep on; they could also bring their own sleeping bags. The city restricted SH to ninety-five people in that first-floor space. Father Mike told me, in a way that reminded me of Tom at SFC, that people wanted to stay at SH because they felt "safe" and knew they would be treated well.

I thanked Father Michael for the informative tour, telling him sincerely that I was impressed by what they were doing for the less fortunate of our city. He said he'd pay us a visit at SFC. Samaritan House clearly practiced the discipline of compassion.

The race for a new mayor of Denver heated up in the early part of 2003. All the major candidates were invited to a forum at the St. Francis Center on April 17. SFC and our neighborhood association sponsored the meeting jointly, a slight suggestion of an improving relationship between the two parties. The candidates who showed up were Phil Perington, Ari Zavaras, and John Hickenlooper. Three others couldn't make it.

Hickenlooper said that homelessness was a problem we could solve, a problem we could do something about. He also proposed to extend the tax on the Broncos' football stadium. *Maybe he read the editorial and my letter to the editor about extending the tax and creating a Housing Trust Fund.*

It was clear to me that Hickenlooper was the most thoughtful of the candidates, at least on the issues important to me. He expressed his love for the city and his "frustration with tired old politics." He said he would break with the practices of the past, would take a new approach. He mentioned appointing a city commission to deal with homelessness. He said "aggressive panhandling drives tourists away and hardens people." He also said he would encourage the business owners of downtown Denver to realize their interest in solving the problem. He talked about chits or vouchers for food and shelter and said he would ask business to match the city's contributions. I decided to vote for him and recommended him to others as well.

A Vincentian volunteer named Ben, one of many working at SFC, was coming to the end of his year of duty and wanted to comment on his experience for the record. I interviewed him for forty minutes in May 2003. *Community,* he said, was the key word, adding that he hadn't done his work as a full-time volunteer as well as he could have until he learned the meaning of that word. The guests want to come where they don't feel like an outcast. They seek instead understanding and acceptance. He was proud of how some of the guests took ownership of SFC, relating the example of a man who volunteered to sweep the sidewalks in front of the building, not for a clothing slip, but to make the place look better. Ben found that moving. "You see guys breaking up a fight; they stop people from stealing a stick of deodorant."

"I was encouraged from the beginning to assume more responsibility; they were grooming me, and I became a coordinator at the age of twenty-two.... As a place to work, I tell people I love it, I enjoy the staff and volunteers—we have a sense of community. We have sharing and prayer every day. Tom [the executive director] does laundry with us in the morning, helping us share the responsibilities. Without trying to be a sensationalist I would be a ten on a one-to-ten scale on community."

Hickenlooper won the election in May in a landslide.

On a Friday in June 2003, one of the first guests I helped was a middle-aged white man of halting speech. Once he had his bag, he stopped on his way out of the storage room to give me a smile as the introduction of a speech. He said he was happy. An employment agency had referred him to a company who had interviewed him the day before, Thursday, June 5, for a job as a machinist. "The interview was going well until I sensed they were reluctant to give me the job because of my age. So I said, 'Let me do the job for a day, and if you like my work and get the contract, I'll have a job. If you don't like my work, you don't have to pay me, and you'll have one day of free work.' He shook my hand on it."

He accepted my congratulations and good wishes with a sincere smile. Not five minutes later I heard one of the staff members announce the man's name over the public address system and then say "You have a phone call." I saw him running toward my counter with a puzzled look, asking me without words where he could take the call. I pointed at the phone at the other end of the counter. He picked up the phone to take the call while maintaining eye contact with me. He was listening in an active, engaged way, nodding his head. Our eyes were locked. He said something I couldn't hear, put the phone in its cradle, and said to me, "They got the contract, and I got the job." I told Mike; he asked me to tell the story at the 2:00 meeting.

The Education Committee of Housing Justice! was holding its meetings at SFC, and at a meeting in May 2003, I presented a summary of the mayoral forum meeting. Tom Luehrs put some numbers on the blackboard:

10,000 Homeless People in Denver
3,000 Kids

He also mentioned that the housing vacancy rate in Denver was 13 percent. Rabbi Joel Schwartzman reported that unemployment in Denver was at 10 percent.

On Tuesday, June 10, 2003, we had another memorial service, this one for William Maurice "Bill" Driscoll: February 7, 1952–June 1, 2003. I helped move chairs and a table to the chapel corner of the big room. There were thirty-five to forty people for the service. Tom opened the service with a reading of scripture. He said he'd known Bill for twelve years. It was always "Hi, Bill" and "Hi, Tom." Bill came to SFC, he said, because "he knew we cared about him. We need each other, need to hear our name spoken by others, and [need to know] that the relationship is everything."

Tom said Bill had been "worn down" during the past year. He didn't know whether Bill had been sick, but he looked worn down—"the streets are hard. He was worn down but we still called him by name, and we'll put his name on the wall." Tom gestured toward the memorial plaques on the wall behind him. This was a manifestation of the collective discipline of compassion.

CHAPTER TWELVE
CHARITY VERSUS JUSTICE

On February 1, 2003, the sky fell. The Space Shuttle *Columbia* came apart during reentry from its earth orbit. Greg Desilet, a close friend, called to tell me the sad news because he knew I had been involved in the space program during the Apollo program of the 1960s, serving as a faculty consultant in organizational communication to Wernher von Braun, director of NASA's Marshall Space Flight Center in Huntsville, Alabama. The Marshall Center had the responsibility for the research and development on the *Saturn V*, the moon rocket. My job was to find out via participatory observation and in-depth interviews what communication practices worked and what practices did not. As mentioned previously, I came to identify with the organization and the remarkable philosophy and techniques of organizational communication they employed. I wrote articles about the organization.

When the Space Shuttle *Challenger* exploded in 1986, I was depressed, and as I read newspaper accounts of the accident it was clear to me that it couldn't have happened if NASA and the Marshall Center had been using the philosophy of organizational communication of the Apollo era. I read the Rogers Commission Report and returned to Huntsville in order to interview some top and middle managers about their practices. Claude Teweles, the founder and owner of Roxbury Publishing Company of Los Angeles, had persuaded me to write a book about the *Challenger*.

I heard from a few people suggesting I write a book about *Columbia*, but I wasn't interested in doing so. I thought I was about to write a book about homelessness and SFC. Yet I found that I couldn't stop reading about the accident and the investigation of it. In April 2003, I was invited to give a lecture via telephone to students in an organizational communication class at Michigan State University who were reading my *Challenger* book, and they wanted to know what I had to say about *Columbia*. As I prepared for the lecture, I heard what Dr. Sally Ride called an "echo" of the *Challenger* accident and realized that part of what I had said about the first shuttle accident would apply to the second one. Claude Teweles called to ask me to write the book, but still I held off, until one day, when I was walking down the Sixteenth Street Mall, I could see in my mind the title of the book and the chapter divisions.

That meant that much of the year 2003 and part of 2004 were dedicated to *Apollo, Challenger, Columbia: The Decline of the Space Program*. My field notes for September 19, 2003, indicate I had missed going to SFC four weeks in a row but was happy to be back. Tom asked each of us that day to comment on the ways SFC affected our spirituality. Cecil, both a priest and a New Testament scholar, said that his work as a volunteer had been one of his most important activities over the preceding ten years or so.

Mike, our Friday coordinator, welcomed me back along with other staff members. "The whole community welcomed me back," I noted. While working at mail/storage the guests thanked me, one saying "God bless you," and a wave of the old feeling rolled over me. Some of the guests noticed my beard, another symbol of my commitment to the book, because I had vowed not to waste time shaving until I finished it.

November of 2003 was a tough month for homeless persons in Denver. There were one hundred fewer beds available to them because the First Baptist Church in downtown Denver closed for remodeling. The housing advocates were trying to get Mayor Hickenlooper to open the Human Services Building for beds that the Denver Rescue Mission could supervise. I wrote in my morning pages that I was almost sure he would open the building. And he did, bringing cots into a city building.

He made an even bolder move, appointing a Commission to End Homelessness in Denver within the Decade. Later we would learn from a federal official that he was one of the first mayors in the country to make such a commitment. He appointed our own Tom Luehrs to the commission, which was to be chaired by Roxane White, manager of Denver's Department of Human Services and the former director of Urban Peak, an effective service agency and shelter for homeless teens. Hickenlooper also appointed several homeless people to the commission, notably Randle Loeb, an occasional guest at SFC and a writer for the Denver *Voice*. Significantly, the mayor also appointed several men representing downtown businesses and the tourist trade. I recalled that he had said during his campaign appearance in the mayoral forum at SFC that the downtown business interests had to realize the stake they had in ending homelessness in Denver. There were forty-two members, or "cats," as Roxane White would later call them after trying to herd them. I admired the ambition of the mayor and the commission's charge—to end homelessness within ten years. It was highly unlikely, I thought, to end homelessness, but that was also a noble and inspiring goal.

I decided to include parts of my keynote address at the annual meeting of the Rocky Mountain Communication Association in *Apollo, Challenger, Columbia* because I decided to put NASA's organizational decline in the context of other contemporaneous corporate failures and scandals. I wanted a couple of organizations to use as a contrast to the failed and disgraced corporate entities; I had one in ACIPCO, the cast iron pipe company that operated with such great financial and human success by accepting the Golden Rule as its guiding philosophy of management. I needed another, and having thought hard and interviewed people at the shelter about its philosophy, I decided to include a section on SFC.

I observed that the shelter functioned by means of the ultimate in value rationality, the Golden Rule. I described the building, mentioning the portraits of St. Francis and Martin Luther King, Jr., hanging on the walls. I also mentioned the deep satisfaction the volunteers derived from their work and their identification with SFC. After the book was published it was gratifying to hear from staff members and other volunteers that Tom had read this section of the book aloud during a sharing discussion.

My wife Elaine and I had become members of the Trinity United Methodist Church in downtown Denver, just across the street from the historic Brown Palace Hotel. We joined the Missions Committee of the church, and I continued meeting with Mary Hupp and the CHUM advocacy group. After a few meetings of the Missions Committee, a minister at Trinity who advised the group, Robert Carlisle, drew me aside for a conversation. Some years before he had organized a forum series at Trinity that was successful in raising the consciousness of the congregation. He called it the "Faces of Poverty." He said it was time to have a new forum series, the "Faces of Homelessness," and he asked me to organize it.

Because of the liturgical cycles of the church, he thought that the fall of 2004 would be the best time, and I responded that it was also the most difficult time for homeless people. Churches also have weekly cycles, leading Bob to suggest four consecutive Thursday nights. I accepted his call because it was an exciting time. The mayor's commission was at work, and I would try to get members of it who could share their thinking with us. Bob and I had many meetings about a general plan for the forum series.

Although it would take me some time before realizing its significance, a truly important program to battle homelessness was launched in February 2004. I first learned of it when I clipped a column published later in the *Denver Post,* on December 19, 2004, by John Parvensky, the president of the Colorado Coalition for the Homeless. He wrote of the then current housing crisis, and then he presented the good news: CCH had opened its Housing First Collaborative Program (HFC) for chronically homeless people. In its first ten months HFC moved sixty people—homeless for an average of 5.7 years—into safe housing with support services. The bad news was that there were six hundred people on the waiting list.

Housing Justice! had decided to organize the People's Walk for Housing. It would begin on June 5, trying to raise statewide support for a Colorado housing trust. One member of the organizer, Blake Chambliss, an architect and one of the founders of HJ!, would walk the entire 850-mile loop, from Pueblo in the south to Fort Collins in the north, a western leg to Grand Junction on the Western Slope, and an eastern leg back to Denver. Elaine and I would do the 5K Walk in downtown Denver, having persuaded friends to commit to contributing to HJ!

We went to the Capitol Building at 10:45 on August 21 to hear the speeches celebrating the end of the People's Walk. Blake gave an excellent speech on the steps of the state Capitol Building, saying that when he started everyone asked "why worry about the rest of the state? All the homeless people are here in Denver." And at every city and town across Colorado, people said that he had come to the right place. The homeless people are here.

We were surprised when Chris, our coordinator of volunteers, who had trained me to clean the showers, toilets, sinks, and drains, announced he had taken a job as a counselor at the University of Denver. I made a short speech relating how our careers were the exact opposite because I had retired from the academic world to work at the shelter. I predicted that he would have the best customers in the world, but said that my guess was that he would always remember the people he had helped at SFC. And a month later we again had mixed feelings when our Friday coordinator, the wise young Mike, let us know that he would be accepting a similar position at the University of Denver. We were happy for him, but we were entering a period of profound organizational change with the loss of young but experienced leaders.

Tom Luehrs opened the sharing discussion on Friday, September 3, 2004, and I had never seen him so optimistic. During the six years I'd known him, he seemed to bear the increasing weight of homeless people on his broad shoulders, but on this morning he expressed his hopeful belief that the Commission to End Homelessness would make some important recommendations to Mayor Hickenlooper and that he would act positively on them. He asked us to ask our guests—ones we know well—to tell us what would be the most important thing the city could do to make their lives better.

I had a private meeting with Tom after the sharing so that he could give me greater detail about the commission: It had taken Philadelphia as something of a model because business leaders there had led an effort to clean up a blighted section of the city and help the homeless people who spent time there. Denver's Downtown Denver Partnership, a coalition of business leaders, was finding inspiration in the Philadelphia model. Tom recommended that I invite John Desmond of that organization, and a member of the commission, to participate in the forum series, volunteering to make the first contact on the matter for me. He also recommended Jim Ryan, a local minister and official in the Colorado Council of Churches, saying we would want to involve the faith community.

During the rest of the day I followed through on Tom's suggestions, asking guests what the government of Denver could do for them. While cleaning the showers, I had three guests working hard to help me from 1:00 to 1:15. One was scrubbing a toilet, another was cleaning a sink, and the third was brushing the shower walls we had sprayed with disinfectant. I was scrubbing the floor with a stiff broom. We had worked together before and had developed a feeling of friendship and solidarity.

"Gentlemen," I said while leaning on the handle of my floor brush, "if the city of Denver could do something to help homeless people, what would make life better?"

"Housing," said Hank, without a pause. "Jobs. And vocational training." The other two men agreed. The man working in the showers added a fourth suggestion: that people who had a birth certificate should have it and other information such as Social Security numbers entered into a national database. I nodded, knowing our guests and staff members spent an inordinate amount of time trying to assemble such information for employers and applications for housing assistance.

I talked to Tom a week later, on September 10, and he had more ideas about participants for Trinity's forum series. I wanted a homeless person to speak, and Tom had a suggestion: Randle Loeb, a homeless man who wrote for the *Denver Voice* and served on the mayor's commission. I asked Tom to approach Roxane White, the mayor's chief adviser on homelessness and chair of the commission, to ask her to participate and to help us persuade Mayor Hickenlooper to participate himself. I was spending a great deal of time on the Faces of Homelessness forum and was running out of time. I was consulting with Reverend Carlisle and the Missions Committee throughout this period, and we decided to delay the forum series until late January and early February of 2005.

I stopped by SFC the next Thursday to ask Tom to make a couple of phone calls on behalf of the forum series. I also asked him and Bernie O'Connell for color photographs I could use in promoting the forum series. Tom had recommended Bernie so I made a point of talking to him about his work. He worked out of SFC on a grant from the Downtown Denver Partnership as an outreach worker, trying to encourage panhandlers and derelicts on the Sixteenth Street Mall and environs to apply for services, even housing. Bernie and Tom both agreed to speak at the first week of the forum, and I had penciled in Tom Jensen and myself as the third and fourth speakers.

Tom Jensen was a neighbor and friend who knew of my interest in abating homelessness in Denver. He called me with a need to see me. Tom is a musical conductor who had previously led the Joffrey Ballet and Colorado Ballet companies. Recently he had been conducting a series of concerts called Inside the Orchestra, during which he would have elementary school students from the Denver Public Schools sit in the center of a circle of players from the Colorado Symphony Orchestra, putting the students inside the orchestra. I was enthralled by the three concerts I had attended.

Tom introduced the sections of the orchestra and the instruments to the students. He had a student no older than those in the audience play a movement from a Haydn piano concerto. He taught them how to conduct, actually letting a student lead the orchestra. Many of the pieces he played were from the classical repertoire, but some were symphonic arrangements of music they knew from Saturday-morning cartoons.

At a concert at a school just off West Colfax Tom said, he had played the opening movement of Beethoven's Fifth Symphony. As usual, he asked the audience of students if anyone knew how many symphonies Beethoven had composed. A hand went up at the back of the audience; Tom called on the smiling face below it.

"Nine," said the boy.

"Correct. You can take the rest of the day off from school." The children howled with laughter, but then they began to applaud the boy with the right answer.

Tom said no one ever gets the right answer, but in this case a teacher came up to talk to him after the concert, saying that she was pleased that he called on Loren, an eleven-year-old boy. She told him Loren was a gifted student, and the recognition and applause would do him a world of good because he was a bit embarrassed by the fact he and his mother were homeless. Tom's story brought tears to my eyes.

Tom then showed me a copy of a letter from Loren's teacher. He loved music so much that he went to the library to listen to recordings and read about music and musicians. He tried to play his mother's old clarinet with broken reeds in the shelter where he and his mother, Berenice, lived. Tom made a commitment to get the musician's union to provide Loren with a clarinet teacher and some new reeds. Without much understanding of what I was getting into, I said that I would get housing for him and his mother. I brought the letter home with me to show Elaine, and, of course, she was moved as well. I decided to tell the story at the first forum as a way of personifying the topic and of developing human interest. Tom and I agreed to protect his identity by calling him Sam.

I arranged to meet Loren at his school after talking to his mother. She told me he was interested in space and black holes and rockets, so I gave him a copy of *Apollo, Challenger, Columbia,* and asked him if I should sign it. "Yes," he said. (Later, when some of his poems came out in a school publication he gave me a copy, asking if he should sign it. "Yes," I said.) We had a talk, and he gave me a tour of the school as we waited for Berenice to arrive from her job as a teacher's assistant at another school. Not only was he precocious, but he was also a handsome boy who seemed to charm everyone he met. He told me how to pronounce his last name, Tenorio, by saying, "Just say ten Oreo cookies without the cookies." I told Berenice and Loren that I would like to help them find housing so they could move out of the shelter. They appreciated my offer. They gave me the name and number of the caseworker at their shelter.

Tom Jensen accomplished his mission quickly, having the clarinet repaired and getting Loren both new reeds and a teacher, an accomplished clarinet player herself. They all agreed to let me sit in on his first lesson. By the end of it Loren was making wonderful sounds, and the teacher was shaking her head. Never, she said, had a student picked up her teachings with such lightning speed. By contrast, my troubles were just beginning. While talking to their caseworker, I learned they were allotted only ninety days in the shelter, and the end of their stay was coming up. Instead of trying to find housing for them, my job was now to *prevent* them from winding up on the street. Berenice said they could live in her ancient, smoky car, which Loren named "La Cucaracha." (Berenice told me she was half Native American and half Hispanic.) I talked to Missy and Carla, two caseworkers at SFC, asking for guidance. Although they had heavy caseloads, they did help with general advice, plus the names and phone numbers of other shelters to apply to for admission.

We somehow got them into a motel room on Colfax (yes, "Cold Facts") Avenue. My wife Elaine was helping me with lists of agencies that could provide transitional housing, but Berenice, and sometimes Loren, would have to apply in person, a difficult requirement because she had a job and he was in school, and their problems had begun when her unreliable car got her fired from a good job in security at the Denver International Airport. Furthermore, they were now running out of time at the motel. I got some money from Trinity United Methodist Church, with help from Reverend George Brunner, to extend their stay, but the motel would only accept city vouchers, not the church's or my money. Berenice showed up to apply for vouchers to extend their stay, but a bureaucrat said she should have brought Loren. Making this more complicated, one can only appeal for renewal vouchers at the last minute of the last day of the allotted stay. When Berenice got off work one day to apply for housing, the agency had a fire drill, ending all possibilities for interaction that day. Moreover, although we got her into another motel, telephone calls from the motel were so expensive she couldn't call me, making our coordination even more difficult. The stress began to take a toll on me. I talked to Missy, and she diagnosed my problem as an advanced case of "compassion fatigue," a common problem among social workers.

When Berenice did hear about houses or apartments or duplexes that might be available, Elaine and I drove Berenice and Loren around the city to examine them. Elaine was also coaching her on agencies to apply to for assistance. A friend of mine, E. L. VanLaningham, gave me a check to help them. So did the St. Francis Center. So did Trinity United Methodist Church. So did the Junior Symphony Guild, the sponsor of the Inside the Orchestra concerts Tom Jensen conducted. With all these contributions I now had enough for a "balloon" payment, enough money to pay for a deposit and the first month's rent, if we could only find an agency willing and able to subsidize the rent.

The phone rang one fall afternoon in my loft. It was Berenice, calling from the housing office of Catholic Charities. "Our prayers have been answered," she said, turning the phone over to Sister Mary, the administrator for the organization, who was wonderfully warm in our conversation. I assured her that I had the money, and she assured me that Berenice's salaries—she now had two jobs—would be enough to afford a two-bedroom apartment in a building the Catholic Charities owned. Catholic Charities would also supplement her rent with a subsidy.

When we later met to complete the rental transaction, I sat across the table from Berenice, with Loren across the room. An administrator explained that there would be inspections of the apartment from time to time and that a caseworker would be assigned to the family. I produced the checks, Berenice signed the lease, and Loren ran across the office to hug and kiss his mother.

Another friend and neighbor, David "Dougal" McDougal, who then had a catering company in Denver, had been following the case with us; he volunteered to let us use a couple of men and a large van his company owned. We met at a Catholic Charities furniture store to help select and move their furniture into the new apartment. It was a day of celebration. I told Berenice that I would like to talk about Loren, and the struggle to find housing for them at the forum series, and that I would change his name. She wouldn't hear of it: "We're real people with real names." She seemed proud of what we had accomplished. Indeed, she wanted to attend the forum and have the two of them introduced.

In late October 2004, I learned from Tony, a new staff member from Texas, that one of our guests would start a new job the next week as global director of infrastructure for a firm in Denver at an annual salary of $120,000. The guest had fallen down and out when he lost his job at IBM, after pleading guilty to a charge of assault. He wound up in prison. When he got out, he found his way, as many do, to the St. Francis Center and connected with an employment agency that specializes in finding jobs for people with a prison record. He kept our employment office informed of what was happening, making a special trip to the shelter to tell us about his success. Tony was proud that William B. was one of ten people we placed in jobs that week.

While composing the entry in my field notes that Friday at the Broker Restaurant, a lawyer at the Stout Street Clinic named Dan sat next to me. I told him about the success of our guest.

"Sounds like a bipolar story."

"You think he made it up?"

"I'd like to believe he got the job but I had a bipolar guy tell me today that he spent the week in Egypt."

On the following Monday I went to SFC to find out how to approach the mayor. Tony was greeting so I told him about Dan's reaction.

"I know he got the job," he said with a quiet intensity, "I called the company, and they confirmed it."

On Friday of that week, November 4, 2004, I met a new staff member who flew in from California on Monday to accept a job on the staff of the shelter. He said he would work on the night shift. *The night shift!* I was dumbfounded. We had always been a day shelter. How could we do both? The Denver Rescue Mission got the people who slept in their emergency shelter up and out early in the morning. So did the Samaritan House, urging people to look for jobs and housing. How did this happen?

I had missed Tom's announcement of the change at the Volunteer Appreciation Dinner while Elaine and I were on vacation. The initiative for this came from the homeless community. A group of homeless people formed a movement to back their request for a tent city in Denver that was denied by the Commission to End Homelessness (because, as I later learned, Mayor Hickenlooper told them he would not support such a plan). Their second choice, the opening of SFC at night, was accepted as a compromise. The city provided funds so that we could begin with three staff members on duty at night. The guests would not be allowed to lie down on the floor because the zoning code prohibited it, but our guests were practiced in the somnambulistic arts of sleeping in a chair with one's head on a table or dozing in a chair leaning against a wall. *This,* I thought, *will be another significant organizational change, made more difficult by the loss of some key staff members.*

On the last Friday in December 2004, I experienced shock at walking into a full house at 7:00 in the morning. I mentioned to a member of the night shift going off that a woman had criticized SFC to one of our ministers at Trinity, saying that we were being mean to our guests because we wouldn't let them sleep. He smiled, saying they now let them use two chairs, warning them "just don't let anything touch the floor." I opened the showers at 8:00, and one of the men waiting for me said they now open the showers for one hour during three nights of the week. He said it helps relieve the "odor."

"Yeah," said another man, "when they take off their shoes it gets pretty bad." That added a new malodorous source to the saying I heard from a guest describing why he didn't like to sleep in the emergency shelters: "They're all armpits and assholes."

I had arrived at SFC on Christmas Eve the week before. Carla led the sharing period that day, whose topic was charity/justice. She gave each of us a document she had copied from the Office for Social Justice of the Archdiocese of St. Paul/Minneapolis. I was so stimulated by the discussion that I wrote an essay, "Communication, Charity, Social Justice, and the Abolition of Homelessness," which was published in a book edited by Omar Swartz.[1] My reasoning was a modified form of deconstruction. The handout Carla had given gave us during her sharing period was set up as a series of oppositions, whose main heading was Charity/Justice. Others can be paraphrased in this way:

> charity = social service vs. justice = social change
> private, individual acts vs. public, collective acts
> responds to immediate need vs. responds to long-term need
> provides direct service vs. provides social change in institutions
> requires repeated acts vs. resolves structural injustice
> directed at effects vs. directed at root causes of social injustice

Examples of charity listed in the handout were keenly relevant to my interests: "Homeless shelters, clothing drives, emergency services" were places and activities I engaged in. Examples of justice were "legislative advocacy, changing corporate policies or practices, congregation-based community organizing." These were activities I engaged in as an advocate for homeless people.

By using the work of such scholars and theologians as Marcus Borg, William Stringfellow, Walter Wink, and William Sloane Coffin, I came to the conclusion that charity and justice are on a continuum. We need both, but justice is the deeper, more important goal.

My essay was published in 2006. Working my way through it made me an ardent abolitionist, making the efforts of the commission all the more important to me: It was trying to find ways to end homelessness.

CHAPTER THIRTEEN
THE FACES OF HOMELESSNESS

Although the keeper of his schedule thought Mayor Hickenlooper would accept my invitation to speak in the forum series at Trinity United Methodist Church, the mayor begged off, saying that he didn't want to make any more public statements about homelessness until his commission made its recommendations to him. That made sense to me. We pushed ahead with the forum series, dedicating it in honor of the ministry of Reverend Robert Carlisle, who had announced his decision to retire.

Forum I: Who Are the Homeless People of Denver?

The first forum began at 7:00 p.m. on Thursday, January 20, 2005, in Fellowship Hall of Trinity United Methodist Church. Reverend Carlisle introduced me as the moderator and organizer. The first speaker was Tom Luehrs, executive director of the St. Francis Center for thirteen years and also the head of the Metro Denver Homeless Initiative, the coalition of service or provider agencies that conducts the annual point-in-time census of homeless people. He spoke about the growing numbers and changing makeup of the population. He reported that the Denver metro area had more than ten thousand homeless persons, and he stressed that we were seeing more and more homeless families and children.

Bernie O'Connell, the outreach worker from the St. Francis Center, was the second speaker. Bernie reported the results of his interviews with panhandlers and loiterers on the Sixteenth Street Mall, the central artery of the downtown area limited to pedestrians and free bus shuttles. Significantly, his work was funded by the Downtown Denver Partnership, a combination of some five hundred urban business owners who were coming to realize what candidate Hickenlooper had said repeatedly, namely, that homelessness had a negative impact on commerce, and who taxed themselves to keep the Sixteenth Street Mall clean for tourists and shoppers. O'Connell's results encouraged the business community and members of the commission, reinforcing them in the belief that homelessness was a problem that could be solved. In fact, O'Connell's grant had just been renewed for a second year. He explained that the Housing First concept had allowed them to move chronically homeless persons off the mall and into housing; others were recommended to the St. Francis Center for a variety of services and to the Stout Street Clinic for diagnosis and medications.

The third speaker was Tom Jensen, the music director of the Junior Symphony Guild Orchestra, which gave the Inside the Orchestra concerts. He related how he had discovered a precocious homeless boy in a school where he conducted a concert, one of one thousand homeless students in the city's schools. Jensen made a commitment to get him free music lessons. He explained how he had introduced Loren to me, and the commitment I made. As the fourth speaker, I admitted to the audience, Jensen was able to accomplish his goals quickly. Not so for me. I explained the long, laborious process of getting the family into an apartment, reporting to them my experience with compassion fatigue. I also confided that his mother wanted me to use his and her real name and wanted to be introduced.

"Would you like to meet them?" The audience shouted "Yes" in unison. I asked each of them to stand as I introduced them to an applauding, sympathetic, and admiring audience. "Would you like to hear Loren play?" Again, they shouted an affirmative answer. Loren came forward, after only four lessons, to play a Native American spiritual song, then sang the lyrics, and finished the performance by repeating the song on the clarinet. The moderator lost control of the situation when the audience of 120 people gave Loren a standing ovation, then moved to get in line to shake hands with him and his mother.

Forum II: What Is the Stance of the City of Denver on Homelessness?

The second forum was held on Thursday evening, January 27, 2005. The first speaker was Roxane White, manager of the Denver Department of Human Services and chair of the Commission to End Homelessness in Denver within the Decade. She got to work by explaining the eight major strategies the commission would recommend:

1. Invest in housing
2. Increase shelter beds
3. Prevent people from becoming homeless
4. Provide twenty-four-hour outreach and enhanced public safety
5. Provide adequate support services to help people leave the streets and maintain housing
6. Provide education, training, and employment to provide stability
7. Improve community awareness and create a coordinated response to the issue of homelessness
8. Address zoning, urban design, and land use to support housing.

There were too many specific, tactical proposals in the plan for White to discuss, but the audience of 120 got a handout and, more importantly, a preview of what the commission was going to recommend to Mayor Hickenlooper. I knew from interacting with people for seven years about homelessness that even compassionate citizens worried that if we made it too comfortable for homeless people, they would come here from all over the country. This is the so-called magnet theory of homelessness. I made sure that Roxane White got a chance to answer this during the question-and-answer period.

She replied that the commission had been in communication with the political leaders of Denver suburbs stretching up and down the front range of the Rockies, and that these entities were actively cooperating with each other. She could also have said that some 150 other cities in the United States were also coming up with action plans, a requirement HUD imposed on cities that wanted to receive future financial support from the federal government.

I introduced the second speaker, Randle Loeb, by saying that he reminded me we had first met when he entered the St. Francis Center as a guest. He too was a member of the commission. Loeb gained the rapt attention of the audience as he identified himself as a "chronically homeless person" and explained the cause of his status: "I am bipolar." After explaining that he couldn't sleep in shelters because of their overcrowded conditions, he let us know how he coped, by working nights cleaning up offices and sleeping in a church where he was a caretaker. He also took a scholarly approach, recommending that the audience read Kusmer's history of homelessness, *Down and Out, On the Road,* discussed earlier in this book. Loeb also plaintively asked the audience this question on behalf of the homeless community: "Why can't we accept each other as brothers and sisters?"

The third speaker of the evening was Richard Scharf, a member of Trinity United Methodist Church. In addition, he was the president and CEO of the Denver Metro Convention and Visitor's Bureau and an expert on tourism, an important source of income for Denver and Colorado. He was also a member of the Commission to End Homelessness. He expressed the commercial concern that panhandling on the Sixteenth Street Mall affected tourism. He got my attention by expressing his support for the recommendations Roxane White had discussed earlier. I pressed him in the question-and-answer period to talk about group processes, trying to get a better understanding of why a man representing business interests would agree to a plan that would raise taxes. He admitted that during the first two meetings of the commission, he doubted that they would ever be able to agree on much of anything. But he kept going to the meetings, heeded the chair's instruction to listen, and tried to be open to solutions and compromises.

Forum III: What Is the Stance of the Faith Community on Homelessness?

It was only fitting that the faith community be given an opportunity to speak out on Thursday evening, February 3, 2005. The first speaker was Warner H. Brown Jr., resident bishop of the Rocky Mountain Conference of the United Methodist Church (UMC). Bishop Brown, an African American, had long been active in housing and social justice ministries, and he pledged a commitment to the goal of ending homelessness. Reverend George Brunner, executive minister of Trinity UMC, the host of the forum, spoke second. He proved by example the commitment of the church, explaining that he had been the director of programs at the Denver Rescue Mission from 1992 to 1996, the period in which he completed his studies for the ministry. He informed the audience that Trinity helped achieve one of the commission's eight strategies of *preventing* homelessness with a fund dedicated to rent assistance for those who might otherwise be out on the street.

The third speaker was Mary Hupp, a person I had worked with on advocacy when she was the community minister for Capitol Hill United Ministries (CHUM). She had recently accepted a position as executive director of Housing Justice! She spoke about working with the faith community of Colorado to achieve goals, including the creation of a state housing trust, or investment fund, and discussed how the faith community could participate in advocacy and in empowering people to meet local needs.

Reverend Jim Ryan was council executive of the Colorado Council of Churches. He presented a statewide perspective of the faith community's commitment to ending homelessness. He quoted the Colorado Council of Churches' Public Policy Statement on Poverty: "Strong themes in scripture indicate that poverty exists because of people's life conditions (widows and orphans), but also because of the greed and unjust practices of those who 'trample on the poor.'" He also submitted that the Colorado Council of Churches supported all efforts and legislative priorities that "seek a just, sufficient, sustainable livelihood for all." The faith community was united in seeking justice and an end to homelessness.

Forum IV: Bringing the Sectors Together
for the Last Word on Homelessness

The fourth and final forum was held on February 10, 2005. The purpose of this session was to hear from ecclesiastical, business, and political leaders. First we heard the words of the Right Reverend Robert O'Neill, bishop of the Episcopal Church in Colorado. He had established a ministry in Honduras that feeds, clothes, and educates homeless boys. Bishop O'Neill gave a thoughtful, provocative theological justification for ending homelessness.

The second speaker was John Desmond, director of the Downtown Environment section of the Downtown Denver Partnership. He was also a member of the commission. Desmond repeated that the business community was concerned about surveys that revealed pedestrians and tourists feared aggressive panhandlers on the Sixteenth Street Mall. He stressed that these fears were perceptions and were not based in reality, conceding that the downtown area was no doubt one of the safest areas in the metropolitan area. Desmond admitted he had shared Scharf's fear that the commission would get nowhere, but he continued to attend the meetings and listen to the others and somehow the group was able to achieve agreement on strategies and recommendations.

The final speaker of the fourth forum was the Honorable Andrew Romanoff, then the recently elected speaker of the Colorado House of Representatives, a dynamic and popular leader in Denver. He had been successful as a member of the house and was among the youngest men ever to be elected speaker when Democrats took control after the election of 2004. He told the audience of 140 people to get behind two referenda that would help the state and the city be able to afford the commission's recommendations. To advance that aim he repeated several times the (Republican) governor's telephone number, asking us to call his office with appeals to support the referenda. (The governor did, and the voters subsequently approved the referenda, improving the state's fiscal situation significantly.)

I concluded the series by expressing the consensus of the business, faith, homeless, and political communities of Denver: We were the new *abolitionists*. We sought to abolish homelessness in our city and metropolitan area.

Reverend Carlisle was pleased with the forum series dedicated to his ministry at Trinity. So was I, but a doubt developed in my mind from the forum series. The doubt was first seeded in a conversation on the dais after the forum devoted to the faith community. One of the clergy members remarked that the Commission to End Homelessness hadn't included a single member of the faith community. I brooded on the observation.

The St. Francis Center was experiencing strains and pressures. The night program was becoming more and more popular with homeless people. Bernie got some help with additional outreach workers who told street people about SFC. At first there were just a handful of people who came in for the night, but the number would steadily grow until it reached a peak of 320 people! The highest intake number during the day was over a thousand, experienced in late 2004, not long after Chris and Mike left for their new jobs. It was difficult to keep the big room as clean as we had in the past. Small things, such as the toilet-paper holders in the men's shower, broke and had to be repaired with duct tape.

Duane, a middle-aged man and one of the brightest guests I ever met at SFC, said he would avoid coming in at 8:00 when the night crowd was still in the building and other guests were arriving after having slept at Jesus Saves, the Sally, their camps, and the streets. I asked him why.

"Because there is a limit to the number of sardines you can get into a can." He went on to say he feared the overcrowding could lead to violence.

The overnight program came to an end with a mild surprise. The city had made a deal with the Curtis Park Neighborhood Association that the decision to allow the overnight program would be reconsidered after one year. At the end of that year, in December 2005, despite the absence of any difficulties with our neighbors, the board members of the association voted narrowly to recommend that we close. The city honored their recommendation, and SFC prepared to close at night in April 2006.

The commission's plan was presented to Mayor Hickenlooper in mid-May 2005, with intense media coverage. Hickenlooper had by this time become fabulously popular and accepted the recommendations with praise for the commission members.

How did this remarkable consensus develop? This was not the paradigm case of a speaker persuading a like-minded audience to adopt a simple program. The original composition of the commission was diverse, even including representatives of conflicting interests: Three staff members, including Roxane White; seven representatives of nonprofit organizations; seven elected members of city councils representing different neighborhoods; seven people from government; three people from neighborhood associations; ten members of the homeless community; and eight members of the business community. Neighborhood associations were generally opposed to shelters and low-income housing in their backyards; business people were generally opposed to the higher taxes and greater government intervention required to invest in more shelters and affordable housing and to subsidize those who couldn't afford it; as always, it is risky to generalize about homeless people, but their grassroots advocacy group was known to favor a tent city in Denver.

It is clear in retrospect that the members of the commission didn't share the same goals and decision premises when they came together for the first time. They lacked the homogeneity assumed by the classical theories of persuasion, which taught that one should find those common value premises among the audience and link one's proposal to them deductively. Politicians typically practice the art of the possible, avoiding hard choices that might alienate voters. Service providers operate with humanitarian value premises and more familiarity with the homeless people. The business leaders wanted what was good for business, making the homeless denizens of downtown go away and become invisible to tourists and shoppers. And as mentioned above, most of the commission members had differing views on taxation. How could they overcome these patent differences to recommend abolition of homelessness?

More than twenty-five years ago Donald Cushman and I offered a theory of rhetoric—that is, persuasion—for contemporary society. Noting that the conditions of homogeneity experienced by the ancient Greeks and Romans no longer existed in the late twentieth century in the United States, we set about to explain how agreement and consensus can be produced in today's conditions of heterogeneity. That heterogeneity was itself a result of three trends we saw in 1980: "(1) an increased tolerance for a plurality of cultural positions; (2) an increased interdependence between nations, groups, and individuals; and (3) an increased need to manifest respect for diversity as an antecedent for coordinated action."[1] I stress the phrase *coordinated action* as the descriptor for the new rhetoric. In addition, the theory takes a pluralistic position on reasoning with others; at the same time it is pragmatic. Instead of doing audience analysis to find a common value set and appealing in a one-way direction to the group to accept a packaged proposal, today's conditions call for coordinated action, precisely the process employed by the commission.

The pluralistic and pragmatic theory also argued that the modern test of achieving coordinated action—as opposed to one-way persuasion—"is whether those who are interdependent in regard to some problem form a *rational consensus* that they have understood and manifested respect for each point of view."[2] Recall that some members of the commission originally strongly doubted that they would be able to reach any kind of agreement with the others. But they were encouraged to listen, understand, and respect each other's point of view. They learned that all recognized a problem they desired to eliminate—too many homeless people on the streets of Denver—but instead of having a common set of value premises, they had *different reasons* for reaching agreement. This can create in the individual a sense of obligation. As Cushman and I put it:

> When one must act in cooperation with others who hold divergent ideologies and must as a condition for cooperation understand and respect those differences in selecting an appropriate principle for guiding collective action, then in order to do what is wanted, *one has to do things that he or she does not want to do for their own sake.*[3]

Although homeless persons and service providers desired more shelters and affordable housing for their *own sake,* business people might not. However, having more shelters open during the day for education and training would draw homeless people away from the Sixteenth Street Mall, an outcome that would be desirable to merchants for its own sake. The director of a shelter might not want to be open day and night because it puts an additional strain on the staff and facilities, but additional support from the city for the shelters, education, and affordable housing could ultimately reduce the population of homeless persons, a goal desirable for its own sake. Politicians wouldn't want to raise taxes for their own sake, but creating an improved business climate and helping destitute people get jobs are desirable outcomes in their own right. Members of the commission had an obligation to listen to others and accept what they didn't want in order to get what they did want for its own sake. An obligation to solve the problem seems to have been a key factor in achieving consensus and a coordinated action plan inside the commission.

I decided to test this theoretical explanation on the best possible person: Roxane White. She graciously granted me an interview on July 11, 2006, in her office at the Department of Human Services, of which she was the manager. She stood five feet one inch tall at age forty-two, and she welcomed me with a dazzling smile. Her programmatic assistant, Jamie Van Leeuwen, sat in on the interview. A bust of Martin Luther King Jr. graced her office.

After asking some general questions, I explained to her the rhetorical theory of coordinated action, asking if it explained the success of the commission.

"Absolutely," she said. "Absolutely correct."

She immediately grasped the essence of the theory and began to come up with illustrations from the commission's activities. She also explained that she had been trained as a professional group facilitator, and in an unusual choice served the commission in that capacity in addition to serving as its chair. Among other leadership functions, she insisted that all forty-two members had to listen carefully to each other.

"Some of the business leaders had never sat down with a homeless person before. Now they were at the same table and listening to their perceptions and ideas. They began to understand the perspectives of people very different from them. While discussing whether to outlaw panhandling, they agreed not to decide, to delay action until outreach workers could try to help the panhandlers," she said.

White used a textbook on group facilitation written by one of her mentors, Sam Kaner: *Facilitator's Guide to Participatory Decision Making.*[4] I would stress the word *participatory* in the title because she used a consensus model and a scale with gradients of agreement from the book. She distributed the eight-point scale on *every important issue* the commission faced. All forty-two "cats" signed off on each strategy and recommendation to make sure there was acceptance by every member—at least at the "I can live with this" level—before sending the recommendations to the mayor. Members no doubt gave acceptance to recommendations they did *not* want for their own sake. The chair led the group to this accomplishment with a group facilitation theory that is consistent with, and highly similar to, the rhetorical theory of achieving coordinated action.

While preparing a lecture on this process, I asked Roxane White some questions via e-mail. One was about the need to step out of her role as chair to explain the mayor's positions. She said yes, she did sometimes have to speak not as the chair but as the mayor's representative—for example, to explain that Mayor Hickenlooper would not support a tent city. He also asked the commission to recommend a mentoring program with the faith community, and he, the mayor, took a position on funding the program. I said that as a candidate, the mayor hadn't mentioned a ten-year plan to end homelessness. Her answer: "After I was appointed we had a meeting with Philip Mangano [executive director of the U.S. Interagency Council on Homelessness] who asked the mayor to create a ten-year plan." She also acknowledged that the plan followed fairly closely a "blueprint" to end homelessness produced by the "provider community." (Providers are the shelters and other organizations that provide services to homeless people.) That reminded me that the blueprint had been written by a group of providers who called themselves People in Public Places. They met in the St. Francis Center to come up with the first version of the vision.

She also gave credit to the Colorado Coalition for the Homeless because it brought to Denver the housing first model, the practice of providing housing to people *before* they can, for example, break their addictions. Indeed, in a conversation with the director of CCH, John Parvensky, on June 2, 2008, he told me they had been experimenting with the concept before there was such a model. Once the model became public in the 1990s, they learned from the experiences of people in New York.

I asked another question: "Why didn't you appoint anyone from the faith community to the commission?"

She admitted that that had been an oversight, a mistake. And she volunteered other mistakes. She learned from experience on the commission that people from the real estate industry and the city's Department of Parks and Recreation would have provided experience and helpful information. By the time she recognized the mistakes, however, there wasn't any room for more members—and there was no one on the commission she wanted to remove. I give Roxane White high marks for her informed leadership skills.

Mayor Hickenlooper made it clear that he wanted to solve the problem and that he was confident it was possible. He and Roxane White appointed people to the commission who had a direct, if at times narrow, interest in solving it. The leadership created an ambiance or culture of respect for others, a willingness to listen to differing ideas and ideologies, and the obligation to accept what one did not want in order to get what one did want. This was a rational process to all when data were presented to prove that doing little or nothing was *more expensive* than providing shelters, education, affordable housing, and rehabilitation programs. *Incarcerating people in jails, detox facilities, and hospitals is an expensive way of making undesirables invisible.*

During the process of moving toward a coordinated action plan, the commission also moved beyond charity to justice. Justice can, therefore, be achieved within a heterogeneous culture if there is a felt interdependence in regard to problems, a willingness to listen and respect other points of view, and a rational sense of obligation to participate in a little horse-trading. Such coordinated action need not require ontological agreement about the essence of the homeless human being. That is, one can agree to accept twenty-four-hour outreach plans to monitor homeless people whether one believes them to be autonomous authors of their own fate or helpless, dependent beings who are what they are because of economic factors, physical handicaps, addictions, and mental illness.

*   *   *

In February 2006 we were surprised to read an article about Denver in the *New Yorker* magazine: "Million-Dollar Murray: Why Problems Like Homelessness May Be Easier to Solve Than to Manage,"[5] by Malcolm Gladwell, a best-selling author of books dealing with social scientific topics, such as *The Tipping Point*. After seeing his article, I recalled that Gladwell had visited the St. Francis Center on a Friday I was working there.

The Murray of Gladwell's title was a charming, well-liked bear of a man, an alcoholic homeless man who lived and died in Reno, Nevada. After his death, Reno officials calculated that he had cost the city over a million dollars to pay the bills for picking him up when he was passed out drunk, taking him in ambulances to detoxification centers and hospitals, and paying for the doctors and nurses who took care of him.

Gladwell used Murray to illustrate the findings of a graduate student at Boston College who lived in a homeless shelter for seven weeks while working on a doctoral dissertation. The student, Dennis Culhane, returned to the shelter a few months later to find that he didn't know most of the people there. He began gathering data and learned that 80 percent of the homeless people were in and out of the shelter quickly. Another 10 percent were episodic users of shelters. The final 10 percent were the chronically homeless people. Collectively, they didn't represent a normal bell-shaped distribution; they made up a power-law distribution shaped more like a hockey stick. That is, the small percentage at the end of the stick stuck up in the air because they cost society more than the others.

Others seem to have sensed this distribution. For example, I recently heard a minister say that clergy are aware of an 80/20 rule: Eighty percent of the work performed in churches is done by 20 percent of the members. *Another crucial fact about the homeless population is that most are homeless for only one night. The second highest number is of people who are homeless for two nights.*

Many of the *chronically* homeless people are mentally ill or physically handicapped, and they sometimes have addictions. They are the ones found lying in alleys or on the grates and passed out on the sidewalk. They make up some of the most aggressive panhandlers. They wind up with virulent pneumonia or abscesses of the lungs, they get hit by buses and cars, and they *cost the taxpayers more on the streets and in hospitals than they do in subsidized housing.* Pushing the power-law distribution and the concept of Housing First is Phillip Mangano, appointed by President Bush in 2002 to be the executive director of the U.S. Interagency Council on Homelessness, overseeing twenty federal agencies. He has since then been traveling across the country persuading mayors to save some of their city's money by paying for apartments for chronically homeless people. His success has been perhaps the brightest light in George W. Bush's administration.

Gladwell visited the old YMCA building in downtown Denver in late summer of 2005, calling it a "handsome" six-story building erected in 1906. It has several hundred apartments and efficiencies that have been owned and operated by the Colorado Coalition for the Homeless since 1999. Gladwell said that even by big-city standards, Denver has a serious homelessness problem. He explains that fact with a variation of the magnet theory: He is not saying that Denver takes such good care of homeless people that they travel from around the country to enjoy the treatment. Rather, his is a meteorological version: The winters are relatively mild, the summers are not so hot as in neighboring states, and therefore, for Gladwell, the weather in Denver is the magnet that attracts vagrants from other parts.

Gladwell said Mayor Hickenlooper signed up with Mangano eighteen months before Gladwell's visit in 2005 to try the Housing First, power-law distribution theory. Using a combination of federal and local money, CCH has been moving the chronically homeless people off the Sixteenth Street Mall and into efficiencies and apartments. Gladwell didn't report the St. Francis Center project started by Bernie O'Connell that has expanded to employ six outreach workers who can recommend people for housing. He did interview Rachel Post at the YMCA, the director of substance treatment at the CCH facility. Post was quoted as saying they have to keep the ratio of staff to clients at one to ten, meaning that there is a limit to the number of people a caseworker can keep track of, making sure they live by the rules. The staffing ratio is quite close to the classical span of control in organization theory, the limit of how many persons a single supervisor can keep track of. Ten caseworkers meet in the YMCA for ninety minutes every morning, Monday through Friday, trying to coordinate their charges. They provide a kind of social capital their charges would otherwise lack, a communicative link to society and a source of support.

I also interviewed Rachel Post at the YMCA. We talked about Gladwell's visit and her plan to leave her job in Denver for a similar one in Portland, Oregon. She had come to Denver to set up the plan and get it going before returning to Portland. She was quite proud of her work, saying that Denver is one of eleven cities to get federal support for Housing First, was the first to get started, and was well ahead of all the other cities.

After she replaced Reverend Carlisle as a minister for missions, Miriam Slejko followed up on the momentum of the forum series, Faces of Homelessness, by deciding to pursue what became the Transformational Housing Project. After taking a tour of the project at 2595 Larimer Street, I became enthusiastic about the project. It was an attractive structure with twenty-three residential units for low-income families. There were a one-bedroom unit, three two-bedroom units, and nineteen three-bedroom units. The units were well built and attractive. Mile High United Way, the state of Colorado, St. Charles Town Company, Charitable Housing, Inc., the faith community, and others combined to provide this affordable housing.

Some families had already moved in, but enough units were still empty, so we saw a good sample of them. They were available to families who were graduates from transitional housing, ready to step up to transformational housing, so called because it is supposed to improve the residents' quality of life and ability to cope. Low income was defined as between 30 percent and 60 percent of the area's median income; rents would range from $408 to $695. The program would require tenants to open individual development savings accounts with matching funds from public and private sources. Tenants would leave the program after five years, potentially with five to seven thousand dollars in restricted savings and four thousand dollars from an individual development account for use in purchasing a home. Thus, the rent payments didn't have to cover mortgage payments, but instead went to maintenance and salaries for case workers

I was enthusiastic, but while taking the tour given by a representative of Mile High United Way, I asked her, "How do we know this won't become a 'project' like those in St. Louis and Chicago?"

"Look around," she said, and she continued to say that the Volunteers of America had a facility across the street to help with day care. There was to be a coordinator there five days a week as well as experts to provide counseling on managing finances and employment. I was sold.

A subcommittee of Trinity's Missions Committee headed by Ken Whitney, inspired by Reverend Slejko, and including Nancy Green and Elaine Tompkins organized the effort and recruited Donald C. Lewis to head the fund-raising effort. Lewis was extremely effective: The group raised sixty-five thousand dollars for the Transformational Housing Project, five thousand more than the goal. Thus, Trinity was able to pay for one unit. Other churches have done the same, leaving tenants' rents to cover maintenance, salaries for case workers, and the restricted savings and individual development accounts. This is additional evidence that the Commission to End Homelessness might have improved its stellar performance by involving the faith community of Denver earlier in their deliberations—and by asking them to do more.

Denver's Road Home relies on the coordinated efforts of levels of government, business interests, and nonprofit organizations. Raising money to solve the problem is crucial, but it may save society money by avoiding the almost invisible taxation of the Million Dollar Murrays, the tax bills society pays for hospitals, detox units, doctor bills. Housing First also provides these chronically homeless people with something they lack, a link to society, a helping hand in the form of a case worker.

CHAPTER FOURTEEN
DENVER'S ROAD HOME

In January 2008 I received an invitation to deliver the Josephine Jones Colloquium at the University of Colorado at Boulder. This is an annual public lecture on social issues sponsored by the Department of Communication. Although members of the department knew I had been working with homeless people and writing essays about my experiences with them, I had never given them a formal report on the topic, so the director of the colloquium encouraged me to speak on the topic of homelessness. I prepared a lecture with this title: "Who Is My Neighbor? Toward Ending the Injustice of Homelessness" for delivery at 7:00 p.m. on Tuesday, April 15, 2008. I couldn't relate all of what I had learned over the preceding ten years, but the process of preparation did force me to review what I had learned and come up with a summary appropriate to this final chapter.

I am happy to report that Betsy Anne is still working and domiciled; I am elated that she and her estranged daughter have had a heartwarming reconciliation. Mother, daughter, and granddaughter are reunited. Berenice and Loren Tenorio are also comfortably housed. Loren won a scholarship to a private school for the arts. Tom Jensen serves as his Big Brother. In the spring of 2008, I got a tour of Boulder's new, handsome shelter built near where the inadequate structure was. Greg Harms, executive director, gave me a tour of the facilities; his pride was evident.

I also have good news to report from Waco. While doing the final editing on this book, I received the first issue of the Waco newspaper on homelessness. It mentioned that the "Angel" of Waco, Teri Holtkamp, had received eleven awards for her efforts to reduce homelessness in that city. I immediately fired off an e-mail to Teri, asking if she remembered our conversation in 2006. That was when I began writing the first draft of the book and needed to check on statistics. Unlike during my first inquiries in 1999, Waco had an official responsible for the problem: Teri Holtkamp, the brand-new administrator. We had a long talk not only about the numbers but also about her new job. Her reply came on Wednesday, October 22, 2008:

> Hi Phil in Denver,
>   Yes I do remember you and our conversation. You were the first person I spoke with that didn't make me feel crazy for actually going out into the field and visiting one on one with the homeless. You were also the one who helped me link my interviews with homeless coming from federal prisons to finish out terms in some of our privately owned jail systems and ending up on our streets.

Congratulations to Teri Holtkamp and to the city of Waco, proving again that both national and local strategies are required to reduce homelessness.

While being socialized and assimilated by the St. Francis Center, I had no idea that I would become immersed in a murder mystery—rather, a mass-murder mystery. I regret to say that no one has ever been charged with the murder of Joe Mendoza and Denver's other headless, homeless men. I do feel that I understand the processes—depicted in Lonnie Athens's theory of "violentization"—that produce virulent killers such as the person or persons who perpetrated these gruesome crimes.

The history of homelessness in America and Denver demonstrates cycles of ups and downs. Deinstitutionalization of the mentally ill and deindustrialization are two recent causes of spikes in the population of houseless people.

Stigmas, such as missing "pickets," have been a constant problem, both a cause and an effect of houselessness. The ancient Greeks called everyday equipment *pragmata*. Shopping carts, plastic bags, and backpacks are part of the *pragmata* of street people as well as stigmas. People look down on houseless people because they attribute to them fewer of what Kenneth Burke calls degrees of being. Public attitudes toward the tramp have changed over the years. Charlie Chaplin's film character won considerable sympathy for the stereotype, but today homeless people seem to be regarded as the Other and are to be avoided and made invisible if possible.

My first research effort—gathering data from Boulder, Lawrence, and Waco—led me to stress the economic factors in producing houselessness: "Income too low and/or housing costs too high." After reading the structural analysis of researchers such as Doug Timmer and D. Stanley Eitzen, however, I learned the crucial lesson that oversimplifying the problem necessarily oversimplifies the solution: It is not enough to say that Congress and the White House ought to pass the proper legislation to correct economic problems.

Relative deprivation is nearly as important as absolute deprivation. In the dynamics of the hierarchy of organizations and society, orders and demands come down, creating stress and domination. Some poor and houseless people do resist the powers that be, and the art of graffiti is a good example of visual backtalk that requires a response from the city.

SFC was described as operating from the Golden Rule, from what Weber called value rationality. It is a listening organization, attentive to messages up the line as well as down. That makes it an adaptive organization that could go from a day shelter to a twenty-four-hour shelter, from three hundred to seven hundred and more guests a day. Now it is open from 7:00 to 7:00, seven days a week. It practices the collective discipline of compassion. The creation of a union—AHSVA—became a running joke, ironic evidence of no need for one.

There is a culture of houselessness. It departs from the linear time regimentation of the larger culture, the nine-to-five day. In Elberta's words, the houseless people doubt that a new or better time will ever come. Linear time is replaced by space: Maybe a change of place will make life better. And yet most houseless people do ultimately find a home.

Since developing my Existential theory of homelessness—we are *all* "thrown" into existence and seek a homecoming—I discovered that the people of India use the term *roofless* instead of *homeless*, and this term is consistent with my preferred term, *houseless*. That is, the real or basic difference between the homeless with houses and those without can be summed up by saying that the latter are houseless.

The police harassment of houseless people and the SFC shelter as practiced by the previous city administration ended with the new Hickenlooper administration. The new mayor gave hope to many with the appointment of a Commission to End Homelessness within the Decade. Many of us became abolitionists. Perhaps we can move from charity to justice.

We finally got the first glimpse of what the commission would recommend to the mayor at the Trinity forum series, The Faces of Homelessness. The chair of the commission, Roxane White, reported what would be sent on. Other members in the forum series said they had doubted that any progress would be made when they first sat down with people of deeply different interests. But Chair White, a trained group facilitator, made them listen patiently to each other. She agreed later that the rhetorical theory of coordinated action explained the success of the group.

As I said in the Josephine Jones Lecture on April 15, 2008, "Denver's Road Home is now in its third year of implementation. It is too early to say whether or not it will achieve its goals. An independent count shows that two years into the plan, there was an 11 percent overall decrease in houselessness and a 36 percent reduction in the category of chronically houseless people. Mayor Hickenlooper also claims there has been a significant reduction in the number of panhandlers on the Sixteenth Street Mall, a claim I can corroborate as I live on Fifteenth Street."

We are also learning more about houselessness and benefits that the plan has brought about. Malcolm Gladwell mentioned Denver's Road Home in his well-known article "Million Dollar Murray." Murray cost the city of Reno one million dollars in hospital and detox visits and in doctor fees. The hope is that subsidizing housing for the chronically houseless people like Murray can actually save society money. This will only work, however, if we can also provide them with caseworkers and counselors. Houseless people have either lost touch with their primary group of family and loved ones, or that group was antisocial. The result is that they don't have that crucial communication network called social capital. A substitute must be provided if we are to prevent isolated people from sliding into houselessness.

Earlier in the book I referred to Carla's explanation of a homeless couple—she said they lacked social support—as the "catcher in the rye" hypothesis, an allusion to J. D. Salinger's novel of the same name. The narrator, a sixteen-year-old-boy named Holden Caulfield, is depressed and flunking out of prep school for the third time. His precocious younger sister Phoebe asks him what he wants to be, a scientist or a lawyer. No, instead he recalls a line from a poem by Robert Burns: "If a body catch a body comin' through the rye." Phoebe corrects him, "It's 'If a body *meet* a body coming through the rye!'" Holden replies:

> I thought it was "If a body catch a body," I said. Anyway, I keep picturing these little kids playing some game in this big field of rye and all. Thousands of little kids, and nobody's around—nobody big, I mean— except me. And I'm standing on the edge of some crazy cliff. What I have to do, I have to catch everybody if they start to go over the cliff—I mean if they're running and they don't look where they're going I have to come out from somewhere and *catch* them. That's all I'd do all day. I'd just be the catcher in the rye and all. I know it's crazy, but that's the only thing I'd really like to be. I know it's crazy.[1]

Ironically, Holden himself is falling, but his family catches him. He speaks to us directly in the final, short chapter, about getting sick and about "a psychoanalyst guy they have here." I, for one, think he will get better.

There is the new approach called Housing First. It originated in the Pathways to Housing program founded in New York in 1992. The guiding premises of the program are two: The first is that housing is a human right, a basic right for all people; the second is that the decision to change one's ways must be made by the consumer.[2] The consumer doesn't have to come "clean" in order to get subsidized housing. She or he must live by the rules all other renters have to follow. It often happens that an alcoholic person cuts down consumption or quits after receiving housing and case management—the crucial communication link with society being the caseworker. In fact, deinstitutionalization was a failure in large part because the case management communication link was not provided at the community level as originally conceived. The St. Francis Center, like Hope Communities, uses transitional housing and a modified approach to Housing First with caseworkers and outreach workers who help the houseless get the services they need.

We also need catchers in the rye to *prevent* people from falling into houselessness. We need organizations that will support caseworkers to help the vulnerable. We need them to *prevent* foreclosures and *prevent* the working poor and fragile elderly people without social capital from losing their housing.

I believe abolition is working; I know people who have experienced the "new time" Elberta feared would never come. "I regret to say," I said in the Josephine Jones Lecture, "I regret to say to you, however, that a few weeks ago I discovered a serious threat to the plan. I discovered the trend from an outreach worker, Bernie O'Connell, attached to the St. Francis Center, and it has been confirmed by others. I call it 'Deinstitutionaliza-tion II.' It seems that the penitentiaries of Colorado are so full that the state is releasing inmates in record numbers." Unemployment, inflation, and the subprime mortgage crisis are also threats.

I was president of the Board of Directors of a nonprofit organization called Housing Justice! at the time of the Josephine Jones Lecture.

> We and a coalition of organizations support the creation of the Colorado Housing Investment Fund, or CHIF. Thirty-eight states have such a fund. Colorado is one of the twelve without one. We also have one of the highest percentages of citizens spending more than 30 percent of their income on housing. My studies have convinced me that we have not understood how the ratio of income to housing cost has changed in the past thirty years. We are paying significantly more of our income for housing than previous generations did.

Since then, we were forced to admit that we didn't have the time and money to get CHIF on the ballot by November 2008. The good news is that on July 31, 2008, President Bush signed the Housing and Eco-nomic Recovery Act, H.R. 3221. This is the first major piece of housing legislation passed in eighteen years. The act includes the establishment of the Housing Trust Fund, a major victory for affordable housing advocates. In conversation with me, a Denver lawyer, John Waters, explained that he had been taught in law school that while the federal government establishes the floor on such matters, the states provide the ceiling. Colorado will need to continue its work to establish a state housing trust or investment fund.

Before closing, I want to stress two points. The first is that this book, unlike most, is as concerned with *solving* the problem as with diagnosing it. That is why in the end I decided not to promote the oversimplified economic approach. Denver's experience has shown us that we must include all interests—the houseless, the clergy, the politicians, the providers, the business people, contractors, workers, banks—in a rational, coordinated action. We need to coordinate nonprofits such as Hope Communities with these interests, and with legislation at all levels of government. The second point is about the prevention and elimination of houselessness. The relatives and friends with whom we are most intimate can nurture us; they can make us productive, law-abiding citizens. They can also turn us into virulent killers. As Hagan and McCarthy discovered while researching street kids in Canada, the dysfunctional family can either kick kids out or make life so miserable they run away. A new "family" on the streets will no doubt teach them survival skills, many of them antisocial and illegal. My observations over ten years have convinced me that while chronically homeless people may have friends and informal group membership, they have *little social capital*. The only substitute for such support, for such communication links, is provided by, well, the providers, the shelters and service agencies and their caseworkers who monitor and control their clients. We must support such shelters and service agencies with our own personal gifts: time, money, expertise. It is not enough to sit back and call for the federal government to "fix" the problem.

Denver's Road Home has served as a model for other cities. When the Democratic National Convention met in Denver from August 25 to 28, 2008, my daughter Kari in Houston called to tell me that MSNBC was broadcasting live from 4:00 to 9:00 a.m. in Sam's #3, a popular diner across the street from our loft. She told me to go there for breakfast so she could see me. I went in at 6:40 the next morning for breakfast at the counter, in view of the television camera. Several politicians worked the diners. Howard Dean, for example, shook hands with me after his interview. Mayor Hickenlooper shook hands with me before his interview. I said I had a book coming out on Denver's Road Home. He expressed his satisfaction, adding, "We're very proud of that program." I told him the title, *Who Is My Neighbor?* I added that it was from the Gospel Luke. "I know that section of Luke well," replied Hickenlooper.

As I explained in the preface of this book, that passage in Luke contains the Parable of the Good Samaritan, a powerful story about a man who asks, "And who is my neighbor?" It is about a foreigner who cared for an injured man on the road and took him to an inn for shelter. The injured man's ethnic group despised Samaritans, and yet he considered him a neighbor who needed housing. The Samaritan provided the houseless man with social and financial capital. It has been suggested that the St. Francis Center can also serve as a model for homeless shelters of its nature. As I close this book, the center has released an annual update on its activities and is planning a celebration of its twenty-fifth anniversary. In 2007, the center had 166,299 visits. Over 535 different guests were welcomed on an average day. The SFC health clinic served 1,282 patients. The social services staff gave assistance to nearly 1,000 guests in need. Guests were placed in 2,617 jobs. The outreach staff had 8,674 contacts with individuals on the streets, individuals who needed access to shelter and emergency services. All of this was possible because of 11,800 volunteer hours.

On Friday, May 9, 2008, Lee Hemminger, the director of health services at SFC, gave a report to volunteers during our lunch period. Support from Denver's Road Home will allow the clinic to expand to three nurse practitioners. They will continue to diagnose illnesses; they will also prescribe, sell, and subsidize prescription drugs. The most common ailments they see in the guests are respiratory problems—allergies, asthma, infections, and pneumonia. They see people with diabetes who don't have a place to refrigerate their insulin. Guests with high blood pressure are encouraged to exercise, to walk briskly. They reply, of course, "We walk all the time." The nurses follow up by asking whether they saunter or walk rapidly. "Well, I guess I saunter."

Speaking during the second week of May 2008, Lee said, "This is the beginning of the trauma season." It was becoming warm enough to drink outdoors. This leads to "encounters" that can sometime become fights. The combatants show up the next day with wounds to be treated. She is also seeing the evidence of bites and infections from scabies and bedbugs, often a byproduct of houselessness.

When I first walked to work in 1998 as a volunteer, the shelter had the look of a warehouse on skid row. SFC was the second building on the left side of Curtis Street as I approached it. The first building, on the corner, was a starkly seedy structure, the Alpine Hotel, 110 years old. We could hardly ignore the drug busts conducted there by the police. Across the street from SFC was a decrepit old house; I heard some refer to it as a "crack house."

The mayor of Denver then was Wellington Webb, an African American man who accomplished much for the city. In a recently published auto-biography, Webb listed his major accomplishments. Among them was what he called the South Platte River Project: "In 1995, my administration began a grand goal of transforming a ten-and-a-half-mile stretch along the South Platte River from an eyesore of abandoned railroad lines and homeless shanties to new park space and recreation areas. I brought to-gether city, state, and federal resources to make the dream become reality." To balance that effort, he also mentioned leasing a city office building to the Colorado Coalition for the Homeless. "The coalition converted the building to provide about 100 apartments for the homeless."[3]

Nonetheless, it seemed at times that parts of his administration were hostile to homeless people. Part of the attitude derived from his desire to sweep homeless people away from the river valley. I reported in a previous chapter that SFC had experienced police harassment during this period. The police during the Webb administration were reactive, sensitive to what the neighborhood associations wanted and didn't want. The direc-tor of the center, Tom Luehrs, and his staff worked hard with the police and the neighborhood association to change the situation. Candidate

Hickenlooper said in his appearance at the St. Francis Center that he would change the city's policy toward homeless people, would move to a more proactive stance.

The decrepit house across the street was recently torn down and replaced by a building of expensive lofts. The St. Francis Center bought the Alpine Hotel on the corner, shut it down, letting the police use a room on the ground floor as a drop-in center and letting the neighborhood association use a room for its meetings! But the hotel will soon be razed, and during the twenty-fifth anniversary celebrations there will be a groundbreaking ceremony for the Cornerstone Residences at St. Francis Center. It will be a handsome, five-story structure costing $12.4 million, and all but $500,000 has already been raised from public and private sources. It will house fifty-one people who need rent subsidies and that powerful communication link called case management. (Since 2002 SFC has provided similar facilities and case management to forty-eight other people down on their luck.)

St. Francis Center Cornerstone Residences will also include space for onsite case managers and a resident manager. It will remove an eyesore, as did urban renewal, but it will also avoid the mistake of not providing affordable housing to replace what was torn down. Residents will have a chance to transform their lives through increased stability and counseling. They will have to pay 30 percent of their income in rent, maintain their units at a specified standard, and participate in building upkeep through weekly chores. The Cornerstone Residences will also help reverse the trend of NIMBYism and will no doubt win additional support from the neighborhood association.

In a brochure about the St. Francis Center Cornerstone Campaign there are two quotations. One is from the Reverend Bert Womack, the founder of SFC, who reminds the reader of the contributions made by the faith community, specifically the Colorado Episcopal community. He praises the "core values" driving the activities of the center and promises a "swifter end to homelessness in metro Denver."

The other quotation:

> St. Francis Center is an important partner in the City of Denver's Road
> Home Initiative. The "Cornerstone Residences" are strategically aligned

with the City's vision for ending homelessness, and this project will serve as a model for other residential communities.

I am personally grateful to St. Francis Center for its leadership and compassion for people who can't get into a home on their own.

John Hickenlooper
Mayor of Denver

Notes

Note to Preface

 1. Quotations are from the *New Oxford Annotated Bible, New Revised Standard Version* (Oxford: Oxford University Press, 1994, 97NT).

Notes to Chapter One

 1. Robert D. Putnam, *Bowling Alone* (New York: Simon and Schuster, 2000), 19.

 2. Alice Baum and Donald Burnes, *A Nation in Denial: The Truth about Homelessness* (Boulder, CO: Westview Press, 1993), 163.

 3. Herbert Simon, *Administrative Behavior*, 3rd ed. (New York: Free Press, 1976; originally published 1945), 26–28.

 4. Lars Eighner, *Travels with Lizbeth: Three Years on the Road and on the Streets* (New York: St. Martin's Press, 1993), 167–68.

 5. George Orwell, *Down and Out in Paris and London* (Orlando, FL: Harcourt, n.d.; originally published 1933).

Notes to Chapter Two

 1. Michel Foucault, *Discipline and Punish: The Birth of the Prison*, trans. Alan Sheridan (New York: Pantheon, 1977).

2. Fredric Jablin, "Organizational Entry, Assimilation, and Exit," in *Handbook of Organizational Communication: An Interdisciplinary Perspective,* ed. F. Jablin, L. Putnam, K. Roberts, and L. Porter (Newbury Park, CA: Sage, 1987), 679–740.

3. Herbert Kaufman, *The Forest Ranger: A Study in Administrative Behavior* (Baltimore, MD: Johns Hopkins University Press, 1967; originally published 1960).

Notes to Chapter Three

1. Kenneth L. Kusmer, *Down and Out, On the Road: The Homeless in American History* (New York and Oxford: Oxford University Press, 2002). Much of the content of the national history of homelessness in this chapter follows Kusmer closely.

2. George Orwell, *Down and Out in Paris and London* (Orlando, FL: Harcourt, n.d.; originally published in 1933).

3. Peter Rossi, *Down and Out in America: The Origins of Homelessness* (Chicago: University of Chicago Press, 1989).

4. Jack London, "The Road," in *London: Novels and Social Writing,* ed. Donald Pizen (New York: Literary Classics of the United States, 1982), 189–314.

5. Jack Kerouac, *On the Road* (New York: Penguin Books, 1991; originally published 1957).

6. Kusmer, *Down and Out,* 37.

7. Louisa Arps, *Denver in Slices: A Historical Guide to the City* (Athens, OH: Swallow Press and Ohio University Press, 1998; originally published 1959), 15.

8. Ibid.

9. Christopher Gerboth and Marcia Kehl, "Historical Perspectives on Homelessness in Colorado, 1858 to the Present," in *Address Unknown: The Human Face of Homelessness,* ed. Christopher Gerboth (Denver: Colorado Endowment for the Humanities, 1995), 20.

10. Ibid., 21.

11. Kusmer, *Down and Out,* 221–22.

12. Kerouac, *On the Road,* 35, 264.

13. Ted Conover, *Rolling Nowhere: Riding the Rails with America's Hoboes* (New York: Vintage Books, 2001; originally published 1981), 281.

14. Eddy Cotton, *Hobo: A Young Man's Thoughts on Trains and Tramping in America* (New York: Harmony Books, 2002), xxvii.

15. Mike Yankoski, *Under the Overpass: A Journey of Faith on the Streets of America* (Sisters, OR: Multnomah Publishers, 2005).

16. Richard Campbell and Jimmie Reeves, "Covering the Homeless: The Joyce Brown Story," in *Reading the Homeless: The Media's Image of Homeless Culture,* ed. Eungjun Men (Westport, CT: Praeger, 1999), 23.

17. Kusmer, *Down and Out,* 178–79.

18. Ibid., 188.

19. Ibid., 243.

20. William Julius Wilson, *When Work Disappears: The World of the New Urban Poor* (New York: Vintage Books, 1997; originally published 1996).

21. Franklin James, "People and Policy: A Profile of Homelessness in Colorado," in Gerboth, *Address Unknown*, 52.

Notes to Chapter Four

1. Mother Teresa, quoted in Kathryn Spink, *Mother Teresa: A Complete Authorized Biography* (New York: HarperCollins, 1997), 187.

2. Ibid., 251.

3. Ibid., xiii.

4. Karen Armstrong, foreword to Adrian House, *Francis of Assisi: A Revolutionary Life* (Mahwah, NJ: HiddenSpring, 2000), ix.

5. Erving Goffman, *Stigma: Notes on the Management of Spoiled Identity* (New York: Touchstone Books, 1986; originally published 1963), 1.

6. Ibid., 4, 5.

7. Erving Goffman, *The Presentation of Self in Everyday Life* (Garden City, NY: Doubleday, 1959).

8. Kenneth Burke, *Dramatism and Development* (Barre, MA: Clark University Press, 1972).

9. Richard Freeman, *The New Inequality: Creating Solutions for Poor America* (Boston: Beacon Press, 1999), 3.

10. Robert Reich, foreword to Freeman, *The New Inequality*, x.

11. Doug A. Timmer, D. Stanley Eitzen, and Kathryn D. Talley, *Paths to Homelessness: Extreme Poverty and the Urban Housing Crisis* (Boulder, CO: Westview Press, 1994), 173.

12. Peter Rossi, *Down and Out in America: The Origins of Homelessness.* (Chicago: University of Chicago Press, 1989).

13. Romesh Ratnesar, "Not Gone, but Forgotten?" *Time,* February 8, 1999, 30–31.

14. Irving Rein and Ben Shields, "Communication and Sports: Language of the City," in *The Urban Communication Reader,* ed. Gene Burd, Susan Drucker, and Gary Gumpert (Cresskill, NJ: Hampton Press, 2000), 175–90.

15. Kenneth Burke, *Attitudes toward History,* 3rd ed. (Berkeley and Los Angeles: University of California Press, 1984; originally published 1937), 264.

16. Quoted in Spink, *Mother Teresa*, 87.

17. Phil Goodstein, *Denver in Our Time,* 2 vols. (Denver: New Social Publications, 1999), 1:276–99.

18. Kim Hopper and Jim Baumohl, "Redefining the Cursed Word: A Historical Interpretation of American Homelessness," in *Homelessness in America,* ed. Jim Baumohl (Phoenix, AZ: Oryx Press, 1996), 3.

19. Ibid., 6.

20. Ibid., 5.

Notes to Chapter Five

1. Henry David Thoreau, *Walden* (New York: Washington Square Press, 1963; originally published 1854), 8–11.

2. Adam Smith, *An Inquiry into the Nature and Causes of the Wealth of Nations,* Great Books, vol. 39 (Chicago: University of Chicago Press, 1952; originally published 1776), 383.

3. John Cassidy, "Relatively Deprived," *New Yorker,* April 3, 2006, 46.

4. Ibid.

5. Jared Jacang Maher, "He Made His Mark," *Westword,* July 17–23, 2008, 27.

6. Phillip K. Tompkins, *Apollo, Challenger, Columbia: The Decline of the Space Program* (Los Angeles: Roxbury/Oxford University Press, 2005).

Notes to Chapter Six

1. Douglas McGregor, *The Human Side of Enterprise* (New York: McGraw-Hill, 1960).

2. Phillip K. Tompkins and George Cheney, "Communication and Unobtrusive Control in Contemporary Organizations," in *Organizational Communication: Traditional Themes and New Directions,* ed. Robert D. McPhee and Phillip K. Tompkins (Beverly Hills, CA: Sage, 1985), 179–210.

3. Jack Kerouac, *On the Road* (New York: Penguin Books, 1991; originally published 1957), 180.

4. Kenneth Burke, *A Grammar of Motives* (New York: Prentice Hall, 1945), 504.

5. Kenneth Burke, *Dramatism and Development* (Barre, MA: Clark University Press, 1972), 28.

6. John Hagan and Bill McCarthy, *Mean Streets: Youth Crime and Homelessness* (Cambridge: Cambridge University Press, 1998; originally published 1997), 231.

Notes to Chapter Seven

1. Richard Rhodes, *Why They Kill: The Discoveries of a Maverick Criminologist* (New York: Alfred A. Knopf, 1999).

2. Lonnie Athens, *The Creation of Dangerous Violent Criminals* (Urbana and Chicago: University of Illinois Press, 1992; originally published 1989).

3. Ibid., 59.

    4. Ibid., 69.

    5. Phillip K. Tompkins, "In Cold Fact," *Esquire,* June 1966, 125 et passim.

    6. David A. Snow and Leon Anderson, *Down on Their Luck: A Study of Homeless Street People* (Berkeley and Los Angeles: University of California Press, 1993).

    7. Walter Wink, *The Powers That Be: Theology for a New Millennium* (New York: Doubleday, 1998).

    8. David Wagner, *Checkerboard Square: Culture and Resistance in a Homeless Community* (Boulder, CO: Westview Press, 1993).

    9. Wink, *The Powers That Be,* 75.

    10. Wagner, *Checkerboard Square,* 18.

    11. Caley M. Orr, "Street Ecology: The Demographics, Adaptive Strategies, and Nutritional Status of Homeless Youth in Denver, Colorado" (unpublished undergraduate honors thesis, anthropology, University of Colorado at Boulder, 2000).

    12. Ibid., 15.

Note to Chapter Eight

    1. Louisa Arps, *Denver in Slices: A Historical Guide to the City* (Athens, OH: Swallow Press and Ohio University Press, 1998; originally published 1959), 15.

Notes to Chapter Nine

    1. Elberta, "Time," *Denver Voice,* August 2000, 8.

    2. Ibid.

    3. Martin Heidegger, *Being and Time,* trans. John Macquarrie and Edward Robinson (New York: Harper and Row, 1962; originally published 1926), 219ff. See also Michael Inwood, *A Heidegger Dictionary* (Oxford: Blackwell, 2000), 218ff.

    4. Jennifer Toth, *The Mole People: Life in the Tunnels beneath New York City* (Chicago: Chicago Review Press, 1993), 87.

    5. Ibid., 78.

Notes to Chapter Ten

    1. Phillip K. Tompkins, "Establish Housing Trust to Help Needy," letter to the editor, *Denver Post,* July 2, 2001.

    2. Elizabeth Axelrod, "Who to Turn To? Connections and Ties among the Homeless" (unpublished honors thesis, sociology, University of Colorado at Boulder, 2001).

    3. Peter Rossi, *Down and Out in America: The Origins of Homelessness* (Chicago: University of Chicago Press, 1989).

4. *Denver Post,* December 27, 2001.

5. Kenneth Kusmer, *Down and Out, on the Road: The Homeless in American History* (New York and Oxford: Oxford University Press, 2002), 247.

6. Richiko Ikeda and Eric Mark Kramer, "*Furoosha* (Bums) and *Hoomuresu* (Homeless): Living in the Shadow of Wealth," in *Reading the Homeless: The Media's Image of Homeless Culture,* ed. Eugjun Min (Westport, CT: Praeger, 1999), 198.

7. Lars Eighner, *Travels with Lizbeth: Three Years on the Road and on the Streets* (New York: St. Martin's Press, 1993), 160–61.

8. Ibid., 161.

9. Ibid., 162.

Notes to Chapter Eleven

1. Phillip K. Tompkins, "Translating Organizational Theory: Symbolism over Substance," in *Handbook of Organizational Communication: An Interdisciplinary Perspective,* ed. Fredric Jablin et al. (Newbury Park, CA: Sage, 1987), 70–96.

2. Nicholas Gane, *Max Weber and Postmodern Theory: Rationalization versus Reenchantment* (New York: Palgrove, 2002).

3. Max Weber, *Economy and Society,* vol. 1, edited by Guenther Roth and Claus Wittich (Berkeley and Los Angeles: University of California Press, 1978), 26.

4. Phillip K. Tompkins, *Apollo, Challenger, Columbia: The Decline of the Space Program* (Los Angeles: Roxbury/Oxford University Press, 2005).

5. Ibid.

6. George A. Theodorson and Achilles G. Theodorson, *A Modern Dictionary of Sociology* (New York: Barnes and Noble, 1969), 12.

Note to Chapter Twelve

1. Phillip K. Tompkins, "Communication, Charity, Social Justice, and the Abolition of Homelessness," in *Social Justice and Communication Research,* ed. Omar Swartz (Mahwah, NJ: Lawrence Erlbaum, 2006), 53–75.

Notes to Chapter Thirteen

1. Donald P. Cushman and Phillip K. Tompkins, "A Theory of Rhetoric for Contemporary Society," *Philosophy and Rhetoric* 13, no. 1 (Winter 1980): 47.

2. Ibid., 58, emphasis in original.

3. Ibid., 47, emphasis added.

4. Sam Kaner, *Facilitator's Guide to Participatory Decision Making* (Gabriola Island, CA: New Society Publishers, 1996).

5. Malcolm Gladwell, "Million-Dollar Murray: Why Problems Like Homelessness May Be Easier to Solve Than to Manage," *New Yorker*, February 13 and 20, 2006, 96–98; 101–7.

Notes for Chapter 14

1. J. D. Salinger, *The Catcher in the Rye* (New York: Little, Brown, 1991; originally published 1951), 173.

2. Sam Tsembelis, "'Housing First' Approach," in *Encyclopedia of Homelessness*, ed. David Levinson (Thousand Oaks, CA: Sage, 2004), 277–81.

3. Wellington Webb, *Wellington Webb: The Man, the Mayor, and the Making of Modern Denver*, with Cindy Brodsky (Golden, CO: Fulcrum Publishing, 2007), 386.

INDEX

ABOUT THE AUTHOR

Phillip K. Tompkins is Professor Emeritus of Communication and Comparative Literature at the University of Colorado, Boulder. He is the author of a number of books, including *Apollo, Challenger, Columbia: The Decline of the Space Program*. He has published articles in such journals as *The James Joyce Quarterly, Esquire, Philosophy and Rhetoric* and *Communication Monographs*. He is the past president and fellow of the International Communication Association and won the Peacemaker Award from the Rocky Mountain Conference of the United Methodist Church in 2006. He is president of the board of directors of Housing Justice!, the mission of which is to "give voice to the struggle for decent housing, affordable to all."